THE UNIVERSITY OF CHICAGO

# SERVICE CENTERS AND
# CONSUMER TRIPS

## Studies on the Philadelphia Metropolitan Fringe

---

DEPARTMENT OF GEOGRAPHY
RESEARCH PAPER #113

By

**John E. Brush**
*Rutgers University*

**Howard L. Gauthier, Jr.**
*Ohio State University*

1968

297308

**Research Papers**
1101 E. 58th Street
Chicago, Illinois 60637


*Library of Congress Catalog Card Number: 67-25274*

## ACKNOWLEDGEMENTS

These studies in the Philadelphia metropolitan fringe were made possible by financial grants from Rutgers--the State University of New Jersey and from the Pennsylvania-New Jersey-Delaware Metropolitan Project, Inc. (Penjerdel), which formerly existed in Philadelphia. The authors take this opportunity to thank John E. Bebout and Marshall M. Stalley, respectively Director and Assistant Director of the Rutgers Urban Studies Center, for generous financial support which released us from teaching duties and covered office and travel expenses and to Guido G. Weigend, Chairman of the Geography Department, for his patience and administrative support. We are grateful to John W. Bodine, formerly President of Penjerdel, for his persistent interest in the project and to the Penjerdel Board for grants to pay certain expenses.

The authors express their sincere appreciation to the research advisory committee, composed of Barbara Terrett, who was Research Coordinator for Penjerdel; David Popenoe, Director of Research in the Rutgers Urban Studies Center; Ernest C. Reock, Jr., Director of the Bureau of Government Research at Rutgers; and Robert Koch, Associate Professor of Agricultural Economics in the Rutgers College of Agriculture and Environmental Science.

Thanks are due also to Franklin Wood, Director of the Bucks County Planning Commission with offices in Doylestown, Pennsylvania; to Henry Fagin, former Director of the Penn-Jersey Transportation Study, with offices in Philadelphia, and to David Longmaid, subsequent Executive Director of the Penn-Jersey Transportation Study, for making available the data used for our analysis of consumer travel.

The senior author was responsible for the field inventories of stores and service establishments while the junior author was largely responsible for obtaining and analyzing the travel data. We were assisted by Bernard P. Geizer, now Economic Analyst in the Port of New York Authority, and James A. Perry, now Director of Urban Renewal for the City of Elmira, New York, when they were graduate students in the Geography Department at Rutgers.

Professors Arthur Getis, Bruce E. Newling, and Barry J. Garner of the Rutgers Geography Department kindly read the whole monograph or parts of it in draft form and offered valuable suggestions.

Finally, we express our thanks to Professor Brian J. L. Berry of the University of Chicago for the opportunity to publish our findings as a Research Paper of the Department of Geography.

John E. Brush

September 1967                          Howard L. Gauthier, Jr.

# TABLE OF CONTENTS

LIST OF TABLES

## LIST OF ILLUSTRATIONS

# CHAPTER I

## INTRODUCTION

Centrality is a basic principle in human affairs. In every inhabited area, where the economy is advanced above a purely self-sufficient subsistence level, there must be places for the exchange of goods and services. Social and political development require personal contact and communication. Division of labor and specialization of production form the economic basis of population concentration in towns and cities. Further concentration of services is induced and each central place becomes both a market outlet and a service center for people living in the surrounding territory. These reciprocal relationships of central places with adjacent market or service areas have been accepted as axioms in geography and in certain related social sciences.[1]

In the United States today rising income, decentralization of population and the use of private automobiles seem to be altering our settlement pattern. In general the central parts of metropolitan cities are stable or declining in population and, while tertiary activity in the central business district may continue to increase in absolute terms, the relative and absolute concentration of people and economic activity is increasing on the metropolitan fringes. These changes raise questions as to their impact on the spatial distribution and relationships of central services. Perhaps there is a need to reconsider some of our traditional concepts and interpretations of centrality.

### Conceptual Framework

The theory of centrality, which is largely traceable to the work of Christaller[2]

---

[1]The most exhaustive listing of references to the growing body of research is to be found in Brian J. L. Berry and Allen Pred, Central Place Studies, A Bibliography of Theory and Applications. Philadelphia: Regional Science Research Institute, Bibliography Series No. 1, 1961; Supplement through 1964 by H. G. Barnum, R. Kasperson and S. Kiuchi. Philadelphia, 1965.

[2]Walter Christaller, Central Places in Southern Germany. Translated from Die zentralen Orte in Süddeutschland by Carlisle W. Baskin. Englewood Cliffs, N. J.: Prentice-Hall, 1966.

and Lösch[3], has been tested by empirical analysis. The existence of functional grades of centers has been demonstrated repeatedly in studies of areas in Europe and Anglo-America, in some countries of Asia and in areas of overseas European settlement in South Africa, Australia and New Zealand. Questions remain as to the determination of the discreteness of functional classes and of achieving objectivity in ranking of centers, problems treated recently by Berry and associates[4] and by Davies[5]. A more controversial aspect of central-place theory is the spatial pattern, i.e., the integrated system of equidistant centers and hexagonal service areas, which is a logical geometrical construct found nowhere on the real earth. Yet, some evidence of a recurring spatial pattern has been found in more or less uniform agricultural areas of Anglo-America and Europe.[6] Dacey[7] and Medvedkov[8] have experimented with techniques of statistical analysis which show that under some conditions the distribution of service centers is more regular than random.

For the purposes of this study it is necessary to consider only certain fundamental concepts in the theory of centrality which bear directly on the problem at hand.

---

[3] August Losch, The Economics of Location. Translated from the second revised edition of Die raumliche Ordnung der Wirtschaft by William H. Woglom with the assistance of Wolfgang F. Stolper. New Haven: Yale University Press, 1954, See also, August Losch, "The Nature of Economic Regions," Southern Economic Journal, Vol. 5, 1938-39, pp. 71-78.

[4] Brian J. L. Berry, H. Gardiner Barnum and Robert J. Tennant, "Retail Location and Consumer Behavior," Papers and Proc., Regional Science Association. Vol. 9, 1962, pp. 65-106. See also, B. J. L. Berry and H. G. Barnum, "Aggregate Relations and Elemental Components of Central Place Systems," Journal of Regional Science, Vol. 4, 1962, pp. 35-68; and B. J. L. Berry, "Cities as Systems with Systems of Cities," Papers and Proc., Regional Science Association, Vol. 13, 1964, pp. 147-163.

[5] Wayne K. D. Davies, "The Ranking of Service Centres: A Critical Review," Transactions, Institute of British Geographers, No. 40, 1966, pp. 51-65.

[6] John E. Brush and Howard E. Bracey, "Rural Service Centers in Southwestern Wisconsin and Southern England," Geographical Review, Vol. 45, 1955, pp. 559-569.

[7] Michael F. Dacey, "Order Neighbor Statistics for a Class of Random Patterns in Multidimensional Space," Annals, Association of American Geographers, Vol. 53, 1963, pp. 505-515. _____, "Modified Poisson Probability Law for Point Pattern More Regular than Random," Ibid., Vol. 54, 1964, pp. 559-565. _____, "A Compound Probability Law for a Pattern More Dispersed than Random," Econ. Geography, Vol. 42, 1966, pp. 172-179. _____, "A Probability Model for Central Place Locations," Annals, Association of American Geographers, Vol. 56, 1966, pp. 550-568.

[8] Yuriy V. Medvedkov, "The Regular Component in Settlement Patterns as Shown on a Map," Soviet Geography: Review and Translation, Vol. 8, 1967, pp. 150-168.

Many years ago Galpin[9] conceived of the service area around a rural center as bounded by a circle which he said would overlap with the circular boundaries of six adjacent service areas. (See Figure 1, A.) According to Christaller and Lösch the ideal shape of a service area is hexagonal because of the geometric relationships of any seven centers when overlap is eliminated on the boundaries. (See Figure 1, B.) A similar conclusion regarding the hexagonal arrangement of areas was reached by Lösch in his development of a general equilibrium location model for centers of production and consumption. The logic of Christaller-Losch geometry results in a perfect system of centers and complementary areas, allowing for stepwise increases in the ranges of specialized goods and services supplied in centers of each of three successively higher functional orders with their respective areas arranged in an interlocking hexagonal point lattice.[10] (Figure 1, C and D.)

Deviations from the idealized pattern are to be expected. There are variations in location due to historical chance which result in the growth of centers at points not expected on the basis of theory. In addition, it seems the higher-order centers dominate the immediately neighboring centers in low-order functions, as well as complementing them in those goods and services which are offered only in the higher centers. This possibility was first recognized by Kolb[11] and it has been noted in empirical studies by Brush[12], Bracey[13], and Davies[14]. Since the service areas of all lower-order centers are reduced with respect to that of any higher-order center there is a tendency towards clustering of the lower-order centers, producing belts or wedges of territory with many such centers, (Figure 2, B) rather than six-point rings as postulated in the Christaller-Lösch theory. Another feature abundantly demonstrated in field investigations is the vagueness of boundaries between service areas. Precise lines are difficult to draw because the

---

[9]Charles J. Galpin, Social Anatomy of an Agricultural Community. University of Wisconsin, Agricultural Experiment Station, Research Bulletin 34, 1915.

[10]Michael F. Dacey, "The Geometry of Central Place Theory," Geografiska Annals, Human Geography, Series B, Vol. 47 B, 1965, pp. 111-124.

[11]John H. Kolb, Service Relations of Town and Country. University of Wisconsin, Agricultural Experiment Station, Research Bulletin 58, 1923.

[12]John E. Brush, "The Hierarchy of Central Places in Southwestern Wisconsin," Geographical Review, Vol. 43, 1953, pp. 380-402.

[13]Howard E. Bracey, "English Central Villages," The International Geographical Union Symposium in Urban Geography, ed Knut Norberg. Lund, Sweden, 1962.

[14]Wayne K. D. Davies, "Centrality and the Central Place Hierarchy," Urban Studies, Vol. 4, 1967, pp. 61-79.

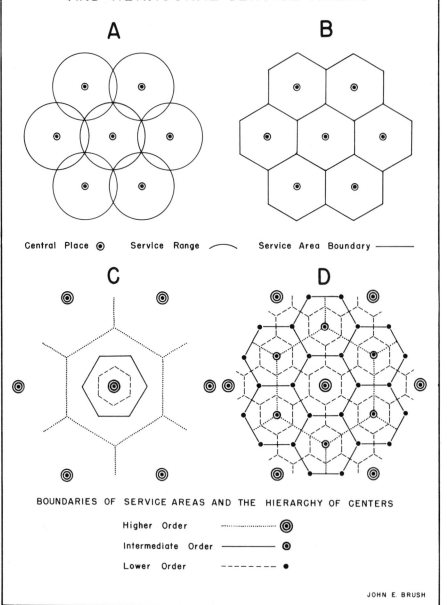

## EQUIDISTANT CENTRAL PLACES
### AND HEXAGONAL SERVICE AREAS

A

B

Central Place ◉    Service Range ⌒    Service Area Boundary ———

C

D

BOUNDARIES OF SERVICE AREAS AND THE HIERARCHY OF CENTERS

Higher Order ............ ◎
Intermediate Order ——— ◉
Lower Order – – – – – ●

JOHN E. BRUSH

Figure 1

# EMPIRICAL PATTERN OF CENTERS AND SERVICE AREAS

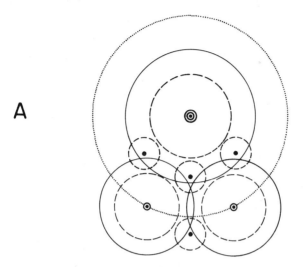

A

CENTERS AND LIMITS OF SERVICE AREAS

Lower Order ● ⎯⎯⎯ Intermediate Order ◉ ⎯⎯⎯ Higher Order ◎ ⋯⋯⋯

B

Service Areas of Intermediate Order ▢　　　Areas of Overlapping Services

JOHN E. BRUSH

Figure 2

boundaries represent areas or zones of overlap and competition.

There is general agreement[15] that gradients of economic nature and social and political influence exist around any central place. One example is a rent gradient which reaches some maximum intensity in a central business district and declines away from it although frequently interrupted by many minor peaks associated with secondary centers. In similar fashion the attraction or influence of a metropolitan city in terms of the volume of commodity shipments or frequency of travel and communication in its regional hinterland is seen to decrease according to some exponent of distance.[16] The relation can be expressed graphically as a general exponential gradient of concave form (Figure 3, A). The intensity or level of the attraction varies according to the size of the center. (Note gradients 1, 2, and 3, Figure 3.) Where the attraction derives from two cities there is overlap and a boundary of intersecting gradients beyond which the attraction of one city is relatively less than that of the other city (Figure 3, B).[17]

If one considers socio-economic gradients in relation to a hierarchy of central places in rural territory, an interpretation can be offered for the distortion of the perfect equidistant pattern of centers. The stronger attraction of a higher-order center makes it unlikely that any low-order center could survive in close proximity to it. Conditions more favorable for low-order centers are found in locations well away from any high-order place. This consideration of central places and interacting socio-economic gradients permits one to explain the clustering of centers of the same functional rank in the broad troughs far from the peaks of the gradients at places of the next higher order rank. The vagueness of boundaries is accounted for by the weakness of gradients and interpenetration near boundaries of service areas.

Support for the above inferences comes from analysis of local vehicular traffic

---

[15] See August Lösch, The Economics of Location, p. 106, and Walter Isard, Location and Space Economy. New York: Technology Press and John Willey and Sons, 1956, pp. 200 ff. See also Edgar M. Hoover, Jr., The Location of Economic Activity, New York: McGraw-Hill, 1948, p. 96. Analysis of land value and economic rent in relation to market originated in the 19th Century work of Johann Heinrich von Thünen, Cf., Von Thünen's Isolated State. An English edition of Der Isolierte Staat. Translated by Carla M. Wartenberg. Edited with an introduction by Peter Hall. Oxford: Pergamon Press, 1966.

[16] J. Douglas Carroll, Jr., "Spatial Interaction and Urban-Metropolitan Regional Description," Papers and Proc., Regional Science Assoc., Vol. I, 1955, p. D-2.

[17] An example of such interaction is provided by Howard L. Green, "Hinterland Boundaries of New York City and Boston," Economic Geography, Vol. 31, 1955, pp. 283-300.

in southwestern Wisconsin[18] and bus services in Great Britain[19]. The effects of attraction on density of vehicles travelling along a highway which passes from one high-order center to another through centers of two lower orders can be seen in the traffic profile (Figure 4, A), which represents the cumulative flow of vehicles on the highway with lesser gradients of lower-order centers (located at points marked II and III) superimposed on the stronger gradients of the higher centers (located at points marked I). Mapping of frequencies and destinations of services on scheduled bus routes reveals similar patterns which correlate with the relative influence exerted by rural towns on local travel in rural Britain. The boundaries bus services emanating from centers of higher order tend to be displaced towards the centers of lower order in accordance with the above-mentioned features of socio-economic attraction. Underlying these aggregate flow patterns of vehicles in rural Wisconsin and local bus service in Britain are the patterns of trips with destinations at several centers of varying rank in the functional hierarchy, the progressive higher density of trip destinations being associated with the successively higher-order centers. (See Figure 4, B.)

Another significant deviation from the idealized equidistant pattern of central places results from geographic variation in population density. The concepts of classical central-place theory are based on an assumption of relatively uniform population distribution. But this assumption poses serious problems in a metropolitan region, where population density increases towards the central city. Although Lösch attempted to consider the impact of urbanization economies, he failed to show unequivocally how service areas would be affected if his assumption of uniform population distribution were to be changed.[20] As Isard has observed[21] the Löschian scheme needs to be modified to allow for the concentration of market and service areas in and around the central city with its greater population density and spatial concentration of demand. One pattern suggested by Isard (Figure 5) represents the impact of non-uniform population distribution and urbanization

---

[18]John E. Brush, "The Hierarchy of Central Places in Southwestern Wisconsin," Geographical Rev., Vol. 43, 1953, p. 401.

[19]Frank H. W. Green, "Urban Hinterlands in England and Wales: An Analysis of Bus Services," Geographical Jour., Vol. 116, 1950, pp. 64-88. _____ and J. B. Fleming, "Some Relations between Town and Country in Scotland," Scott. Geographical Mag., Vol. 68, 1952, pp. 2-12. See also, map entitled, Local Accessibility: The Hinterlands of Towns and Other Centres as Determined by Analysis of Bus Services. Great Britain: Ordnance Survey, scale 1:625,000, 1955.

[20]August Lösch, The Economics of Location, pp. 124 and 125.

[21]Walter Isard, Location and Space Economy, pp. 271-73.

# SOCIO-ECONOMIC GRADIENTS

A  PROFILES OF INFLUENCE GRADIENTS

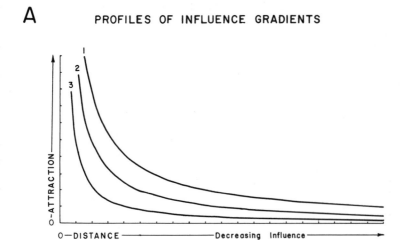

B  INTERACTION OF TWO UNEQUAL GRADIENTS

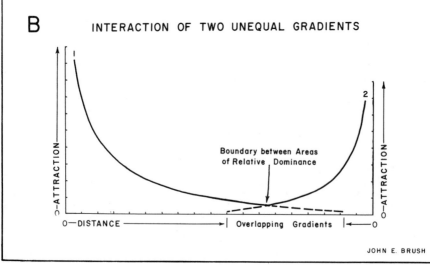

JOHN E. BRUSH

Figure 3

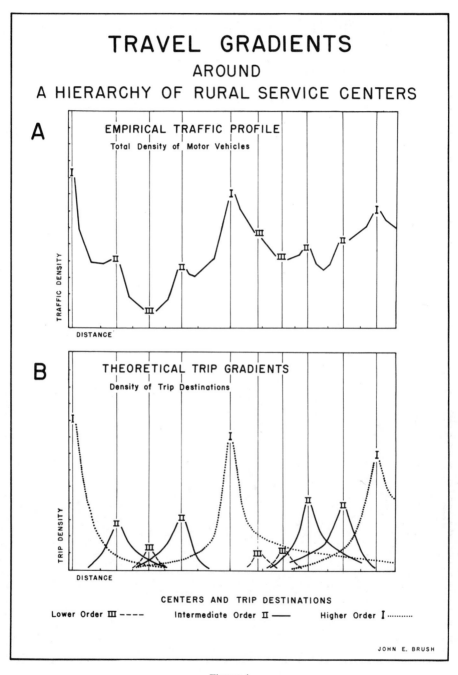

# TRAVEL GRADIENTS
## AROUND
## A HIERARCHY OF RURAL SERVICE CENTERS

**A**

EMPIRICAL TRAFFIC PROFILE
Total Density of Motor Vehicles

TRAFFIC DENSITY

DISTANCE

**B**

THEORETICAL TRIP GRADIENTS
Density of Trip Destinations

TRIP DENSITY

DISTANCE

CENTERS AND TRIP DESTINATIONS

Lower Order III ----    Intermediate Order II ——    Higher Order I ··········

JOHN E. BRUSH

Figure 4

10

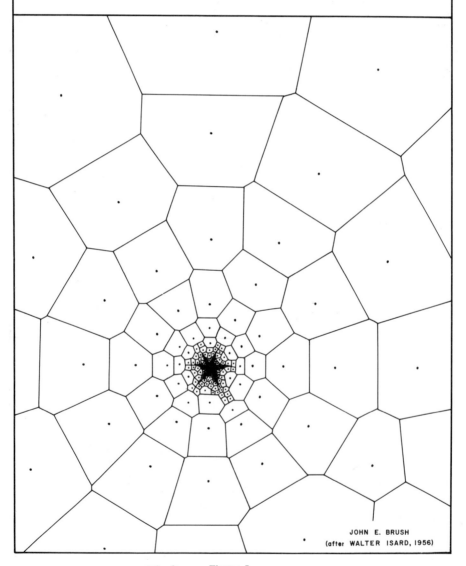

# A PATTERN OF CENTRAL PLACES
## MODIFIED BY POPULATION CONCENTRATION
## AROUND A METROPOLITAN CITY

JOHN E. BRUSH
(after WALTER ISARD, 1956)

Figure 5

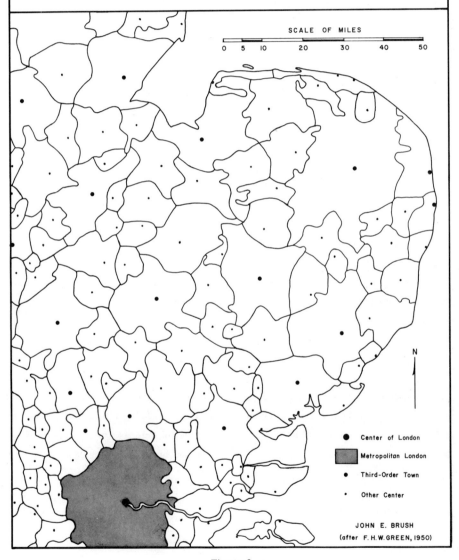

Figure 6

economies on the spatial distribution of central places and their service areas. The pattern is one of distorted hexagons which decrease in size concurrently with population density increase as the metropolitan center is approached from any direction. This reduction of areal dimensions of the service areas permits the growth of greater numbers of central places than would be possible under conditions of uniform population distribution. An éxample which may be regarded as an illustration of this Isardian pattern is the map of bus service areas in southeastern England. (See Figure 6.) Note the clustering of centers and shrinkage of service areas in the periphery of Greater London and the contrast between this tendency and the previously-mentioned locational tendencies in areas of more nearly uniform rural population densities in the region 35 or 40 miles distant from London.

### The Problem

Some students of urban phenomena do not find any system of local centers and service areas on the fringes of metropolitan cities. In Lösch's scheme there is an hiatus on the urban periphery. Indeed, the suggestion is made by Stewart and Warntz that near a major city the general gradient of socio-economic "gravitation" exceeds any local peak created by a small city and "unless its internal cohesion is very great the would-be small city can have no independent . . . existence. "[22]

Yet it might be true as Gottmann, the French geographer says, that "a new order in the organization of inhabited space"[23] is evolving in Megalopolis, a term which he applies to the urbanized Atlantic seaboard region spread from Boston, Massachusetts to Washington, D. C. There are so many people on the move and so many relationships between people and the places where they work and conduct their shopping or personal business or where they seek social and recreational contacts that they do not fit known theoretical patterns. "Perhaps the best comparison . . . would be the structure of a nebula. The expression is apt to convey the confusion spreading before us in place of a neatly organized system to which we were accustomed in the past. "[24]

Webber, the social ecologist and city planner, writing on future land use in metropolitan areas, asserts that, ". . . spatial patterns of American urban settlements are going to be considerably more dispersed, varied and space consuming than they ever

[22] John Q. Stewart and William Warntz, "Physics of Population Distribution, " Journal of Regional Science, Vol. 1, 1958, pp. 99-123. Specific citation is on page 119.

[23] Jean Gottmann, Megalopolis: The Urbanized Northeastern Seaboard of the United States. New York: The Twentieth Century Fund, 1961, p. 7.

[24] Ibid., p. 736.

were in the past..."[25] Never before has it been possible for people to maintain contact and economic interchange so easily and cheaply over distance with the result that cohesive forms which mark contemporary settlement may be replaced by drastically different forms. He does not predict homogeneous dispersion, but rather "order in diversity" on the growing edge of the metropolis..." while centers and sub-centers of various compositions and densities persist and grow in a range of sizes spanning the whole spectrum from 'center' to 'sprawl'."[26] Furthermore, Webber thinks that "Spatial separation or propinquity is no longer an accurate indicator of functional relations: and, hence, mere locational pattern is no longer an adequate symbol of order."[27]

It may be postulated that the freedom of movement which is possible in America is diffusing the force of centrality and producing a more or less random pattern of consumer travel. Of course, there must be ultimate limits of time and cost, but such limits are ill-defined. In many of our new metropolitan cities, especially in the western United States, there is low population density and maximum use of private automobiles on a network of freeways. These urban areas should be ideal testing grounds for such a notion. In Megalopolis around the fringe of an old major city such as Philadelphia one also would seem likely to find the "...'almost' colloidal pattern...which seems to be shaping."[28]

In our analysis of service centers and consumer interaction in selected peripheral areas of metropolitan Philadelphia we attempt to discern basic spatial patterns which existed in the past and to understand currently evolving relationships. The results of these local studies, it is hoped, will elucidate the functional pattern of central places, not only around Philadelphia but also in other American metropolitan areas. The conclusions may have application to city and regional planning as well as some significance in social ecology.

### Four Study Areas

Research is confined to four representative areas in the Philadelphia

---

[25] Melvin M. Webber, "Order in Diversity--Community without Propinquity," pp. 23-53, in Cities and Space, edited by Lowdon Wingo, Jr., Baltimore: The Johns Hopkins Press, 1963, p. 23.

[26] Ibid., p. 24.

[27] Ibid., p. 49.

[28] Jean Gottman, Op. cit., p. 737.

metropolitan region.[29]

One of the study areas, designated A on the map (Figure 7) is Middle Bucks County, a piece of beautiful countryside some 20 to 30 miles from the center of Philadelphia.  Land use is largely agricultural and population is dispersed.  This is "exurbia," a farm and estate area populated by writers, artists, journalists, business executives and other <u>intelligentsia</u> whose livelihood is largely tied to metropolitan Philadelphia or New York.  However, the majority of the residents do not travel daily to work in the central cities and Middle Bucks County is representative of the outer metropolitan fringe.

The second study area is Lower Bucks County (Fig. 7, B) in the inner metropolitan fringe, astride the main transportation corridor between Philadelphia and Trenton, crossed by the Pennsylvania Turnpike and fronting on the navigable Delaware River.  This area was transformed abruptly in the 1950's from farmland into an urban landscape,

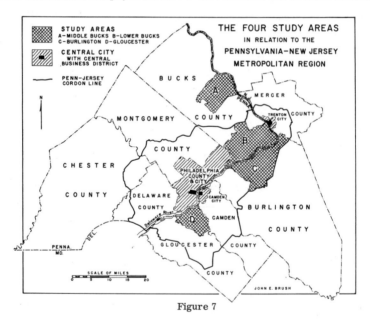

Figure 7

triggered by the building of the Fairless Works of the U. S. Steel Corporation below Trenton on the Delaware.  Levittown and other large-scale housing developments

---

[29] The study areas are located within the region designated by the U. S. Census Bureau as the Philadelphia, Pa. - Camden, N. J., Standard Metropolitan Statistical Area. If the Trenton, N. J., S. M. S. A. is included, and Burlington County, N. J., added, the term Pennsylvania-New Jersey Metropolitan Region is applicable (Fig. 7).

burgeoned and Lower Bucks County is now considered by the United States Census Bureau
as an "urbanized area."[30]  The influx of large numbers of young, middle-income families
of varied occupations and the expansion of local retail trade and services on the highways
and in shopping centers give this part of Bucks County a prime position in the urban
growth of the Philadelphia region.

The third and fourth study areas (Fig. 7, C and D) are in Burlington and
Gloucester counties, respectively, on the New Jersey side of the river.  The land is
intensively farmed, more than half being in agricultural use.  But few people are farmers.
These New Jersey areas are partly urbanized and lie well within daily commuting range of
Philadelphia and Camden or Trenton.  Some 40 miles of industrial waterfront as well as
major highways and sections of the New Jersey Turnpike are included.  There is another
Levittown in Burlington County and all the features of metropolitan sprawl are to be seen
in incipient or advanced stages of development in the New Jersey study areas, best described as parts of the inner metropolitan fringe.

## Objectives and Procedures

The objectives of analysis may be stated as a series of questions:
1. In what manner were the existing service centers created?
2. What, if any, are the functional grades and spatial patterns of centers?
3. Are consumer service areas identifiable and, if so, how are centers and areas related?

Thus, attention is directed first (Chapter II) to settlement history in the
Philadelphia metropolitan region and to tracing the origins and development of local service centers.  The present variations in size and geographical arrangement of retail
stores and establishments engaged in finance or personal and professional services are
treated (Chapter III) in terms of a functional and spatial hierarchy of centers.  Analysis
of data of origin and destination of consumer trips is related (Chapter IV) to distribution
of population and income and to location of the service centers.  A probability model is
developed in an effort to replicate the general pattern of consumer travel.

A field inventory of stores and service establishments in each of the four study
areas was conducted by the Rutgers Geography Department during the spring and fall of
1962.  The senior author, John E. Brush, and two research assistants, Bernard P.
Geizer and James A. Perry, traversed the highways and side roads, recording the location of business establishments on large-scale topographic maps.  Estimates were made
of the square footage of enclosed floor space devoted to commercial purposes in order to

---

[30]See map of Philadelphia Urbanized Area, pp. 40–46, 47, United States
Census of Population: 1960, Vol. I, Characteristics of the Population, Part 40,
Pennsylvania, Washington, D. C., 1963.

determine the relative size and concentration of business facilities. Historical and current census data and other kinds of information were assembled in order to gain knowledge of the origin and current status of settlement.

The analysis was enriched by certain supplementary studies carried forward by the research assistants. Bernard Geizer undertook an intensive study of the evolution and location of central places in Middle Bucks County as a thesis to qualify for the master's degree at Rutgers University in 1963. James Perry conducted a special food shopping survey in Woodbury, Gloucester County, in connection with a graduate seminar at Rutgers during 1962-63.

The choice of study areas depended not only upon obtaining suitable representation of the outer and inner metropolitan fringes but also upon obtaining consumer travel data for analysis in relation to the inventory of stores and services. Travel data come from two sources: (1) the Bucks County Planning Commission with offices in Doylestown and (2) the Penn-Jersey Transportation Study with offices in Philadelphia. Study regions A and B encompass areas of Bucks County for which data on travel for food shopping were readily available from household censuses conducted in 1961 and 1962. In that county the Planning Commission supervises and collates local municipal censuses carried out every third year in connection with property taxation and school enrollment. Among the several questions asked of a householder is one as to the location of stores where food is regularly purchased. Locations of households and food stores could be rendered easily into cartographic form, using maps and records available in the Bucks County Planning Commission office. Study regions B, C and D lie within the Cordon Line (Figure 7) which bounds the area within which travel data were gathered by household interviews conducted during the period, beginning in September, 1960 and ending in March, 1961, by personnel of the Penn-Jersey Transportation Study. These extensive data, which were gathered to ascertain travel for all purposes, including work, personal business, shopping, school attendance and social or recreational activities, represent stratified random samples of four per cent of the households in Lower Bucks County and 10 per cent in the New Jersey counties. All information, classified by origin and destination, purpose, mode, distance, and various household characteristics, had been coded and transferred to punch cards for computer analysis. The junior author, Howard L. Gauthier, was largely responsible for obtaining and analyzing the Penn-Jersey travel data required for our purposes. Extraction of this data was carried out at the Rutgers Center for Computer and Information Services. Our analysis of consumer interaction, therefore, is based on more or less contemporaneous travel data, pertaining to the period from 1960 to 1962, a time closely following the date of United States Census of Population (April 1960) and preceding the field inventory.

# CHAPTER II

## ORIGIN AND EVOLUTION OF SERVICE CENTERS

The first step in analysis is elucidation of the origin and evolution of service centers in the four study areas. The stage is then set in Chapter III for analysis of the current status of both the old and the new developing centers. In the ensuing chapter the spatial relationships between existing service centers and consumers living within the study areas are treated. Thus, it is possible to understand service centers and service areas in terms of the dynamics of locational equilibrium, influenced by the successive modes of transportation, changes in population distribution, rising mobility and increasing specialization of trade and services.

### Settlement in the 17th and 18th Centuries

In order to trace the beginnings of settlement in the lower Delaware valley we may look to the 17th Century. The first Europeans arrived about 1630 and the first permanent settlement occurred when the region was under the rule of Sweden (1638-55) and the Netherlands (1655-64) and subsequently under English rule. A small Dutch post for trade with the Indians was established briefly in the early 1630's on an island below the Delaware Falls (Trenton) near the head of navigation for seagoing vessels. During the next three decades some scattered Swedish and Dutch farmers lived on or near the river in territory now included in Bucks, Burlington, and Gloucester counties, while the principal centers of trade and government came into existence at sites situated down the river at Upland (now Chester) on the west bank in present Delaware County and other places in the state of Delaware.[1] (See Figure 8.)

Major settlement did not begin in the study areas until the 1870's on the Jersey side of the river and the 1680's in Pennsylvania. The influx of people proceeded rapidly thereafter, flowing northward from the alluvial lowland of the Coastal Plain below Trenton

---

[1] A general summary of settlement history is found in Monograph No. 1, of the Penjerdel Governmental Studies, entitled "Historical Development of Local Government in the Penjerdel Region, " Philadelphia, Pennsylvania Economy League, 1961, pp. 1-14.

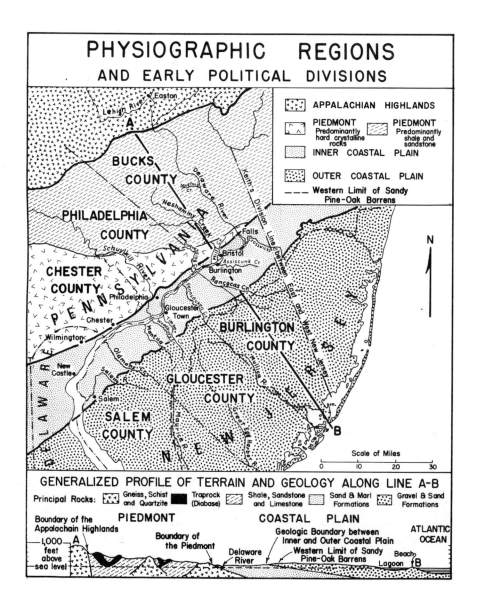

PHYSIOGRAPHIC REGIONS
AND EARLY POLITICAL DIVISIONS

Figure 8. West New Jersey consisted of the area lying west of Keith's Division Line and fronting on the Delaware River.

into the rolling hills of the Appalachian Piedmont of Middle Bucks County by the second decade of the 18th Century. At the same time the frontier of settlement expanded eastward across the Coastal Plain in Burlington and Gloucester counties.[2]

In general, it can be said that farms were well established everywhere in the study areas and population had become well disseminated by the third decade of the 17th Century. The study areas contain no physical deterrents to farming such as large topographic barriers or belts of infertile soil, although there are rugged bluffs of sandstone along the Delaware River in the Piedmont of Bucks County and sandy pine-oak "Barrens" are reached in the outer Coastal Plain of southern Burlington County within 10 miles of the limits of study.[3] (See Figure 8.)

The terrain of the Burlington and Gloucester study areas is very nearly flat, consisting of terraces of loamy soils near the river and slightly undulating sandy loam and rising 20 to 100 feet above the level of the Delaware and its local tributaries. The river and many of the creeks are subject to tidal fluctuations of two or three feet and are bordered by swampy flood plains. Thus, while the waterways constitute natural routes of ingress and became the earliest channels of commerce, they form narrow barriers which necessitated ferrying and eventually bridging for overland travel.

Similar topographic and hydrographic relationships obtain in Lower Bucks County south of a line drawn from Morrisville through Fallsington and Newportville to Andalusia, but northward, the Piedmont rises progressively to an undulating upland of sandstone, shale and limestone some 200 to 300 feet above sea level in Middle Bucks County. The highest elevations are coterminous with quartzite rock outcrops, e.g., Buckingham Mountain, 530 feet above mean sea level. Here streams are rapid with valleys incised 100 feet or more below the general upland surface. None of the small Piedmont streams are navigable, and the Delaware River above Trenton is too rocky and shallow to be of value for navigation today, although it was used commercially during the 17th and 18th

---

[2]Many details of settlement history in each county are to be found in: W. W. H. Davis, History of Bucks County, Pennsylvania..., Doylestown, 1876; J. H. Battle, History of Bucks County, Pennsylvania..., Philadelphia, 1887; Thomas Cushing and Charles E. Sheppard, History of the Counties of Gloucester, Salem and Cumberland, New Jersey..., Philadelphia, 1883; E. M. Woodward and John F. Hageman, History of Burlington and Mercer Counties, New Jersey..., Philadelphia, 1883.

[3]See George H. Ashley, Geologic Map of Pennsylvania, Harrisburg, Dept. of Internal Affairs, Topographic and Geologic Survey, 1931, Scale: 6 miles to one inch, 1: 380, 160, and J. Volney Lewis and Henry B. Kümmel, Geologic Map of New Jersey, Revised by H. B. Kummel, 1931, Trenton, Division of Geology and Topography, Atlas Sheet, No. 40, Scale: 1: 250,000 (approximately 4 miles to one inch).

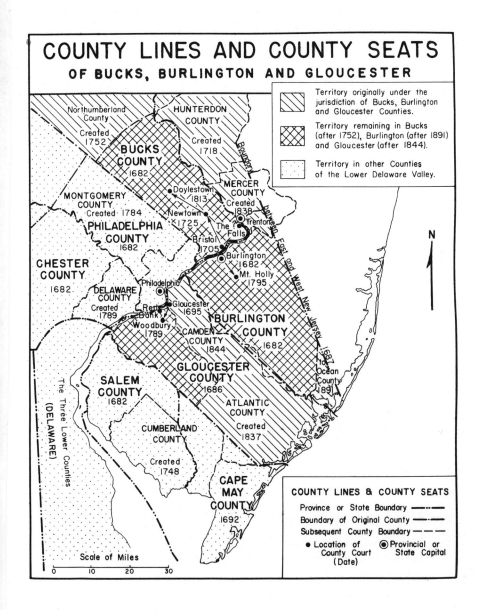

Figure 9. Boundary changes resulted in reduction of the areas of Bucks, Burlington, and Gloucester counties, while the county seats were shifted inland from original waterfront locations.

Centuries to float down rafts and was traversed by Durham boats which had a maximum draft of two feet and were propelled by poles or sails.

The English colonial proprietors both in New Jersey and Pennsylvania, conceived from the outset that there should be centers of trade and government to serve the needs of people taking up grants of land in the Western Division[4] of New Jersey and the three original counties of southeastern Pennsylvania: Chester, Philadelphia, and Buckingham (Bucks). William Penn was given authority by Charles II in 1681 to divide his domain into "... Towns, Hundreds of Counties and to erect and incorporate Towns and Boroughs into Cities and to make and constitute fairs and markets therein...."[5] Before settlement in 1682 Penn gave instructions for laying out Philadelphia as a major port and town to become the seat of his government.[6] The plan was effected the next year with immediate success. In Bucks County, Newtown and Wrightstown were conceived as rural towns laid out in a systematic pattern during the 1680's with a central tract, or townstead, to be taken up by house-lots and commons for persons receiving land within the bounds of each town.[7] But Penn's intentions regarding rural settlement were not carried out fully in these instances, and elsewhere in Bucks County no attempt was made to follow his instructions, the usual land grant being one or more large tracts of 400 to 500 contiguous acres.

Execution of Penn's plan for Philadelphia had been antedated five years by the Quaker proprietors of West New Jersey at Burlington in 1677 when a centralized settlement of 20 one-acre lots for the first twenty shareholders was laid out with frontage on High Street as soon as it had been out through the woods on Chygoes "island" on the east bank of the Delaware and before any of their respective 400-acre tracts had been surveyed in the territory beyond which was later to become Burlington Township.[8] The Burlington

---

[4]The Western Division of New Jersey was Lord Berkeley's moity of the province granted in 1664 by the English King Charles II to him and Sir George Carteret, who controlled the Eastern Division. West New Jersey, purchased by Quaker proprietors in 1673, was separately administered from 1677 to 1703 when the province came under a Governor appointed by the English Crown.

[5]William P. Holcomb, "Pennsylvania Boroughs," John Hopkins Studies in History and Political Science, Fourth Series, IV, 1886, p. 135.

[6]John W. Reps, "William Penn and the Planning of Philadelphia," Town Planning Review, Vol. 27, 1956, pp. 27-39.

[7]W. W. H. Davis, Op. cit., pp. 232-234 and 257-258; J. H. Battle, Op. cit., pp. 454-457 and 464-466.

[8]George De Cou, Burlington: A Provincial Capital, Philadelphia, 1945, pp. 29-31.

Town Bounds were fixed in 1683, and ten years later the original settlement on the Delaware River, covering a smaller area than the present Burlington City, was constituted with certain rights of municipal government. From the outset Burlington served as the headquarters of proprietary government and the place of court sessions. After the termination of proprietary rule in New Jersey during 1702-3 and the creation of provincial government, Burlington served alternately with Perth Amboy as the site of New Jersey's legislative sessions and was chartered as a City in 1734 by King George II.

It remained for the early settlers of Bucks County to choose for themselves the place for their county center of government and trade. By 1697 local landowners in Bristol Township on the west bank of the Delaware opposite Burlington had laid out streets and lots and petitioned for the establishment of a weekly market and two annual fairs. By 1705 Bristol was fully established as the county town with courthouse, jail, and market place and had been granted the privilege of holding annual fairs in May and October. Petition to erect Bristol Borough was made in 1718 and given assent of the Crown in 1720, creating it the third oldest municipal corporation in Pennsylvania after Chester and Philadelphia. The Durham Road, running northwest from the river, was opened to give Bristol access to the interior of the county. There was a ferry to Burlington and considerable shipping to and from Philadelphia and overseas to Britain and the West Indies. [9]

Similarly, Burlington had tradesmen, markets, and fairs and enjoyed the advantages of seaborne commerce. At the end of the 17th Century Burlington, or Bridlington as it was sometimes known, was described as follows:

It is "...a fine Market Town, ... having several Fairs kept yearly in it; likewise well furnished with good stores of most Necessaries for Humane Support, ... of which they freight several Vessels and send them to Barbadoes and other islands."

"There are very many fine stately Brick-Houses built, and a commodious Dock for Vessels to come in at..."

The Agents and Deputy-Governors of the New West Jersey Society are in Burlington, "Which brings their Assemblies and chief Courts to be kept there; and by that means it is become a very famous Town...with a delicate great Market House, where they keep their Market; it hath a noble and spacious hall overhead, where their Sessions are kept, having the prison adjoining to it."

"Likewise in the said Town there are very many fine Wharfs and large Timber-Yards, Malt Houses; and most sorts of Tradesmen...viz., Cloath-Workers, who make very good Serges, Druggets, Crapes, Camblets...and good Plushes, with several other Woollen Cloathes, besides Linnen.

"There are kept also in this Famous Town several Fairs every year; and as for Provisions, viz., Bread, Beer, Beef, Pork, Cheese, Butter, and most sorts of fruit here is great Plenty and very cheap; all those commodities are to be bought every market-day.

---

[9]Ibid., pp. 41 ff.

"There are Water-Men who constantly ply their wherry boats from that Town to the City of Philadelphia..." [10]

Evidently there were few if any retail stores, as we know them today, in any of the 17th and 18th Century centers of the region, but hand trades flourished in Philadelphia, Burlington and to a lesser extent elsewhere. Merchants for the most part were involved in export-import trade and would be considered wholesalers today. Weavers, tailors, bakers, brewers, cabinet-makers, and clock-makers manufactured goods at home or in adjacent shops with the help of family members and apprentices and retailed directly often upon customers' orders. Fresh food was sold in market stalls on one or two specified days each week. Shelters were provided for this purpose not only in Burlington but also in Bristol and subsequently in Mt. Holly. (See Figure 9.)

At the same time no market town existed in Gloucester County, which then included all the territory now comprised in Gloucester, Camden, and Atlantic counties. The courts of Gloucester, beginning in 1686, were held first at Arwamus or Gloucester-town (now Gloucester City) and alternately in Red Bank. [11] At this period court sessions lasted only a few days and were accommodated in local taverns until the erection of courthouse jail in Gloucester-Town during the late 1690's. Evidently no need was felt for public markets, and there was no incorporation of a municipal government in the county during colonial times. The chief factor working against urban development in old Gloucester County seems to have been the overwhelming influence of Philadelphia, merely three miles distance over water. Regular ferry services had been established to the Pennsylvania side in the early 1690's. [12]

Philadelphia, the great objective point of travel and trade by the end of the 17th Century, had become incorporated as a city in 1701 with several thousand inhabitants. There was a constant flow of seaborne commerce and a large street market, held twice a week. Farmers could make ready sale of their grain and livestock or produce and raftsmen their timber by travelling all the way to Philadelphia. Although travel was slow and trips to market were infrequent, Philadelphia seems to have exerted a strong influence in Bucks and Burlington counties, as well as in Gloucester. [13] Most of the main roads in the 17th Century and early 18th Century were opened at the specific request of local inhabitants

---

[10] Gabriel Thomas, An Historical and Geographical Account of the Province and Country of West-New Jersey in America, London, 1698, pp. 15-19.

[11] Frank H. Stewart, Gloucester County under the Proprietors, Woodbury, 1942, p. 16.

[12] Ibid., p. 25.

[13] Thomas Cushing and Charles E. Sheppard, Op. cit., pp. 105-119.

to give direct access to Philadelphia or to connect with the waterways and so permit them
to get to the city.

On the other hand, a need was felt by the scattered inhabitants of each of the
three counties to have closer access to their respective county seats. During the 18th
Century the functions of government in each county were transferred to somewhat more
central locations, although in each case not so far removed from the river as to seriously
hamper connections with Philadelphia. In 1725 the Bucks court was moved to Newtown,
nine miles inland on the Durham Road and seven miles from navigable water in Neshaminy
Creek. [14] The seat of justice in Gloucester was removed in 1789 to Woodbury three miles
from the river on a small creek and about eight miles over water from Philadelphia. [15]
In 1795 the Burlington County seat was relocated by popular vote in favor of Mt. Holly,
seven miles south of Burlington City, at an early mill dam site near the head of navigation
for small craft on the North Branch of Rancocas Creek. [16] While in each instance the
relative location of the court remained strongly off center with respect to the county as a
whole, it was less eccentric with respect to population distribution. Creation of Hunterdon
County from West New Jersey territory lying north of Assunpink Creek in 1714 and of
Northumberland County from the inland part of Bucks County in 1752 gave settlers in these
extremes new seats of courts and records closer to their homes. (See Figure 9.)

Growth of population both in the river and the county towns was sluggish
throughout the 18th Century. In 1784 the population recorded in Bristol was only 295
persons, while that of Burlington in 1797 is recorded to have been 1,714, making it by
far the largest town existing at that time within the limits of study. In 1800, Newtown was
a village of some 30 to 50 houses and 200 to 300 people, but Mt. Holly was much larger
with about 200 houses and 1400 to 1500 people. Woodbury in 1800 was only a roadside
hamlet, stretching along the road between the Friends Meetinghouse and the Courthouse.

The principal reason for sluggish growth of local centers in the hinterland of
Philadelphia in the 18th Century was the primitive condition of life. Trips of any sort
were costly and arduous with the result that rural people remained isolated and largely
self-sufficient. The typical farm of 100 acres or so produced a little more than the basic
requirements of food and fiber needed by the owners. Clothing, furniture, and implements
were produced by local farmer-craftsmen who supplied their services to customers within

---

[14] W. W. H. Davis, Op. cit., pp. 240-247 and J. H. Battle, Op. cit., pp. 455-460.

[15] Thomas Cushing and Charles E. Sheppard, Op. cit., pp. 116, 168-170.

[16] E. M. Woodward and John F. Hageman, Op. cit., pp. 175-179; J. D. Scott,
New Historical Atlas of Burlington County, New Jersey. Philadelphia: 1876, p. 20.

10 miles of their homes. The six main crafts practiced in Bucks County in the period from 1750 to 1800 were: iron working (blacksmithing and wheelrighting), weaving of wool and flax, woodworking, leather working (tanning and shoemaking), tailoring and pottery making. There were also saw mills and grist mills to which farmers brought their own logs to be cut and their own grain (wheat, corn, and buckwheat) to be ground. The local craftsmen and millers supplied services for small returns, often being paid in kind rather than cash.[17] Thus, there was little or no real need of market centers for the local exchange of goods and services.

Merchants and the more specialized shops concentrated in riverine locations, especially in Philadelphia and Burlington, were occasionally visited by rural people. A good occasion might be when a journey was necessary to sell produce or livestock, and cash was available. Farmers could order cloth and hardware, as advertised in the Philadelphia papers, through wagon and coach drivers who served as intermediaries. Peddlers went through the countryside, offering fancy goods for sale at farmhouses. But there was insufficient concentration of demand in typical rural areas to support retail stores.[18]

However, the needs of travellers, especially those who passed through Bucks County and Burlington County en route to Philadelphia and New York, gave rise to taverns and inns in rural areas. Public houses which had had a long history in England prior to the 17th Century were often the first non-farm enterprises to be established in the settled areas of America. From the promulgation of the Duke of York's laws when the English Governor Nicholls assumed control of the former New Netherlands bordering the Hudson and Delaware rivers in 1664, inns and taverns, then called "ordinaries" or "victualling houses," were to be licensed.[19] The earliest of such establishments recorded in the areas of study is Jegou's "ordinary" which stood in 1668 at the junction of Assiscunk Creek and the Delaware River within the present boundaries of Burlington City, nine years before the arrival of the Quaker settlers.[20] Favored locations for public houses established during the late 17th Century were river landings and ferries, and in the 18th Century they had appeared along most of the main roads at bridges and junction points.

---

[17] Shirley A. Martin, "Craftsmen of Bucks County, Pennsylvania, 1750-1800." Unpublished M.A. Thesis, University of Delaware, 1956, pp. 22 ff.

[18] Ibid.

[19] Charles S. Boyer, Old Inns and Taverns in West Jersey, Camden, 1962, pp. 1-2.

[20] Ibid., pp. 27-28.

The roads at best were muddy or stony and rutted surfaces with bridges only at the smaller streams. Springless stage wagons were running between Philadelphia and New York by the mid-18th Century, being supplanted by stage coaches just before and after the Revolution. Two, if not three or more days, were required to travel between Philadelphia and New York or Easton at the end of the 18th Century.

The oldest roads arose from Indian or Dutch and Swedish paths, paralleling the Delaware River and leading to convenient crossings or points of embarkation. The King's Highway from Philadelphia through Frankford across Lower Bucks County, going to the ferry below the Falls at Trenton, passed through Bensalem, Bristol, and Falls townships on the approximate alignment of Bristol Road (now U.S. 13). It was the most important colonial stage route linking Bristol Borough, which was made a post town, to Philadelphia, Trenton, New Brunswick, and other colonial cities.[21] The Burlington Road, connected by stage boat with Philadelphia, went through Bustleton, Hedding, Mansfield Square, and Crosswicks; thence continuing northward to the Raritan River and Bay where stage boat connections were made from New Brunswick or South Amboy for New York. Bordentown provided an alternative stage route by land and water, advertised as the shortest overland and the fastest (one and a half days) between Philadelphia and New York.[22]

Other routes of long-distance travel were laid out at the insistence of the inland English settlers in radial fashion from Philadelphia, extending northwards across Bucks County and Eastward across old Gloucester County from Gloucester and Cooper's Ferry (now Camden). The Easton Road (now U.S. 611) was one such route which passed through Middle Bucks County, intersecting with another road at a place later called Doylestown, where William Doyl opened a tavern in 1745.[23] The tavern not only served travellers between Philadelphia and Easton, but those going eastward on another road (now U.S. 202) to New Jersey and New York by way of Well's Ferry, later Coryell's Ferry (now New Hope).

By the latter 18th Century the tavern, or inn, was the one kind of service establishment which had become ubiquitous in the hinterland of Philadelphia and had assumed some significance in local affairs in addition to accommodating transient persons. In the strict meaning of terms, a tavern should provide only food and drink, while an inn should provide lodging and board, but these words were used more or less

---

[21] W. W. H. Davis, Op. cit., pp. 739-740.

[22] E. M. Woodward and John F. Hageman, Op. cit., pp. 53-56.

[23] J. H. Battle, Op. cit., p. 541.

synonymously for all public houses in colonial times.[24] There was not only much informal social contact and transmission of news amongst strangers and local people gathered for refreshment and entertainment by occasional travelling shows, but some taverns were regularly the places of business dealings, local court sessions, and general township meetings. Here tax assessors sometimes received the residents of the neighborhood to give an account of their ratable land and livestock. The first national system of post offices in 1790 often made use of taverns on stage routes as had the previous colonial post system. Thus, these early public houses served as central places for communication or recreation and sheltered rudimentary governmental services.

The number of taverns had grown surprisingly large by the late 18th Century. In 1784, there were 57 taverns in all Burlington County[25] which then had a population of less than 18,000 persons. That is to say, the ratio was one tavern for some 300 persons. There were 30 taverns in old Gloucester County,[26] or one for every 430 persons. In 1800, 78 public houses were licensed in all Bucks County,[27] a proportion of one to about 350 persons. It must be remembered that Bucks and Burlington taverns along the main-travelled roads were concentrated in excess of the number which could be supported by the local population.

County towns were also attractive places for tavern-keeping because of prolonged court sessions and annual fairs. Although temporary booths and tents provided shelter for many who came to sell or buy and be entertained at the fairs, the local lodgings would be crowded for days. Court trials and other county business often detained persons overnight who had come distances of 10 or 20 miles. The relative concentration of taverns in a county town at the end of the 18th Century is exemplified by Newtown, where we are told that among the 50 dwelling houses one in every 10 had a license to sell liquor.

The countryside at the turn of the century can be visualized as an open landscape with thickenings of the fabric of settlement where tiny hamlets clustered at ferries and river landings or near mills and bridges. The population density averaged between 40 and 50 persons per square mile, representing five or six farmsteads per square mile.

---

[24] Charles S. Boyer, Op. cit., p. 2.

[25] Ibid., p. 7.

[26] Ibid., pp. 7-8.

[27] W. W. H. Davis, Op. cit., p. 842.

Distinctly agglomerated centers of settlement were few and far between. Burlington and Mt. Holly were the only centers with more than 300 inhabitants. During the 18th Century the pattern of roads had taken shape and along them at intervals of three to five miles were the isolated taverns or inns. Here and there were mills and shops of local crafts-men, supplying local needs for processed and manufactured goods. A few religious edifices and schoolhouses were to be seen. With the exception of the county seats this geographic pattern had developed without preconceived plan or policy.

## Development in the 19th Century

After 1800 a series of technological and economic changes fundamentally altered the pattern of population distribution. Not only did central places acquire new roles, but the number of agglomerations multiplied. Construction of turnpikes, canals, and railroads was made possible and supported by increased agricultural production and the rise of industries in the 19th Century. In the northeastern United States great cities such as Philadelphia absorbed much of the natural increase of population of their rural hinterlands, as well as receiving fresh European immigration. In the year 1800 Philadelphia City had a population of some 41,000, while the Philadelphia County had 81,000. By 1900 the population had grown to almost 1,300,000, the city now being coter-minous with the county. Trenton became the New Jersey capital and an incorporated city in the late 1700's and grew from less than 3,000 to 73,000 in the 19th Century. Camden, which had less than 2,000 inhabitants in 1830, two years after its incorporation as a city, grew to about 76,000 in 1900.[28]

At the same time the old river and county towns in the study areas gained population and new centers of population were formed. By the end of the 19th Century there were six urban places,[29] ranging between 3,000 and 7,500 inhabitants, while three other agglomerated settlements in the study areas exceeded 1,000. Burlington and Mt. Holly maintained steady growth rates until 1890-1900 when they became temporarily stabilized at about 7,000 and 5,000, respectively. Bristol and Woodbury showed sharp and somewhat irregular gains, reaching 7,000 and 4,000, respectively. Doylestown expanded rapidly to about 3,000 in 1900, due largely to the transfer of courts and offices to this most central location in Bucks County in 1813. New Hope, which had a population exceeding that of Doylestown during the first half of the century became a fluctuating and

---

[28] Tabulations of population counts from the United States Census for 1800 and thereafter are contained in Monograph No. 2 of the Penjerdel Governmental Studies, entitled "Geographical Development and Population Growth in the Penjerdel Region," Philadelphia, Pennsylvania Economy League, 1962.

[29] According to U. S. Census Bureau definition an incorporated city or borough which has 2,500 inhabitants or more is an urban place. Mt. Holly was then and still is a township, but it should be classified as an urban place.

declining center of about 1,200 after 1850. Bordentown grew erratically before 1850, then stabilized at about 4,000, while Beverly and Morrisville experienced modest growth after 1850 and were approaching 2,000 and 1,500, respectively, by the end of the century.

These local growth trends are evidence of the impact of the urban-industrial revolution, just as the declining population of rural townships in the study areas after 1860 reflects the decrease of farming population due to migration to new land in the West and to cityward movement. Note, for example, the diminution of population in Buckingham and Solebury townships in Middle Bucks County and of Springfield and Mansfield or Westampton and Eastampton townships in Burlington County. The trends of rural population decline in other townships are obscured by boundary changes or the growth of small settlements within existing boundaries. Many small agglomerations came into existence in the rural townships during the 19th Century, chiefly in response to the increasing demands of farm people for goods and services. Typical rural townships in each of the study areas now contained one or more villages and hamlets with a nucleus of stores and service establishments. (See Tables 10 and 11.)

Thus, the cumulative effect of economic changes in the 19th Century was to create a small number of large agglomerations and a large number of small agglomerations in the study areas. Analysis of these population trends and the pattern of settlement requires knowledge of changes in manufacturing, transportation, and functional development of large and small service centers.

The rise of local manufacturing industries had much to do with the initial growth of population centers in the study areas. Early 19th Century industrial development involved direct use of mechanical power from falling water. Local manufacturing of grain, wood, iron, and textiles was greatly expanded at sites suitable for construction of dams and mill races, chiefly on the creeks and some smaller streams of Bucks and Burlington counties. New Hope is the most outstanding example of such industrial development within the study areas. The industrial complex here was based on Aquetong Creek, which had been used for mills and forges as early as the middle 18th Century.[30] Hulmeville and Morrisville are localities where industries flourished in Lower Bucks County.[31] In Burlington County the mill dam at Mt. Holly was rebuilt and a new era

---

[30] Ibid., p. 240.

[31] Tabulations of population counts from the United States Census for 1800 and thereafter are contained in Monograph No. 2 of the Penjerdel Governmental Studies, entitled "Geographical Development and Population Growth in the Penjerdel Region," Philadelphia, Pennsylvania Economy League, 1962.

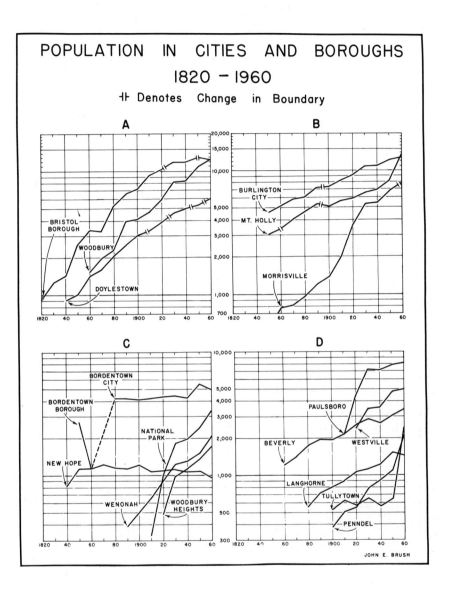

POPULATION IN CITIES AND BOROUGHS
1820 – 1960
-IⱵ Denotes Change in Boundary

A

B

C

D

JOHN E. BRUSH

Figure 10.

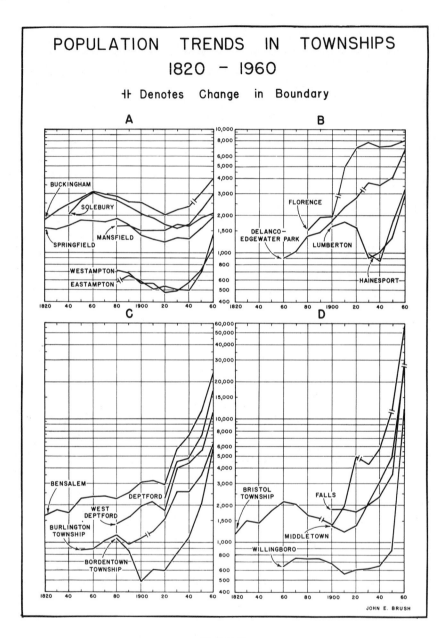

Figure 11.

inaugurated for local industry on Rancocas Creek.[32] Isolated grist and saw mills were built at many other sites in the study areas during the late 18th Century and early 19th Century. A few stores and services clustered around some of these mills were dependent upon trade from farmers. Water power was replaced by steam power but small mills became uneconomic, and by the end of the 19th Century many local industries had declined and disappeared as it became evident that the larger mills in Philadelphia, Trenton, Camden, and elsewhere could produce the same goods more cheaply. Yet, some local manufacturing has persisted into the present century, and some of the population agglomerations to which 19th-Century industries gave rise remain significant features of the settlement pattern.

Transportation went through a series of changes during the 19th Century, beginning with turnpikes and bridges and ending with the railroads dominant, although for a time canals and steamer navigation on the Delaware River and Rancocas Creek played important roles. Turnpikes were built by privately financed companies under franchises issued by the Pennsylvania and New Jersey legislatures.[33] Tolls were levied on persons, vehicles, draft animals, and market livestock in return for improvement and maintenance of the route of travel. Sometimes a new road would be laid out on a direct line between predetermined points, but usually the existing road was merely straightened, the roadbed graded and in part surfaced with stone and gravel. Milestones and toll gates were necessary for determination of distances travelled and for collection of tolls. Toll bridges replaced ferries.

The first phase of turnpike construction effected improvement in long-distance travel between Philadelphia and New York during the second decade of the 19th Century. The earliest was the Bristol Turnpike through Lower Bucks County, more or less along the old King's Highway to Morrisville. This company, incorporated in 1803, completed construction in 1812, connecting by a covered wooden bridge 1,100 feet in length to Lamberton (now part of Trenton City) with the Trenton and New Brunswick Turnpike, previously completed.[34] Another early turnpike was laid out in 1816 from Bordentown to South Amboy along the short route through Hightstown between Delaware and Raritan tidewater, connecting with steamer services to the major cities.[35] These routes were

---

[32] W. W. H. Davis, Op. cit., pp. 676-688.

[33] Ibid., pp. 173-175, 657-663.

[34] E. M. Woodward and John F. Hageman, Op. cit., pp. 176-178.

[35] A good general account of the turnpike era in New Jersey is given by Wheaton J. Lane, "The Turnpike Movement in New Jersey," Proc., New Jersey Historical Society, New Series, Vol. 54, 1936, pp. 19-52.

used by fast stage coaches which made it possible for the traveller to be conveyed from
Philadelphia to New York between sunrise and sunset on a summer day. There was also
heavy traffic of freight wagons especially during the War of 1812 when the seaways between major Atlantic ports were endangered by the British Navy.

The second era of turnpike construction came in the middle 19th Century after
the establishment of the first railroads and canals and continued well into the last quarter
of the 19th Century. During this time Doylestown was linked to Philadelphia by way of
Willow Grove, Bordentown to Trenton, Mt. Holly, Burlington and Woodbury to Camden
and so to Philadelphia by ferry. There were many other short turnpikes built to connect
minor villages and hamlets with the above named towns. Five turnpikes radiated from
Mt. Holly, three from Woodbury, and two from Bordentown. In Middle Bucks County the
Durham, York, and various other roads were turnpiked, not only giving better access to
Doylestown and New Hope from intermediate points, but also joining them in the larger
network of improved roads.

One is impressed by the degree to which turnpikes set the present patterns of
local travel and by their role in creating and drawing support for the local service centers as well as providing access to the larger cities of the 19th Century. It is estimated
that the toll roads of the 19th Century initially lowered land transport costs to the users
as much as 50 per cent, despite the high rates charged. In the words of Wheaton Lane:

"Travel was speedier, delays [were] fewer, and much larger loads
[were] possible on the hard surface of a good turnpike than on the average public road... Cheaper land carriage permitted a more complete exploitation of
the soil than existed before, because its produce could not be marketed profit-
ably. In southern New Jersey especially the use of natural fertilizers [chiefly
marl] became widespread when made available by improved roads. These factors caused a general increase in land values." [36]

Turnpikes proved unprofitable in the long run and they were abandoned or became public roads, although the last ones were not finally abolished until the 20th Century.
At the end of the 19th Century long-distance traffic had been taken over largely by the
railroads. Turnpikes were dependent upon revenue from local traffic and there was
increasing public sentiment against them and for making all roads free. State, county,
and local governmental bodies were now able to take over maintenance and improvement
of the road system.

Canal construction was initiated in the early 1830's at the same time as the
first railroads were being projected and was thought to offer a form of transportation
superior to both turnpikes and railroads. After 1834 coal and other bulky goods could
be moved in barges from anthracite mines in the Lehigh valley by way of Easton and the

---

[36] J. H. Battle, Op. cit., 340-342; Edward W. Hocker, "Highways and Transportation," pp. 403-406, in Southeastern Pennsylvania, Vol. 1, Philadelphia, 1943,
edited by J. Bennett Nolan.

Delaware valley to the major seaboard cities through the Pennsylvania Canal and the Delaware and Raritan Canal in New Jersey. The Delaware Division of the Pennsylvania Canal passed through New Hope, Morrisville, and Bristol, providing water power at the locks and cheap coal in unprecedented volume. [37] Bordentown was the western terminus of the Delaware and Raritan Canal where barges from Bristol and Philadelphia entered from the river. But after 1854 an outlet lock was built at New Hope, permitting transfer of barges across the river to the Delaware and Raritan Feeder Canal at Raven Rock, so shortening the trip to New Brunswick and New York. New Hope was made the sole toll station on the Delaware Division Canal. Coal traffic was heavy during the mid-19th Century, reaching a maximum following the Civil War. The industrial development based on cheap fuel was much greater at Trenton and the major cities than at New Hope, Morrisville, Bristol, or any other place in the study areas, although there were distinct industrial advantages recognized in almost every canal location. Passenger travel on the canals was never important and by the end of the 19th Century the freight traffic had declined markedly.

Expansion of the rail network generally followed the geographic pattern and chronologic sequence of turnpike development. The earliest rail lines were built in the 1830's to connect Philadelphia with New York or intermediate places with steamboat services, while subsequent lines were extended into the agricultural hinterlands during the latter half of the century. The railroads, which at first were flimsy affairs with small engines and light rolling stock, were greatly improved and eventually captured almost all passenger traffic, whenever the tracks paralleled turnpikes or waterways. The Camden and Amboy line was operating north of Bordentown by 1834 and shortly thereafter it was extended through Burlington to the Camden ferry to provide an alternative to the water route in winter from Bordentown to Philadelphia. [38] Meanwhile the railroad across Lower Bucks County from Philadelphia through Bristol and Morrisville, paralleling the old King's Highway and the Turnpike and now traversed by the main line of the Pennsylvania Railroad, was being built to connect across the Delaware by bridge to Trenton, making possible continuous travel to New Brunswick by the late 1830's. [39] In In 1850 the Camden and Amboy Railroad built a branch to Mt. Holly from Burlington[40] and in 1857 connections from Camden to Woodbury were put into operation, replacing a

---

[37] W. M. Woodward and John F. Hageman, Op. cit., p. 56.

[38] Wheaton J. Lane, Loc. cit., p. 52.

[39] Edward W. Hocker, Op. cit., pp. 410-411.

[40] E. M. Woodward and John F. Hageman, Op. cit., pp. 59-60.

primitive horse-drawn line built about 1840.[41]  Both of these lines were extended, and
Mt. Holly and Woodbury were made junction points with other lines, most of which were
eventually consolidated into the Pennsylvania and Reading Seashore systems.  In 1856 a
branch from the railroad between Philadelphia and Bethlehem was extended to Doylestown.[42]
A third main line connecting with Philadelphia and New York now operated by the Reading
Company, was built in 1876 through Middletown Township passing between Langhorne and
Penndel.[43]  Other branch lines and spurs were added in Burlington and Gloucester coun-
ties during the 1870's.  Not until 1891 did rail service reach New Hope which, like
Doylestown, always remained a terminus.[44]

By the last decade of the 19th Century the rail network had been completed
except in Lower Bucks County where the Pennsylvania Company has added extensive
trackage in the 20th Century to facilitate freight operations.  Hauling power and rolling
stock capacity were sufficiently enlarged to carry every type of freight on tracks of uniform gauge over interconnected systems penetrating nearly everywhere within and beyond
the study regions.

### Growth of Central Places in the 19th Century

Increasing population and rising production in factories and on farms created
demands which had not existed for goods and services in the study region during the
18th Century.  Turnpikes, waterways, and railroads now provided cheaper and more frequent access to Philadelphia and enormously stimulated its growth as the regional center
of trade and manufacturing.  But not all growth was concentrated in Philadelphia.  Urban
growth was stimulated, as already pointed out, in Trenton, Camden, and the several
river and county towns in the study areas.  Both the old towns, i.e., Burlington, Bristol,
and Mt. Holly, and the new towns, i.e., Doylestown, Bordentown, and Woodbury, grew
rapidly into urban settlements and strengthened or acquired the roles as the principal
central places in their respective areas.  Additional points of exchange were required,
and during the same time period many villages and hamlets arose as subsidiary central
places in their rural hinterlands.  By the end of the 19th Century no farm in the study
areas was beyond two miles of a central place of some sort.  Contemporary descriptions
provide details of the development of retail trade and services in centers of different
sizes.  Examples are taken from the Gloucester and Burlington study areas.

---

[41] Edward W. Hocker, Op. cit., pp. 412-414.

[42] E. M. Woodward and John F. Hageman, Op. cit., pp. 177-178.

[43] Thomas Cushing and Charles E. Sheppard, Op. cit., pp. 97.

[44] Ibid.

In the third decade of the 19th Century, Woodbury was entering its most dynamic era of development. Turnpikes and rails had yet to come, but in 1834 it was already a center of trade and professional services, according to Gordon's Gazetteer, which reads as follows:

> "Woodbury, ... 8 miles south of Camden... contains a spacious courthouse... and county offices...; 1 Friends meetinghouse... 1 Presbyterian Church..., the upper part of which is used as an academy; and 1 Methodist Church; 2 common schools; 2 public libraries...; 2 Sunday Schools;... 10 stores, 3 taverns, 4 lawyers, 3 physicians... 100 dwellinghouses, and 735 inhabitants." [45]

In the next four decades Woodbury acquired turnpike and railroad connections and became an incorporated municipality (a borough in 1854; and a city in 1870). By 1880 the population had increased more than threefold to 2,298. The county historians now found much to praise here.

> "WOODBURY in 1883. -- Woodbury is second to none of the many county seats in the state. Whatever her facilities were two hundred years ago for going and coming, they are today the best that the art of man, with the help of nature can supply. Her railroad facilities... are all that could be required by the most fastidious. Twenty or thirty minutes [are required] to Philadelphia..."
>
> "From the one broad and well-shaded street, ... she has spread out over a large extent of territory, with broad avenues, along the lines of which are hundreds of beautiful villas and cottages..."
>
> "From the one or two small and dingy stores and blocks of even a century ago, Woodbury now boasts of elegant blocks of buildings and stores..."
>
> "From the five or six country taverns at the beginning of the present century, the number has been reduced to two well-appointed modern hotels..."
>
> "...Woodbury now boasts of her town hall, in which is a store, public library, and a hall of modern size and appointments; also Green's block, one of the largest and best constructed of its kind in the State, in which are four large stores, Common Council Chamber, Printing-Office, [a novelty manufacturing works], offices, and one of the best-appointed opera houses in New Jersey."
>
> "From no manufacturing establishments one-quarter century ago, Woodbury has at present... three establishments [which] employ between five and six hundred persons..."
>
> "From no printing-press at all at the beginning of this century, Woodbury has grown up to support three first-class weeklies..."
>
> "From one place of worship... there have arisen six others..." [46]

However, there were concentrations of population and amenities developing concurrently elsewhere in Gloucester County. One such place is Paulsboro, which was described in the 1830's and 1880's as follows:

---

[45] Thomas F. Gordon, A Gazetteer of the State of New Jersey, Trenton 1834, pp. 365-366.

[46] Thomas Cushing and Charles E. Sheppard, Op. cit., p. 184.

"Paulsboro, ...4 miles west of Woodbury; [in 1834] contains a tavern, store, 10 or 12 dwellings, and a Methodist Church."[47]

"PAULSBORO IN 1883. -- The Paulsboro of today is one of the wide awake industrious towns upon the line of the Delaware River Railroad, and contains two churches;...1 hotel...; 4 general stores...; [2] lumber dealers...on the dock below the turnpike bridge; [2] coal merchants...; [2] wheelwright and blacksmith shops...; [2] boat builders...; [4] physicians, two of whom also keep a drug-store. There are also the usual number of small shops usually found in a town of the size of Paulsboro."[48]

In the span of 50 years, Paulsboro had grown from a hamlet to a village of 750 inhabitants,[49] with an assemblage of stores and services less varied and complete than Woodbury's, serving mainly the farmers living in Greenwich Township west of Mantua Creek and relatively far from Woodbury. Its role as a central place always remained secondary to that of Woodbury, although the building of petroleum refineries at Billingsport on the river incorporated in the borough with Paulsboro (in 1904) caused a sharp increase in population and business activity in the first three decades of the 20th Century.

Wenonah, three miles south of Woodbury, is an example of planned development of a new residential settlement of the sort which was taking place in the study areas during the last half of the 19th Century. It was founded in 1871 by a real estate company on the main line of the West Jersey Railroad from Woodbury to Glassboro on a tract of some 500 acres, extending a mile along the railroad tracks with the depot nearly in the center.[50] Streets and lots were plotted the same year. "The hotel and four cottages were erected in 1872... There were in 1883 about fifty cottages on the tract, and a population of three hundred," when the Borough of Wenonah was incorporated. The first store was open in 1872, the second in 1880, the third in 1883. The Wenonah post office was kept in the rail depot at first and later moved into one of the stores. The Presbyterian Church was built in 1873; the Methodist Church in 1883. "The pioneer resident physician...located here in 1882." Population, which is reported to have been 166 in 1880,[51]

---

[47] Thomas F. Gordon, Op. cit., p. 211.

[48] Thomas Cushing and Charles E. Sheppard, Op. cit., p. 238.

[49] This population count is taken from the listings of unincorporated places in New Jersey, Table III, Statistics of the Population of the United States at the Tenth Census, June 1, 1880, Washington, D.C., 1883.

[50] Thomas Cushing and Charles E. Sheppard, Op. cit., pp. 200-201. All quotations in this paragraph are from p. 200.

[51] See footnote 49 above.

Figure 12

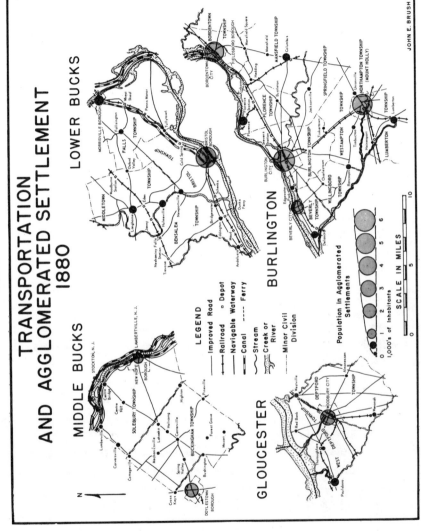

TRANSPORTATION
AND AGGLOMERATED SETTLEMENT
1880

JOHN E. BRUSH

grew steadily but did not pass 1,000 until 50 years later, and there was never a large concentration of business establishments here. Wenonah remained a residential community supported by employment in Camden and Philadelphia and largely dependent upon Woodbury stores and services. (See Figure 12.)

Almonesson was a smaller settlement (originally called Lambtown) in Deptford Township which developed during the 19th Century at a mill dam where power was used to grind flour or manufacture cotton. In the 1880's it was a typical rural hamlet of some 60 to 70 inhabitants with grist mill, store, blacksmith, wheelwright, post office, and a church, but without rail service.[52] Such centers could only exist to serve farmers within one or two miles. Woodbury, only three miles away by direct road, could provide goods not sold in the general store and more specialized services beyond the scope of the local smithy and wheel shop.

In the Burlington study area, it is possible to see the influence of long-distance transportation upon industrial and residential development in Burlington City, Bordentown, Mt. Holly, and the smaller settlements with early rail connections along the route of the Camden and Amboy line and the Delaware River and, at the same time, to discern the pattern of central services evolving into a three-level hierarchy serving rural people in the agricultural hinterlands of the big cities. Burlington grew steadily to 6,090 in 1880 and was enjoying a "healthy trade with the surrounding country in New Jersey and Pennsylvania...," serving as "a shipping-point for large quantities of produce and manufactured goods of various kinds."[53] Bordentown, which had been established as a Borough in 1825, prospered for a time in its role as the junction of river canal and rail transport, but suffered severe retrenchment after withdrawal of the railroad repair shops were closed, the canal traffic declined in the latter 19th Century. Bordentown was re-established a city in 1867, but its population of about 4,000 remained stable. Meanwhile, the development in Mt. Holly gained impetus, despite the conservatism of the inhabitants and the lag in transportation improvements. In this same period several smaller settlements between these three towns were developing into villages or hamlets and assuming their roles in the hierarchy of central places.

Mt. Holly, chosen to be the county seat just before the start of the century, had not experienced much population growth by the 1830's, when Gordon described it, although the number and variety of businesses had increased.

"Mt. Holly, 20 miles, n.e. from the city of Camden, 6 miles s.e. from Burlington, 21 miles from Trenton... At the period of the revolutionary war,

---

[52]Thomas Cushing and C. E. Sheppard, Op. cit., p. 198.

[53]E. M. Woodward and John F. Hageman, Op. cit., p. 123.

the town contained 200 dwellings, and at present, 1833, has not more than 230, ... erected on 7 streets. It contains a courthouse of brick, ... a stone prison, 1 Episcopal, 1 Methodist, 1 Baptist Church, and 2 Quaker meetinghouses; 1 boarding school for young ladies, 4 day schools, 5 taverns, 8 stores, 1 grist mill, a paper mill... A bank was established here in 1816... There run from the village 2 stages twice a day to Burlington... and 6 others... There are two newspapers printed there weekly."[54]

Due to the fact that Mt. Holly remained nominally a township and was never separately incorporated as a borough or city, it is not possible to trace the population growth accurately in the 19th Century; but it would appear that its rise as a center of settlement is reflected in the increase of population in Northampton Township (containing Mt. Holly) from about 3,000 in 1850 to over 4,630 in 1880. It is clear that it was gaining rapidly as a business center during the mid-19th Century, despite contemporary adverse judgment of municipal leadership.

"MT. HOLLY IN 1882. -- This pleasantly-situated town, ... has chosen rather to stand idly by and remain a quiet looker-on... Conservatism has held sway... The county buildings have had their influence, and the Pennsylvania Railroad has done its share towards making the town as large as it is.

"The streets are probably in about the same condition they were one hundred and fifty years ago, only there are a few more of them, and all strangers to improvement, except that portion of Main Street, ... which was paved in 1882."

"An improvement has, however, been made in the number of business-places... In 1800 there were but three stores, and two or three small shops not yet dignified by the title of 'store,' and four or five taverns.

"At the beginning of 1882 there were nearly or quite two hundred places of business of different kinds, some of which we herewith give: There are seven churches, three national banks, two water-wheel manufactories, thread-mill, one creamery..., two dealers in agricultural implements... four bakeries, six barber shops, six blacksmiths...; three carpenters and builders...; one cooper ...; two dentists...; four drug stores...; twenty-four grocery, ten notions, and seven dry-goods stores, two book-stores...; [12] shoe stores, and shoemakers, three carpet-weavers, five cigar stores, two billiard and pool-rooms, seven meat markets, three clothing stores... three coal and wood dealers, six dressmakers, two flour and feed stores, one fruit dealer, two furniture stores and undertakers ...; one gents' furnishing store, two hardward stores, one hat and cap store...; two music stores, two painters, eight physicians...; two plumbers, steam and gasfitters, one produce and commission merchant, one artist...; two harness shops; two saw and planning mills...; one veterinary surgeon...; three jewelry stores...; shoe factory; there was also one liquor store, telegraph office, soap and candle factory, sash and blind factory, six saloons, two tailors, three stove and tin stores, one auction and sales room, several real estate and insurance agents, [one insurance company] , three newspapers, one gristmill, express company, railroad depot, and several other places of business, [including] a fruit canning establishment... and the match factory..., each of which employ a large number of workmen." [Three hotels are kept in Mt. Holly.] [55]

---

[54]Thomas F. Gordon, Op. cit., p. 187.

[55]E. M. Woodward and John F. Hageman, Op. cit., pp. 223-224.

Meanwhile, increments occurred at Columbus, a pre-revolutionary hamlet which had grown up around the site of the Black Horse tavern on the old road from Burlington to Wrightstown, now intersected by the Bordentown-Vincentown road. In 1834 Gordon described it thus:

"Columbus, or Black Horse...7 miles N. E. of Mt. Holly; 5 S. E. from Bordentown ...contains a tavern, store, and about 30 dwellings,..."[56]

In the 1880's the revolution in retail trade as well as in transportation and in agriculture was evident.

"COLUMBUS is the principal village in Mansfield Township ...and on the line of the Kinkora Branch of the Pennsylvania Railroad...contains two steam-mills, one of the largest canning establishments in the country, four large stores, a drug store, a seminary, the usual variety of mechanics' shops i.e., blacksmiths and wheelwrights , a public library, four churches."[57]

Columbus at this time had a population of 750.[58] There was further growth of business enterprises, e.g., a bank and other services, but Columbus always remained an unincorporated village and served mainly rural people within a radius of three or four miles.

On the other hand, Bustleton in Florence Township, failed to attract population in the 19th Century, losing its post office and retaining only the religious function, albeit with a change of denomination. Compare the description of Bustleton in 1834 with that of 1883. The latter description is still applicable today.

"Bustleton. -- hamlet...7 miles n.w. from Mt. Holly and 4 from Burlington City; in 1834 contains a Friends meetinghouse, and some half dozen farmhouses,..."[59]

"BUSTLETON. -- This is a neighborhood of not more than half a dozen houses in 1883 ...Years ago, in the days of staging over the Old York Road, it was at times the scene of considerable activity. A post office was formerly located there. Here is the Providence Presbyterian Church."[60]

Not all hamlets suffered such stagnation in the 19th Century. The development of Three Tuns (now Hedding), about two and a half miles northeast, along the same ancient road from Burlington to Crosswicks is more typical of hamlets in those days. It was described thus in 1883:

---

[56] Thomas F. Gordon, Op. cit., p. 123.

[57] E. M. Woodward and John F. Hageman, Op. cit., pp. 354-355.

[58] Population count from Table III, Tenth Census of the United States, 1883.

[59] Thomas F. Gordon, Op. cit., p. 113.

[60] E. M. Woodward and John F. Hageman, Op. cit., pp. 330-331.

"THREE TUNS is the somewhat odd name of a hamlet...in the northwest part of [Mansfield Township]. It is said that a hotel there formerly bore the sign of three tuns or casks, whence the appallation. It contains one wheelwright and two blacksmith shops, a Methodist Church, and several dwellings."[61]

The census record of June 1, 1880, shows that there were 12 dwellings inhabited by 48 persons in Three Tuns at that time.[62] By the mid-20th Century (1962) there were some 40 residences and an estimated population of 140 to 150 in Hedding, but its role as service center had become vestigial.

The lack of growth impetus in the hamlets of Bustleton and Hedding can be ascribed not only to the disappearance of the stage traffic on the Old York Road in the early 19th Century after construction of the Bordentown and Amboy Turnpike and the fact that the Camden and Amboy Railroad passed them by one or two miles to the north. The depots on the line at Kinkora and Florence Station soon became the starting points for new hamlets.

The township's largest nucleus of population nearby in 1880 was Florence "City" on the high bank of the Delaware River. A village of some 190 dwellings, occupied by more than 800 people, had grown up here, beginning in 1849 when lots and streets were laid out and a wharf built to provide steamboat service to Philadelphia.

"Being but an hour's ride by rail from Philadelphia, Florence soon came to be sought as a place of residence by gentlemen doing business in the city, who were attracted by its beautiful and healthful location, and the promise that it would speedily become a pretty village of country-houses."[63]

But Florence did not grow and it remained for the iron foundry, which was established in 1857 and later purchased by R. D. Wood and Company, to provide an economic basis for its development as an industrial settlement. A rail siding was extended to the foundry on the lower ground by the river. There were in 1883:

"...six general stores...several churches, the usual number and variety of small mechanic shops, and the Florence Iron-Works..., which afford [ed] employment to a large number of hands...and made it one of the most thrifty and enterprising [places] of its size in this section."[64]

In the early 20th Century another industrial settlement came into existence in Florence Township on the river near Kinkora when the steel wire plant of the John A. Roebling

---

[61]Ibid., p. 355.

[62]"Inhabitants of Mansfield Township, Burlington County," Ms. Schedule No. 1, Tenth Census of the United States, 1880, New Jersey. Rutgers University Library, Special Collections.

[63]E. M. Woodward and John F. Hageman, Op. cit., p. 330.

[64]Ibid., p. 330.

Company was established in 1913. Neither Florence "City" nor Roebling, which was a company-owned town, became separately incorporated municipalities, although their combined population reached 6,785 by 1950.[65]

### The Functional Hierarchy of the Late 18th Century

The particular places in Gloucester and Burlington counties so far mentioned represent three functional levels from the standpoint of business and service: (1) towns, such as Woodbury, Burlington, and Mt. Holly; (2) villages, such as Paulsboro, Columbus, and Florence; and (3) hamlets, such as Almonesson, Bustleton, and Hedding. A systematic survey of all centers of population and business establishments in the New Jersey study areas about 1880 reveals the evolving functional and spatial patterns.

There were then four centers to which the generic term town can be applied, including Bordentown in addition to the three places mentioned above. Population ranged from 2,298 in Woodbury to 6,090 in Burlington, with that of Bordentown and Mt. Holly (Northampton Township) falling between with 4,258 and 4,630, respectively. The few examples of central places in this class in the study areas do not permit reliable determination of mean inter-town distance, but it can be observed that no town existed closer to another than six miles (Burlington-Mt. Holly) and that the maximum distance observed is twelve miles (Bordentown-Mt. Holly). The development of Woodbury does not seem to have been hampered by its location only five miles from the City of Camden.

The outstanding feature of towns developed in the late 19th Century was concentration of (a) specialized retail stores, (b) banking and financial institutions, (c) communication and transportation (d) personal services, and (e) professional services. Business activity was sustained on a daily basis and the weekly farmers' markets and periodic fairs were superseded by other modes of commerce. The Burlington fair had been abolished in the early 19th Century, and when the old town hall, standing in the middle of Union Street at High Street and used for markets until about 1860, was replaced by a new structure no space was provided for produce stalls.[66] By the late 1830's the market shed in the center of Mill Street near Main Street in Mt. Holly had fallen into disuse and was torn down.[67]

Retail trade now loomed large in contrast to the previous century when retailing

---

[65] The population agglomeration of Florence-Roebling was identified and reported as an unincorporated urban place in the United States Census: 1950, Vol. I, Ch. 30, Table 6, Washington, D.C., 1952.

[66] George De Cou, Op. cit., p. 111.

[67] J. D. Scott, New Historical Atlas of Burlington County, New Jersey, Philadelphia, J. D. Scott, 1876, p. 20.

had scarcely existed, apart from the shops of the tradesmen and the public markets, where farmers had sold their produce. General stores now had become the most common kind of retail establishment in the study areas, not only in the towns where there might be half a dozen or more, but in the smaller centers. Such stores handled cloth, hardware, and miscellaneous home and farm supplies as well as staple foods. The increasing volume and variety of retail trade in towns demanded separate grocery stores, meat markets, and other stores, specializing in the following types of goods: drugs, jewelry, books, furniture, hardware, lumber, and building supplies. The development of retail stores among the 19th Century is a correlary of the industrial revolution and the larger flow of money in rural areas.

Banks were a new and important feature of the commercial economy in rural America, but they existed only in the four towns of the New Jersey study areas. In addition insurance companies or insurance agents were beginning to appear in towns.

Communication and transportation facilities, the necessary basis of any central-place development, were concentrated in towns. At least two weekly newspapers were published in each of the three largest towns. Post offices, of course, were to be found in almost every outlying village and hamlet as well as in the towns. Coach lines and livery stables were distinctive features of towns, although stage coaches were suffering severe competition from the faster and more comfortable railroad trains. Thus, rail depots tended to replace the stables and inns as foci of transportation. Old-fashioned inns or taverns had now been remodelled or replaced by larger and more elaborate hotels in the towns. Taverns in the countryside were often converted into stores or were remodelled for dwellings. The ubiquitous general stores now had usurped their former role in communication and social contact.

Services of blacksmiths, wheelwrights, and harness makers were essential for the maintenance and repair of the horse-drawn vehicles of the period and were to be found in every town as well as in almost all the smaller centers; but bakers, tailors, barbers, milliners, and photographers tended to concentrate in towns, where their services were demanded by the well-to-do-residents and where they were accessible to those farmers who could afford their services when they came into town to shop.

The most common professional services available at this time were those of physicians, teachers, and clergymen. Elementary schools, whether supported by private subscription or by public funds, were becoming universal in towns and in the smaller centers and even at open-country crossroads by the 1880's. However, privately-supported secondary schools, then known as academies and seminaries, were to be found only in towns and in the largest villages, and did not yet receive public financial support. Lawyers had become established in every town and were attracted to the county seats in largest numbers.  Physicians were widespread, some having their practices centered in villages.  But hospitals were yet to be created.  Churches of several denominations were now to be found in each town, where it was possible to obtain support for full-time clergy-men more readily than in most villages or hamlets.

Concentration of business activity became a dominant physical fact of the 19th Century urban landscape.  The small 18th Century craft shops and elegant town houses of the wealthy inhabitants along the main streets were now being replaced by store fronts, built as closely as possible to the street and/or sidewalk and extended to the full width of each lot, forming solid commercial frontages.  Business entrepreneurs depended more and more upon prime locations on the principal thoroughfares where wagons and buggies would pass most frequently and where pedestrians congregated in largest numbers.  Thus, one or more streets came to be built up on both sides, forming business districts.  Such business districts grew without the benefit of planning along thoroughfares leading to bridges (Mt. Holly and Woodbury) and turnpike gates or giving access to river landings and rail depots (Burlington and Bordentown).  It was not only permissible but desirable to have the railroad tracks running across a business street, e.g., the Camden and Amboy in Burlington, or to allow a turnpike company to improve the main street, e.g., Woodbury. Courthouses, municipal offices, and schools or churches often mingled with business establishments or clustered close at hand.  The water and steam-driven mills which had flourished during the early 18th Century might still be situated in the heart of town. Closely-built residential streets extended in a compact area around such commercial and industrial centers within walking distance of the business establishments or principal public facilities and places of employment.

The geographic pattern of small central places in the New Jersey study areas[68] is clarified by examination of their spatial relationship to the towns in 1880 (Figs. 12 and 13).  Agglomerations of 50 to 80 households, or about 200 to 720 inhabitants, and 12 to 20 stores and services had developed in places situated 4.5 to 5.0 miles from the nearest towns.  Paulsboro, Columbus, and Rancocas could now be described as villages.  The dozen or more smaller clusters of 10 to 20 households and seldom more than four or five business establishments or services, could be classed as hamlets.  They existed as closely as one to four miles from any town or village or from one another.  The outstand-ing exception to this spatial ordering is Lumberton, which was a village less than 2.5

---

[68]Household counts and location of business establishments or service facilities were made from maps in J. D. Scott, Op. cit., and Everts and Stewart, Combination Atlas Map of Salem and Gloucester Counties, N.J., Philadelphia, Everts and Stewart, 1876.  Population and household counts in certain settlements were taken from the manu-script schedules of New Jersey, Tenth Census of the United States, Rutgers University Library, Special Collections.

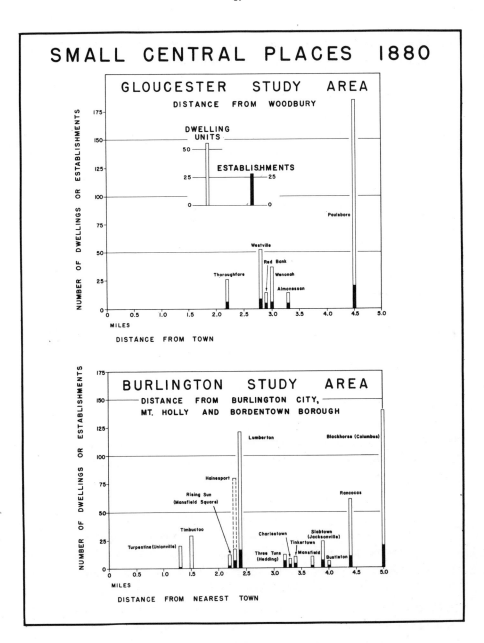

Figure 13.

miles from Mt. Holly on the South Branch of Rancocas Creek. The combined advantages of two intersecting turnpikes, drawing trade from the area southward, and its position at the head of navigation for small freight vessels account for the concentration of population and trade so close to Mt. Holly. Hainesport, an iron manufacturing village with an uncertain number of households (Fig. 13), located still closer to Mt. Holly, is another exception for the general tendency for villages to develop farther from towns than hamlets.

The attraction of a waterway is evident along the Delaware River where settlement was clustering in the 19th Century. Not only was there the industrial village of Florence, previously described, four miles upstream from Burlington, but also the flourishing small town of Beverly, an incorporated city of 1,759 inhabitants in 1880, was located only three miles down the river. Growth of population and trade in Beverly, as well as in the adjacent residential settlements of Delanco and Edgewater Park, was due to the advantage of relatively good transportation for Philadelphia commuters on the main rail line to the Camden ferry and on river steamer directly to the Philadelphia waterfront. Beverly was a poor second to Burlington as a business center, competing for the trade of the agricultural hinterland, although it was the terminus of turnpikes and Dunk's Ferry had provided connection to the Pennsylvania side from Colonial times. The fact that little or no development occurred at the Camden and Amboy rail depots located east of Burlington, i.e., Stevens, Florence Station, and Kinkora, indicates that the existence of rail facilities alone was not sufficient to generate a population agglomeration or service center.

The villages and hamlets situated in the Gloucester study area conform fairly well to the spatial ordering found in the Burlington area. Thoroughfare, Red Bank, and Almonesson, located between 2.0 and 3.5 miles from Woodbury are clearly hamlets, while Wenonah and Westville, respectively located south and north of Woodbury on the main railroad, had acquired larger populations of some 30 to 50 households, but remained hamlets in terms of functional development. Paulsboro, 4.5 miles from Woodbury, was the only well-developed village at that time in the Gloucester study area.

The functional differentiation of villages and hamlets was not strongly marked in 1880. There was a tendency for the villages to provide specialized retailing of drugs, hardware and lumber, secondary education and the services of one or more physicians. A village almost always supported one or more churches and often had acquired facilities such as a township hall or library. In no case had a village become an incorporated municipality, thus gaining territorial separation from the township in order to provide municipal services. Hamlets supported general stores and rudimentary services such as blacksmith and wheelwright shops, grist or saw mills, and elementary schools or churches.

It is possible to ;make some generalizations concerning the hierarchical pattern of centers in the two New Jersey study areas. It can be assumed that the goods sold and services provided in hamlets represent those most frequently in demand by rural people, while the more specialized goods and services concentrated in villages located relatively far from towns. Thus, trips of three or four miles would be required to obtain specialized goods and services. It can also be assumed that towns would attract customers from greater distances than villages because of larger and more numerous establishments of the same types found in villages and more especially because of commodities and services available only in the towns. The proliferation of centers in the 19th Century, together with some key features of functional development and strengthening of travel gradients, stands sharply in contrast to the paucity of centers and slightly developed travel gradients of the 18th Century.

The two Bucks County study areas provide interesting variations of the hierarchical pattern. In Lower Bucks County the Borough of Bristol with 5, 273 inhabitants in 1880 was dominant in the local pattern of trade and services. The only population agglomerations[69] in Bristol Township within a radius of five miles were the hamlets of Newportville on Neshaminy Creek and Tullytown on the Pennsylvania Railroad. In Falls Township the ancient village of Fallsington, which grew up around the Quaker meetinghouse, had a population of 320. Another center was the roadside hamlet of Oxford Valley. No other significant centers of agglomeration were to be found in the vicinity aside from Morrisville, a small and rapidly growing municipality of 968 (Fig. 10, B), which had a minor role as a trade center. Trenton, New Jersey, at the end of the toll bridge opposite Morrisville, greatly overshadowed the latter place and was beginning to contribute to its growth as a residential settlement. Langhorne, situated in Middletown Township at an intersection of main roads seven miles from Bristol and nine miles from Trenton, was now a functional village and in 1880 incorporated as a municipality of 558 inhabitants. The old mill village of Hulmeville on Neshaminy Creek had 378 inhabitants, while Attleboro (later called Penndel) was little more than a depot on the Reading Railroad. It is worthy of note that these small centers formed a cluster within a mile and one half of each other in territory four or five miles from Bristol on the south and Newtown, population 1, 001, on the north (outside the boundary of the study area). Bensalem Township exhibited the weakest agglomerating tendencies in 1880, there being only three small residential settlements in the extreme south along the main line of the Pennsylvania Railroad.

In Middle Bucks County the two functional towns, Doylestown Borough with

---

[69]All population counts in the Bucks County study areas are taken from Table III, Statistics of the Population of the United States at the Tenth Census, June 1, 1880, Washington, D. C. , 1883.

2,070 inhabitants and New Hope Borough with 1,152 and located ten miles apart, were dominant in local trade and services. Doylestown had been increasing steadily in population and business activity since the beginning of the 19th Century (Fig. 10 A), while New Hope had failed to grow after 1850 (Fig. 10 C). The stagnation of New Hope was accompanied by the rise of Lambertville, N. J., situated just across a bridge over the Delaware River and provided with rail connections, a distinction which had not been achieved by New Hope or any place in Middle Bucks County, excepting Doylestown. Meanwhile 15 hamlets had grown up in Buckingham and Solebury Townships (Fig. 12), spaced at intervals of one or two miles from one another and, at most, three miles from the above-mentioned towns. Thus, there was a much closer pattern of small centers in Middle Bucks County as compared with the other study areas, perhaps reflecting the lesser degree of influence from any large town like Bristol or Burlington and the difficulty of local travel in the hill terrain on less well improved roads in the early 19th Century when hamlet formation was most active. Perhaps it was the proliferation of small centers at close intervals which hampered the growth of any one place above the hamlet level. Only Carversville on the northwestern border of Solebury Township is reported to have had more than 100 inhabitants in 1880. Typical hamlets had 20 to 80 inhabitants and provided only rudimentary goods and services. Such centers supplemented rather than impeded the functions of Doylestown.

The spatial pattern is developed without general planning or policy decisions. It is the outcome of innumerable choices made by entrepreneurs and their customers and patrons. The functional hierarchy, which had appeared in the study areas during the 19th Century, bears a fundamental resemblance to the hierarchy of rural service centers previously described by the senior author in his analysis of southwestern Wisconsin during the mid-20th Century.[70] Differences in types and grouping of functional units would be expected on account of the lapse of 80 years, bringing many technological and economic changes. Studies by Bracey in southern England suggests that a similar pattern is basic in two widely separated regions with unlike population density and economic history.[71] Evidence available from many other studies has lent support to the theory of hierarchical patterns of spatial and functional development in all commercial agricultural areas, as noted in the introductory chapter.

However, the radius of travel to the most rudimentary centers appears to be

---

[70] John E. Brush, "The Hierarchy of Central Places in Southwestern Wisconsin," Geographical Review, Vol. 43, No. 3, 1953, pp. 480-502.

[71] John E. Brush and Howard E. Bracey, "Rural Service Centers in Southwestern Wisconsin and Southern England," Geographical Review, Vol. 45, No. 4, 1955, pp. 559-569.

# TABLE 1

## EVOLUTION OF HAMLET AND VILLAGE FUNCTIONS: CENTRAL BUCKS COUNTY

| | 1700 | 1711 | 1750 | 1800 | 1832 | 1850 | 1876 | 1891 | 1900 | 1914 | 1936 | 1950 | 1962 |
|---|---|---|---|---|---|---|---|---|---|---|---|---|---|
| **MANUFACTURING INDUSTRIES** | | | | | | | | | | | | | |
| Grist Mill | | | | 2 | 5 | 6 | 5 | 1 | 1 | 1 | | | |
| Saw Mill | | | | 1 | | 3 | 3 | | 3 | 1 | | | |
| Carriage or Wagon Shop | | | | | | | 1 | ? | 4 | 4 | | | |
| Creamery | | | | | | 1 | | | 2 | | | | |
| Other Food Mfg. | | | | | | | | | | | | | 3 |
| **TRANSPORTATION AND COMMUNICATION SERVICES** | | | | | | | | | | | | | |
| Post Office | | | | 1 | 5 | 3 | 12 | 17 | 19 | | 13 | 13 | |
| Ferry or Bridge | | | | 1 | 2 | 2 | 2 | 2 | 2 | 2 | 2 | 2 | 2 |
| Turnpike Toll Station | | | | | | | 3 | 4 | | | | | |
| Railroad Station | | | | | | | | | 2 | 2 | 2 | 2 | 2 |
| **RETAIL STORES** | | | | | | | | | | | | | |
| General Store | | | | 1 | 6 | 19 | 20 | 15 | 20 | 15 | 12 | | 12 |
| Lumber & Coal | | | | | | | 1 | 1 | 2 | 2 | 2 | 2 | 2 |
| Feed & Grain | | | | | | | | | | 4 | 1 | | 1 |
| Hardware | | | | | | | | | | 2 | 2 | | 2 |
| Butcher | | | | | | | | | | 8 | 4 | | 3 |
| Grocery Store | | | | | | | | | | | 2 | | 2 |
| Eating & Drinking Place | | | | | | | | | | | 4 | | 10 |
| Gasoline Filling Station | | | | | | | | | | | 2 | | 6 |
| Antique or Art Dealer | | | | | | | | | | | 2 | | 26 |
| Apparel Shop | | | | | | | | | | | | | 2 |
| **PERSONAL AND REPAIR SERVICES AND MISCELLANEOUS** | | | | | | | | | | | | | |
| Tavern-inn, Hotel | | | | 5 | 9 | 12 | 12 | 9 | 11 | | 7 | | 6 |
| Blacksmith and or Wheelwright Shop | | | | | 10 | 16 | 24 | 21 | 14 | 1 | 2 | | |
| Automobile Repair Shop | | | | | | | | | | 1 | 3 | | 4 |
| Barber or Beauty Shop | | | | | | | | | | | 2 | | 5 |
| Upholstery Shop | | | | | | | | | | | | | 2 |
| Realtor | | | | | | | | | | | 2 | | 3 |
| **PROFESSIONAL AND PUBLIC SERVICES** | | | | | | | | | | | | | |
| Physician | | | | | 1 | 5 | 2 | 3 | 7 | | 4 | | 2 |
| Church or Quaker Meetinghouse | | | | | 2 | 8 | 10 | 10 | 10 | | 12 | 13 | |
| Elementary School (Private and Public) | | | | ? | | 2 | 4 | 2 | 3 | | | 1 | |
| Volunteer Fire Company | | | | | | | | | | | 1 | | 3 |

Explanation: 1832 — year for which existence of function is reported. Data are reported for 23 agglomerated settlements in 1876 or earlier and for 26 settlements thereafter. Bold face numbers indicate that the number of establishments exceeds half the number of settlements then existing.

━━━ Indicates function in more than half of the settlements then existing.

─── Indicates probable appearance or disappearance of function between dates.

── Indicates existence of function between dates.

Source: Bernard P. Geizer, "Central Places of Central Bucks County, Pennsylvania," Unpubl. M. A. Thesis, Rutgers University Library, New Brunswick, N. J., 1963

significantly less in the New Jersey and Pennsylvania study areas than in southwestern Wisconsin or southern England. The spacing of hamlets at a mean distance of five to six miles in the Wisconsin study area and of service villages at about the same distance in England[72] permits the inference that the maximum radius of frequent travel to such center is 2.5 to 3.0 miles. The spacing of small centers in 1880 in the New Jersey and Pennsylvania study areas is much closer, suggesting that travel conditions and consumer preferences favored trips not more than 1.5 or 2.0 miles. Investigation by the senior author in southwestern Wisconsin has not revealed any closer pattern of spacing during the 19th Century,[73] but it is possible that study of the evolution of central-place hierarchies in England and other regions with long settlement histories and greater population densities than the Wisconsin study area will reveal periods when closer spacing prevailed.

### The Evolution of Service Centers: 19th to 20th Centuries

By the mid-20th Century the rise of income, decentralization of population and use of private automobiles had altered patterns of consumer interaction almost beyond recognition. Yet in the first two decades of the 20th Century, when railroads were still the dominant mode of long-distance transportation, much local movement still depended upon horse-drawn vehicles. Strong centripetal tendencies were still evident in the pattern of population growth and central places, both large and small continued to be maintained by local trade until the decade of the 1920's. In Lower Bucks County and the New Jersey study areas electric trolleys were important means of passenger travel for two or three decades, ending about 1930. The trolley lines formed a network, linking the rural towns on the metropolitan fringe and the numerous residential suburbs now rapidly developing with the major cities. It was not until the 1940's and 1950's that the spread of paved roads and the impact of the automobile on consumer behavior became fully evident. In the decade of the 1960's the diffuse settlement pattern of the metropolitan fringe is to be observed alongside the old pattern. As urban sprawl has encroached, the larger towns and their service areas continue to exist, although not without severe problems of obsolescence and competition from new shopping centers. Meanwhile, most of the villages and hamlets are being transformed into residential settlements, still identifiable in the metropolitan landscape as "fossils" of the previous

---

[72]Howard E. Bracey, "English Central Villages," Proc. International Geographical Union Symposium in Urban Geography, Lund, 1960, Ed. by Knut Norberg, Lund, Sweden (D.W.K. Gleerup), 1962, pp. 169-90.

[73]John E. Brush, "The Trade Centers of Southwestern Wisconsin: An Analysis of Function and Location," Unpublished Ph.D. Dissertation, University of Wisconsin Library, 1952.

53

agricultural era.

Thanks to Geizer's analysis of central places in Bucks County, it is possible to trace the evolution of some 19th Century settlements on the outer metropolitan fringe during this period of change. [74] Summaries of the records of business establishments and services of all types, derived from his studies of Doylestown, New Hope, and some 20 small settlements in Central Bucks County[75] are examined briefly here in order to show the impact of technological and economic changes. The analysis of current relationships of old and new service centers is to be found in the ensuing chapters.

Looking first at the evolution of hamlets and villages (Table 1), it is clear that the small centers had their greatest development during the late 19th Century. In 1876 and 1891 nearly every place had a general store, which, in most instances contained the local post office. Almost all had blacksmith or wheelwright shops. Taverns, grist mills and other local industries still existed at that time, while schools and churches were being acquired. Physicians had come to a few of these small centers, but specialized types of retail trade or personal services were extremely rare. After the turn of the century various types of retail trade appeared, but none except the sale of antiques could be described as ubiquitous in 1962. Local mills were abandoned and processing industries all but disappeared after World War I. After the Great Depression (1936) almost all other types of business disappeared or declined. Today general stores, selling foods principally, and post offices survive in a majority of the centers, while the local religious function is increasing slowly. Thus, villages and hamlets on the outer metropolitan fringe persist as service centers, probably because of the fact that they have viability as residential settlements with slowly increasing population and hence some local demand for the convenience of a food store, post office, and church. Gasoline stations and especially antique shops are concentrated in those places, which are located on main highways, easily accessible to transient travellers.

The decline of population in rural territorial units, e.g., Buckingham and Solebury townships (Fig. 11 A) is a general phenomenon of all the study areas in the late 19th and early 20th Centuries, resulting from diminishing farm labor force and sharply increasing urban employment opportunities. Hamlets and villages undoubtedly suffered loss of business due to the population losses in their trading areas, beginning

---

[74]Bernard P. Geizer, "Central Places of Central Bucks County, Pennsylvania: Their Evolution and Classification," Unpublished M. A. Thesis, Rutgers--The State University, 1963.

[75]Geizer has included in his Central Bucks study area Warrington Township to the east, in addition to Doylestown and New Hope boroughs and Buckingham and Solebury townships.

the middle of the 19th Century. Yet these centers maintained themselves and, in some instances, gained population until the early 20th Century. The most marked decline of their function as central places occurred in the 1930's and 40's when the rural population trend had been reversed and there was a rising demand for goods and services in the outer metropolitan fringe.

Therefore, it seems clear that the transportation revolution is the principal cause for decline of small centers in Bucks County and elsewhere in the rural hinterland of Philadelphia. The declining economic and social role of Lahaska in Middle Bucks County is put vividly by Walter Teller, who describes the change from the point of view of a local resident, as follows:

"When, in 1874, Lahaska became a postal address, it comprised, in addition to fifteen houses clustered around the [road] intersections, a store, hotel, coach factory and scythe and axe works...While perhaps a slightly greater number of persons live here now than ever before, there are those who find the village increasingly lonesome, and perhaps for that very reason. 'People used to stay home more,' Robert Johnson,...clerk of the general store, explained, 'sort of stick together more and help each other out, but now it's everybody off for himself in his car. They come in here and almost knock you down to get a loaf of bread and run right out to the car again. To hook up a horse and go to Doylestown or New Hope or one of those places used to take half a day. It was quite an undertaking. Now they ride down in six or seven minutes and don't think nothing of it. When people came here they generally stayed and chewed the rag a while.'"[76]

The diminished economic role of small centers, such as Lahaska, was compensated by the rise of Doylestown, where many of the requirements and amenities of 20th-Century America became accessible to the farming and "exurban" people of Middle Bucks County. In Teller's words:

"If you live in Lahaska, then Doylestown is where you are like to shop, collect green stamps, eat out, and scatter the years of your prime. Doylestown is where you go to be x-rayed, hospitalized, buy a record, a cigar, cash a check, borrow books, tell the judge, have the car washed or greased or inspected. It is where you face the utility companies, pay on the mortgage, insure the title, pick up airline tickets, go to the movie, to jail or a meeting, register for Selective Service, wait for a haircut, have eyes examined, glasses adjusted, teeth cleaned and drilled and, if more than twenty-one, or look it, step up to the counter of the State Liquor Store. You buy The New York Times in Doylestown, chicken feed and the usual hardward, installment-plan furniture, costume jewelry, standard baked goods, and shoes if your feet are not narrow. You can board a train bound for Philadelphia, hear a tip on the market, have a toaster repaired or a tube replaced—in fact, get whatever is easy to get."[77]

---

[76]Walter Teller, Area Code 215: A Private Line in Bucks County, New York: Athenium, 1963, pp. 25, 26.

[77]Ibid., pp. 75, 76.

TABLE 2

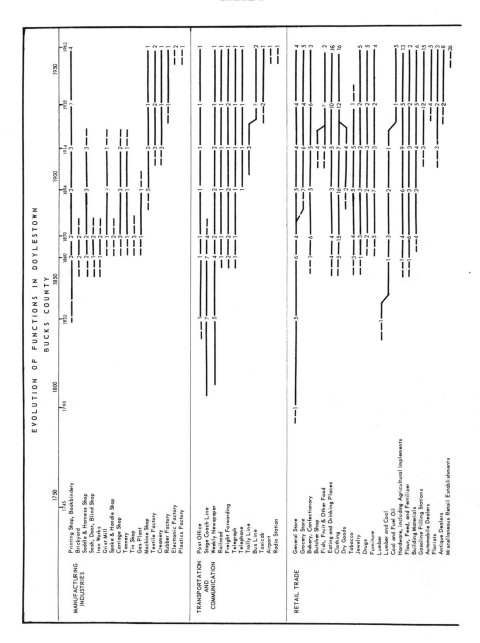

TABLE 2--Continued

56

| PERSONAL AND REPAIR SERVICES | Tavern, Inn, Hotel | 1 —— 2 —— 6 —— 6 —— 6 —— 4 —— 4 —— 2 —— 2 |
| | Rooming House | —— 3 —— ? —— 2 |
| | Blacksmith and/or Wheelwright Shop | —— 1 —— 2 —— 3 —— 5 —— 4 —— 7— |
| | Livery Stable | —— 2 —— 3 —— 4 —— 4 — |
| | Tailor | —— 1 —— 2 —— 2 —— 3 —— 2 —— 2 |
| | Barber, Beautician | —— ? —— ?— —— ? —— ? —— 3 —— 12 |
| | Laundry, Dry Cleaner | —— 3 —— 7 |
| | Undertaker | —— 2 —— 2 —— 2 —— 3 —— 2 —— 2 |
| | Photographer, Artist | —— 3 —— 3 —— 3 —— 3 —— 2 —— 2 |
| | Upholstery Shop | —— 1 —— 3 |
| | Shoe Repair Shop | —— 1 —— 1 —— 1 |
| | Auto Repair Shop | —— 1 —— 6 |
| | Car Wash | —— 3 —— 1 |
| | Miscellaneous Repair | —— 2 —— 9 |

| AMUSEMENTS | Movie Theater | —— 1 —— 1 |
| | Bowling Alley | —— 1 |

| FINANCE AND INSURANCE | Bank | —— 1 —— 1 —— 2 —— 3 —— 3 —— 1 —— 2 |
| | Insurance, Investment Agency | —— 3 —— 3 —— ? —— ? —— 4 —— 9 |
| | Credit Agency | —— 1 —— ? —— 4 |
| | Realtor | —— 1 —— 2 —— 3 —— 3 —— 2 —— 15 |

| PROFESSIONAL SERVICES | Physician | —— 1 —— ? —— 2 — 7 —— 7 —— 11 —— 14 —— 30 |
| | Dentist | —— 3 —— 5 —— 2 —— 5 —— 12 |
| | Veterinarian | —— 3 —— ? —— 2 —— 1 |
| | Hospital | —— 1 —— 1 |
| | Lawyer, Attorney | —— ? — ? —— ? —— ? —— 20 —— 36 |
| | Certified Public Accountant | —— 1 —— 1 —— 1 —— 3 |
| | Architect | —— 1 —— 1 —— 2 —— 2 |
| | Management Consultant | —— 1 |
| | Church | —— 1 —— 4 — 7 —— 8 —— 9 —— 10 —— 13 |

| PUBLIC AND GOVERNMENTAL SERVICES | County Court & Prison | —— 1 —— 1 —— 1 —— 1 —— 1 —— 1 |
| | Elementary School (Public) | —— 1 —— 1 —— 1 —— 1 —— 1 —— 1 |
| | Secondary School (Public) | —— 1 —— 1 —— 1 —— 1 —— 1 |
| | Private School | —— 1 —— 2 — 3 —— ? —— 3 —— ? —— 5 |
| | College | —— 1 —— 1 —— 1 |
| | Library | —— 1 —— 1 —— 1 —— 1 —— 1 |
| | Historical Society | —— 1 —— 1 —— 1 |
| | Museum | —— 1 —— 1 |
| | Borough Government | —— 1 —— 1 —— 1 —— 1 —— 1 —— 1 |

Explanation: 1832 -- year for which existence of functions is reported; number of establishments.

—— — — —— Indicates probable appearance or disappearance of function between dates.    ———————— Indicates existence of function between dates.

Source: Modified from Bernard P. Geizer, "Central Places of Central Bucks County, Pennsylvania". Unpubl. M. A. Thesis, Rutgers University Library, New Brunswick, N. J., 1963.

Doylestown is a prime example of a central place in which the supplying of goods and services is the basic economic activity. It has been a thriving settlement with steadily increasing population ever since its incorporation as a municipality in 1838 (Fig. 10 A). Manufacturing employment has never been an important factor in Doylestown's growth, although small industries did exist in the 19th Century to supply certain local demands, and there are today a few light industries, attracted by local labor supply and low overhead costs rather than local markets. Doylestown's role as a county seat is important, but it is only one of the large variety of functions. The parallel increases in concentration of retail stores, transportation and communication services, personal and repair services, professional services and public or quasi-public facilities (Table 2) bear out the descriptive passage quoted above. Blacksmithing and wheelwrighting shops, livery stables, stagecoaches, and other appurtenances of transportation in the 19th Century have been replaced by auto repair shops, filling stations, bus lines, and taxicabs. Retail trade has been maintained, while undergoing changes due to new types of commodities and business reorganization. Finance, insurance, and real estate business has a strong role and all essential professional services show increasing concentration. Doylestown is well supplied with physicians, dentists, and lawyers and is served by both public and private schools, in addition to having a hospital, a college, a library, an historical society with a small museum of local artifacts, chiefly old agricultural tools, furniture, and transportation equipment. The transportation revolution has enlarged Doylestown's service area, enabling consumers living at distances of five to ten miles to increase the frequency of their trips. Doylestown's outreach eight or ten miles into territory westward and northward is not hampered by competing centers. Even New Hope has felt the inroads of Doylestown in the local trade of adjacent Solebury Township.[78]

The loss of New Hope's early preeminence in the manufacturing and trade of Middle Bucks County is reflected in the functional changes recorded during the past 100 years or more (Table 3). In the mid-19th Century New Hope mills were still using the water power of Aquetong Creek and coal barge traffic on the Delaware Canal was reaching its maximum volume. There had been a bridge over the Delaware since 1816, replacing Coryell's ferry. Construction of the outlet lock on the canal in 1854 enabled barges to cross the river and enter the Delaware and Raritan Feeder Canal, thus making New Hope the only point where all barges had to pass and the only place where tolls were collected on the Pennsylvania side. Thus, in the 1860's when traffic converged on New Hope by

---

[78]A Comprehensive Plan for New Hope Borough, Part I--Community Analysis, New Hope Borough Planning Commission and Bucks County Planning Commission, May 1962, Mimeographed Report, pp. 25-26.

road and canal, its population as well as the number and variety of its stores and services nearly equalled Doylestown's. But the following decades were to witness the aban-
donment of all of New Hope's industries except paper manufacturing and the decline and
disappearance of coal traffic.

New Hope became a stagnant center by the early 20th Century and was to remain so until the decade of the 1930's when the natural beauty of the area began to
attract professional artists, writers, and a few "exurban" commuters from New York
and Philadelphia suburbs. The Bucks County Playhouse was established in the Borough
in 1939, and a small summer trade of theatre devotees began. The archaic quality of
New Hope's dwellings and shops now came to be an advantage to city people looking for
old-fashioned rural surroundings. In the period since World War II, New Hope gained
in fame but nothing in population. Tourists and transient shoppers crowd the streets,
but few stay overnight. They support the summer theatre, numerous art exhibits, and
an unusual concentration of antique and gift shops. Thus, the role of New Hope has
shifted largely to specialized types of trade and recreation drawing patrons from near
and distant parts of metropolitan Pennsylvania, New Jersey, and even New York.
Traffic congestion and preponderance of stores catering to tourists now cause increasing
numbers of local consumers to seek satisfaction of their needs elsewhere.[79]  Much of
the local trade has been lost to Doylestown or to Lambertville, situated at the other end
of the toll-free bridge.

A full analysis of changes in the functions of centers in the other three study
areas undoubtedly would reveal much the same basic evolution as shown in Middle Bucks
County. Large towns, i.e., Burlington, Mt. Holly, and Woodbury, which have had continued population growth, have gained much in retail trade and in financial, personal,
and professional service during the past 70 or 80 years. Most of the functional units
lost by towns during this time period are those types which have become obsolete,
especially in transportation and repair services, or uneconomic as in certain methods
of manufacturing and retailing. In contrast, the stagnation or decline of retail sales
and services in the smaller centers is evident generally and has not been counterbalanced
by the growth of tourism as in the case of New Hope. However, almost all of the 19th-
Century centers are still identifiable as settlement units, and many persist in some
manner as service centers.

During the same time period population growth on the inner metropolitan
fringe has increased the demand for goods and services. Prior to 1930 most of the
growth was concentrated near railroads and trolleys, following a linear geographic

---

[79]Ibid., p. 27.

TABLE 3

EVOLUTION OF FUNCTIONS IN NEW HOPE
BUCKS COUNTY

1700  1750  1800 1798  1832  1850  1860  1871  1894 1900  1914  1936  1950 1962

**MANUFACTURING INDUSTRIES**

Iron Forge and Mill
Fulling Mill
Grist Mill
Saw Mill
Copper
Hatter
Textile Mill
Soap Maker
Agricultural Implement Maker
Carriage Shop
Harness Shop
Paint Shop
Boot Builder
Boot & Shoe Shop
Foundry
Paper Mill
Printing Shop

**TRANSPORTATION AND COMMUNICATION SERVICES**

Ferry
Bridge
Post Office
Canal
Turnpike
Telegraph
Livery Stable
Railroad
Telephone
Bus Line
Forwarding Agent

**RETAIL STORES**

General Store
Grocery Store
Confectionary Shop
Butcher Shop
Eating and Drinking Places
Lumber Yard
Lumber and Coal Yard
Coal & Fuel Oil Dealer
Hardware & Implement Store
Clothing
Dry Goods and Notions
Tobacco Shop
Drug Store
Jewelry Store
Gasoline Filling Station
Antique Shop
Automobile Dealer
Furniture Store
Miscellaneous Retail Stores

## TABLE 3--Continued

**FINANCE AND INSURANCE SERVICES**
- Bank
- Building and Loan Association
- Insurance Agency
- Advertising Agency
- Realtor

**PERSONAL AND REPAIR SERVICES**
- Tavern, Hotel, Motel
- Rooming House
- Blacksmith and/or Wheelwright Shop
- Shoemaker
- Tailor
- Barber or Beauty Shop
- Undertaker
- Stage Playhouse
- Photographer, Artist
- Secretarial Service
- Cleaner, Laundry
- Auto Repair
- Miscellaneous Repair

**PROFESSIONAL SERVICES**
- Physician
- Dentist
- Veterinarian
- Lawyer
- Engineer, Architect
- Church

**PUBLIC SERVICES & GOVERNMENTAL SERVICES**
- Fire Company
- Free Library
- Township, Borough Hall (After 1837)
- Elementary School
- Secondary School

Explanation: 1832 -- year for which existence of functions is reported; number of establishments.

------ Indicates probable appearance or disappearance of function between dates.

——— Indicates existence of function between dates.

Source: Modified from Bernard P. Geizer, "Central Places of Central Bucks County, Pennsylvania", Unpubl. M. A. Thesis, Rutgers University Library, New Brunswick, N. J., 1963.

pattern and resulting in the creation of little residential boroughs in order to provide municipal services which were not supported by townships. Such small population agglomerations, whether separately incorporated or not, seldom acquired significant roles as local service centers, and the inhabitants remained dependent upon the existing towns and major cities. With the exception of Westville and Paulsboro, none of the new municipalities created after 1880 exceeded 2,500 inhabitants until 1960. (See Fig. 10 C & D) After 1930 many of the townships in the four study areas began to show some population gains (Fig. 11) and after World War II the gains became abrupt, especially in Lower Bucks County, where Falls, Middletown, and Bristol increased some 300 to 800 per cent between 1950 and '60 as a result of the enormous house construction enterprise of Levitt & Sons. In Willingboro Township, Burlington County, population gain in the same decade amounted to 1,300 per cent due to same circumstance. Doubling of population occurred in many other townships and in some of the small boroughs during the past decade. (See Table 4).

In no instance has this wave of settlement resulted in the formation of a new municipality in the four study areas. The need to extend streets and water systems, to construct sewage disposal plants and schools, and to provide police, fire, and ambulance protection has been met in part, and sometimes inadequately, through various private and municipal or special public district arrangements. It is not the objective of the writers to analyze the requirements and existing patterns of public or quasi-public services in the study areas.

Shopping centers and highway-oriented business places have developed to serve the needs of newcomers no longer willing or able to find their way to the long-established business centers. Here are circumstances most disturbing to government officials and business entrepreneurs. How can a well-developed town such as Woodbury maintain or regain its place in the trade of Gloucester County? Is it the fate of Bristol, Burlington, and Mt. Holly to become urban slums? Is Doylestown assured of dominance in the future development of Middle Bucks County because of its location somewhat removed from competing centers on the metropolitan fringe? What is the incipient trend of development among the shopping centers in townships with expanding service requirements? The authors address themselves in the next two chapters to clarification of the current locational patterns of retail stores and of financial, personal, and professional services in old and new service centers and to interpretation of the associated consumer interaction.

TABLE 4

POPULATION

MIDDLE BUCKS COUNTY STUDY AREA

| Municipality | Population | |
| --- | --- | --- |
| | 1960 Census | Per Cent Change 1950–1960 |
| Buckingham Township | 4,018 | +34 |
| Doylestown Borough | 5,917 | +12 |
| New Hope Borough | 958 | −10 |
| Solebury Township | 2,972 | +35 |

LOWER BUCKS COUNTY STUDY AREA

| Municipality | Population | |
| --- | --- | --- |
| | 1960 Census | Per Cent Change 1950–1960 |
| Bensalem Township | 23,478 | +107 |
| Bristol Borough | 12,364 | −3 |
| Bristol Township | 59,298 | +387 |
| Falls Township | 29,082 | +822 |
| Hulmeville Borough | 968 | +16 |
| Langhorne Borough | 1,461 | −7 |
| Langhorne Manor Borough | 1,506 | +93 |
| Middletown Township | 26,894 | +438 |
| Morrisville Borough | 7,790 | +15 |
| Penndel Borough | 2,158 | +96 |
| Tullytown Borough | 2,452 | +224 |

BURLINGTON COUNTY STUDY AREA

| Municipality | Population | |
| --- | --- | --- |
| | 1960 Census | Per Cent Change 1950–1960 |
| Beverly City | 3,400 | +10 |
| Bordentown City | 4,973 | −10 |
| Bordentown Township | 5,936 | +192 |
| Burlington City | 12,687 | +5 |
| Burlington Township | 6,291 | +83 |
| Chesterfield Township | 2,519 | +25 |

TABLE 4 (Continued)

POPULATION

BURLINGTON COUNTY STUDY AREA

| Municipality | Population | |
|---|---|---|
| | 1960 Census | Per Cent Change 1950-1960 |
| Delanco Borough | 4,011 | +43 |
| Easthampton Township | 1,402 | +97 |
| Edgewater Park Township | 2,866 | +124 |
| Fieldsboro Borough | 583 | -1 |
| Florence Township | 8,127 | +9 |
| Hainesport Township | 3,271 | +82 |
| Levittown Township | 11,861 | +1,301 |
| Lumberton Township | 2,833 | +114 |
| Mansfield Township | 2,084 | +9 |
| Mount Holly Township | 13,271 | +38 |
| Springfield Township | 1,956 | +25 |
| Westhampton Township | 1,114 | +56 |

GLOUCESTER COUNTY STUDY AREA

| Municipality | Population | |
|---|---|---|
| | 1960 Census | Per Cent Change 1950-1960 |
| Deptford Township | 17,878 | +145 |
| National Park Borough | 3,380 | +40 |
| Paulsboro Borough | 8,121 | +4 |
| Wenonah Borough | 2,100 | +39 |
| West Deptford Township | 11,152 | +105 |
| Westville Borough | 4,951 | +5 |
| Woodbury City | 12,453 | +14 |
| Woodbury Heights Borough | 1,723 | +25 |

Source: U. S. Census of Population: 1960, Vol. 1, Washington, D. C., 1961.

CHAPTER III

ANALYSIS OF SERVICE CENTERS

The objective of this chapter is to analyze the present-day pattern of retail stores and services, first in relation to population distribution and, second, in terms of ranked orders of geographic aggregation. Using data from the Census of Business, it is possible to determine something about the relative local concentration of business activity in certain parts of the study areas. But full and detailed analysis of the study areas depends upon data obtained in field inventory of business establishments. These data, which include the numbers of establishments engaged in various kinds of retail sales or personal and professional services and estimates of size (square footage), are classified in type-of business categories and grouped according to the geographic units employed in the Penn-Jersey Transportation Study in order to relate the results to our subsequent analysis of the travel data collected in the Penn-Jersey Transportation Study.

Concentration of Trade and Services

It is possible to extract certain facts about the concentration of retail trade and services from the Census of Business, [1] which provides the basis for measuring the relative development of nine small cities and boroughs and four townships in the study areas. (See Table 5 and Figure 14.) No data were published in the business census for any municipality not classified as an urban place or considered to be in urban territory. [2]

---

[1] The United States Census of Business: 1958, covers retail trade, wholesale trade and the following services: Personal services, auto repair services, garages, hotels, motels and tourist courts, miscellaneous repair services, motion pictures, amusements and recreational services. (See Footnote, Table 5.)

[2] Urban places, as defined by the Bureau of the Census, include all municipalities and "unincorporated" compact settlements, which have 2,500 or more inhabitants. In New Jersey and Pennsylvania most urban places are cities or boroughs. Townships are also recognized as urban in the census only if they are densely populated. (See United States Census of Population: 1960, Vol. I, Part 32, New Jersey, pp. xvi, xvii.)

TABLE 5

CONCENTRATION OF TRADE AND SERVICES IN SELECTED MUNICIPALITIES:  1958-60

| County and Municipality | 1958 Census of Business[1] | | | 1960 Population Census[2] Employed Persons | Commercial Employment Index[3] |
| --- | --- | --- | --- | --- | --- |
| | Establishments | Sales $1,000's | Proprietors & Employees | | |
| Middle Bucks County | | | | | |
| Doylestown Boro. | 215 | 36,574 | 1,278 | 2,553 | .50 |
| Lower Bucks County | | | | | |
| Bensalem Twp. | 76 | 7,973 | 507 | 8,425 | .06 |
| Bristol Boro. | 365 | 31,126 | 1,396 | 4,782 | .29 |
| Bristol Twp. | 112 | 9,903 | 538 | 18,623 | .03 |
| Falls Twp. | 39 | 9,883 | 447 | 9,721 | .05 |
| Middletown Twp. | 37 | 39,584 | 744 | 3,463 | .21 |
| Morrisville Boro. | 157 | 16,547 | 813 | 3,232 | .25 |
| Burlington County | | | | | |
| Beverly City | 78 | 3,239 | 208 | 1,254 | .17 |
| Bordentown City | 134 | 10,812 | 476 | 2,067 | .23 |
| Burlington City | 311 | 40,894 | 1,225 | 4,820 | .25 |
| Gloucester County | | | | | |
| Paulsboro Boro. | 184 | 11,082 | 755 | 2,901 | .26 |
| Westville Boro. | 105 | 6,943 | 440 | 2,000 | .22 |
| Woodbury City | 317 | 44,040 | 1,782 | 4,855 | .37 |

Sources:   U.S. Census of Business:  1958.  Vols. II, IV, and VI, Washington, D.C., 1961.
U.S. Census of Population:  1960.  Vol. I, Parts 32 and 40, Washington D.C., 1963.

[1] Includes establishments engaged in retail trade, wholesale trade, and selected services; total annual sales or receipts; active proprietors and employees during work week ending November 15, 1958.

[2] Includes all residents who reported employment in any industry or occupation at time of the population census, April, 1960.

[3] The commercial index is obtained by dividing the number of active proprietors and employees (as reported in the Census of Business) by the total resident employed population (as reported in the Census of Population), expressed as a ratio.
See John E. Brush, The Population of New Jersey.  New Brunswick, N.J.:  Rutgers University Press, 1958, 2nd edition, pp. 65-66.

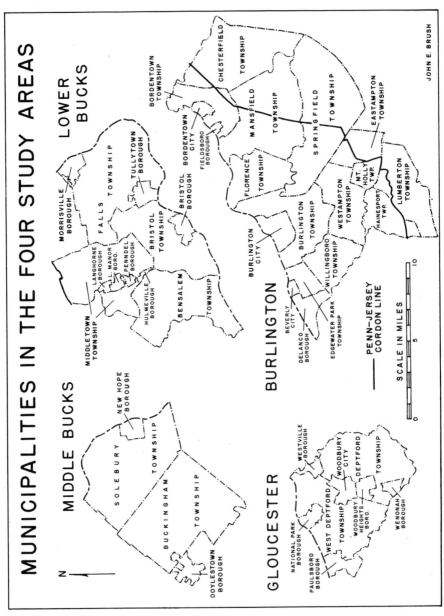

Figure 14.

Thus, no data are available from most of the townships and most of the territory in the study areas. The four townships (Bensalem, Bristol, Falls, and Middletown) in Bucks County, which were reported in the Census of Business, happened to be considered urbanized by the time of the 1960 Census of Population. On the other hand, Northampton Township (Mt. Holly) in Burlington County was omitted because in its legal name the word township is used instead of city or borough, [3] and it was not ruled an urban place. Three other townships in the New Jersey study areas, i.e., Willingboro (Levittown), Deptford, and West Deptford, had become wholly or partly urbanized by 1960 and, thus, should have been included also in the listing of the 1958 business census.

Looking at the aggregates of establishments, sales, and employment, certain conclusions about the magnitude of business concentrations can be drawn (Table 5). Urban places which have been well developed towns since the 19th Century, i.e., Doylestown, Bristol, Burlington, and Woodbury, show groupings of 200 to some 300 establishments and gross sales or receipts of 30 to 44 million dollars. The number of active proprietors and full-time workers varies from 1200 to 1800 in such towns. Smaller urban places vary from Beverly, reporting only 78 establishments, sales of some three million dollars, and about 200 persons employed, to Paulsboro and Morrisville, where there are some 170 to 180 establishments, gross sales and receipts of 11 to 16 1/2 million dollars and 750 to some 800 employed persons.

While there is no overlap in size between these two classes of urban places, the business concentrations in the townships are more variable. Bensalem, Bristol, and Falls have aggregates equaling the sales volume and employment found in small urban places. The fact that less than 40 establishments in Falls and Middletown have as much or more dollar volume as urban places with two or three times as many establishments is a reflection of the larger scale of operation of the businesses existing in the townships. The larger volume of sales per establishment in townships is demonstrated strikingly in Middletown by its sales, approaching 40 million dollars, and its employment of almost 750 persons. Field survey reveals that this is caused mainly by a concentration of auto dealers along U. S. Route One in Middletown Township near Langhorne and, in particular, by one dealer who draws customers from a large trading territory in Pennsylvania and New Jersey, and whose sales must have comprised a large share of the gross sales total of 32 million dollars reported by eight automotive dealers during 1958.

---

[3]While rural townships are not densely inhabited and may provide only minimal governmental functions, all New Jersey townships are incorporated under state law, and any densely inhabited township may assume the role of urban government when and if the need is recognized by the inhabitants. (See Stanley H. Friedelbaum, Municipal Government in New Jersey, New Brunswick, N. J., Rutgers University Press, 1954.

Another way to look at the localization of business in any geographical area is to measure the relative concentration of employment in trade and services. The ratios between the number of persons employed in commercial activity on the one hand and in manufacturing on the other hand has been found useful by the senior author in analyzing the functions of all urban places in New Jersey.[4] The index of commercial employment (Table 5) is calculated by dividing the number of active proprietors and employees working in a given municipality by the total number of employed persons who reside in the municipality. Although it is not possible from the data to determine how many of these persons actually work in the municipality where they live and the application of the method may be criticized because of the time lapse between the date of employment figures reported in the business census (November, 1958) and the date of the population census (April, 1960), it offers a simple and direct measurement of the local concentration of commercial activity.

It is clear from the array of commercial employment indices that two well-established urban places, Doylestown (index .50) and Woodbury ( .37), have unusually high concentrations of business while three newly urbanized townships, Bristol (.03), Falls (.05), and Bensalem (.06), have unusually low concentrations. Middletown Township (.21) ranks below most of the less developed urban places, such as Bordentown and Westville, but has a higher concentration than Beverly. The other urban places fall into an intermediate range of business concentration with indices not exceeding .29. In general, any place with an index in the range between .20 and .30 can be considered to have moderate development of trade and services according to this criterion. Beverly's index of .17 indicates its declining role as a business center. The very low indices of the three Bucks County townships mentioned above indicate the lag in localization of stores and services within their boundaries during the recent period of population growth.

## Data Analysis Zones (Penn-Jersey Transportation Study)

From the standpoint of geographic analysis, the townships are unwieldy territorial units. They range in area from two or three square miles to ten or twenty and from less than 2,000 inhabitants to nearly as many as 60,000 in the study areas. Perhaps it goes without saying that the urban development of formerly rural townships is incomplete and spotty, with the result that local concentrations of businesses may be

---

[4] The explanation of the criteria of concentration of employment in manufacturing and commerce in New Jersey is found in John E. Brush, The Population of New Jersey, New Brunswick, N.J., Rutgers University Press, 2nd edition, 1958, pp. 65-67, with application to 220 urban places for which data were available from 1948-1950.

obscured in the aggregates. The problems of variable township size and of settlement diffusion raise questions regarding the validity of the above-mentioned indices of commercial employment as measures of development in Lower Bucks County. The most meaningful territorial divisions are the old established urban municipalities which are fully built up and form compact settlements around distinct business districts. The use of subdivisions of townships, which are found in the Zones drawn for the Penn-Jersey Transportation Study, is a reasonable solution to the problem because they form territorial units of two to four square miles, roughly comparable to areas of the long-established urban municipalities. (See Figure 14.)

The field inventory provides the information necessary for an analysis of the location and size of stores and services in more detail than the census record permits. (See Table 7.) The inventory does not include data on business volume and employment, but only square footage of floor area enclosed. No account is taken of wholesale trade or service establishments offering lodging and amusements. The field data are arranged in terms of the Penn-Jersey Zones in order to correlate the distribution of stores and services with population and income. (See Table 6.) In this way the authors are able to make use of the Penn-Jersey data on household counts and estimated median annual income of families in 1961 or 1962 in the analysis to follow. No Penn-Jersey Zones exist in Middle Bucks County, so it is necessary to take whole townships in the cases of Buckingham and Solebury. Household counts (1960) and estimated median annual income (1959) are available from the Census of Population: 1960 for these two townships and for the boroughs of Doylestown and New Hope. (See Footnote Table 6A.)

## Relationships of Establishments to Households

It might be assumed that there is a correlation between the geographical distribution of population, i.e., households and the distribution of stores and services. While this is true, in general, it is clear that there is a wide range of variation if the spatial relationship is examined in detail. In old urban places with well developed stores and services the ratio of all establishments to households is usually one to every 10 or 15, with the lowest occurring in Doylestown, where it is one to seven. (Compare Tables 6 and 7.) A minimum of one to four occurs in the small Borough of New Hope, indicating the extreme degree of concentration in proportion to households in any of the areas under study. Tullytown (Zone 3931) with a ratio of 1:7 and Langhorne (3851) with 1:9 are small boroughs in Lower Bucks County with high concentrations of stores and services in proportion to their size. Certain urban places with moderately well developed services have ratios ranging up to 1:20 or more, e.g., Morrisville (Zone 3871) with 22 and Westville

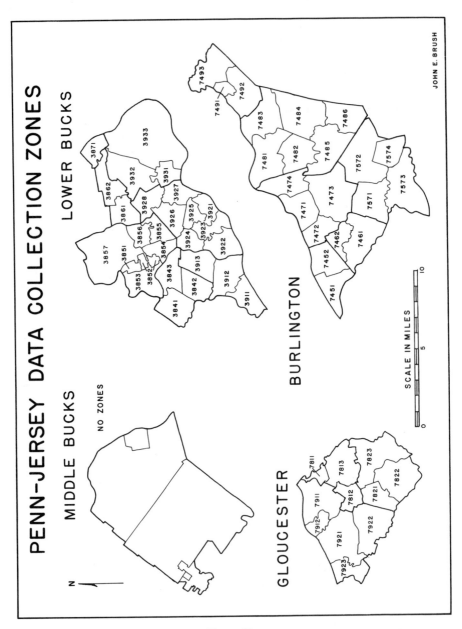

Figure 15.

TABLE 6

HOUSEHOLDS, AREA, AND INCOME: 1959-61

A - MIDDLE BUCKS COUNTY STUDY AREA

| Municipality | U. S. Census Occupied Housing Units | Area Square Miles | Density per Sq. Mi. | U.S. Census Estimated Median Annual Income* |
|---|---|---|---|---|
| Doylestown Borough | 1,981 | 2.3 | 861 | $5,652 |
| New Hope Borough | 392 | 1.3 | 302 | 5,614 |
| Buckingham Township | 1,211 | 33.0 | 37 | 5,882[1] 6,620[2] |
| Solebury Township | 974 | 27.1 | 36 | 6,078 |
| Totals & Mean Density | 4,558 | 63.7 | 72 | |

Sources: Land areas from Bucks County Planning Commission, 1962. Housing and income data from U.S. Census of Population and Housing: 1960. Census Tracts. Final Report PHC (1)-116. Washington, D.C., 1962.

* Income data for 1959 are estimated from 25 per cent sample of families and unrelated individuals.

[1] Median for the portion of Buckingham Township north of Old York Road.

[2] Median for the portion of Buckingham Township south of Old York Road.

TABLE 6--Continued

## HOUSEHOLDS, AREA, AND INCOME: 1959-61

### B - LOWER BUCKS COUNTY STUDY AREA

| Penn-Jersey Zone | Municipality | Penn-Jersey Household Count | Area Square Miles | Density per Sq. Mi. | Penn-Jersey Estimated Median Annual Income |
|---|---|---|---|---|---|
| 3841 | Bensalem Twp.* | 2,301 | 3.68 | 625 | $ 5,865 |
| 3842 | Bensalem Twp.* | 517 | 2.74 | 189 | 7,207 |
| 3843 | Bensalem Twp.* | 492 | 3.07 | 160 | 4,872 |
| 3911 | Bensalem Twp.* | 1,431 | 3.14 | 456 | 6,305 |
| 3912 | Bensalem Twp.* | 1,433 | 4.01 | 357 | 5,694 |
| 3913 | Bensalem Twp.* | 698 | 3.14 | 222 | 5,620 |
| 3851 | Langhorne B. | 457 | .51 | 1,116 | 5,809 |
| 3852 | Penndel B. & Langhorne Manor B. | 718 | 1.11 | 647 | 5,668 |
| 3853 | Middletown Twp.* | 1,063 | 3.57 | 298 | 5,868 |
| 3854 | Middletown Twp.* & Hulmeville B. | 717 | 1.94 | 369 | 5,922 |
| 3855 | Middletown Twp.* | 3,181 | 2.02 | 1,575 | 8,098 |
| 3856 | Middletown Twp.* | 2,231 | 1.90 | 1,174 | 7,878 |
| 3857 | Middletown Twp.* | 708 | 10.19 | 69 | 14,842 |
| 3861 | Falls Twp.* | 1,694 | 2.78 | 609 | 7,541 |
| 3862 | Falls Twp.* | 1,128 | 3.22 | 350 | 7,752 |
| 3932 | Falls Twp.* | 3,774 | 5.80 | 651 | 6,205 |
| 3933 | Falls Twp.* | 154 | 12.53 | 12 | 5,244 |
| 3871 | Morrisville | 2,550 | 1.65 | 1,545 | 6,034 |
| 3921 | Bristol B. | 3,650 | 1.65 | 2,212 | 5,402 |
| 3922 | Bristol Twp.* | 2,471 | 3.00 | 824 | 5,846 |
| 3923 | Bristol Twp.* | 1,070 | 2.15 | 498 | 6,307 |
| 3924 | Bristol Twp.* | 571 | 1.78 | 321 | 6,023 |
| 3925 | Bristol Twp.* | 1,476 | 1.59 | 928 | 5,923 |
| 3926 | Bristol Twp.* | 3,931 | 2.70 | 1,456 | 6,820 |
| 3927 | Bristol Twp.* | 1,741 | 2.22 | 784 | 6,745 |
| 3928 | Bristol Twp.* | 3,440 | 2.82 | 1,220 | 6,839 |
| 3931 | Tullytown B. | 600 | 1.86 | 322 | 6,509 |
|  | Total & Mean Density | 44,197 | 86.77 | 509 |  |

* Portion only of municipality

Sources: Area from Bucks County Planning Commission, 1962. In portions of munici-
palities estimated by Geography Department, Rutgers, The State University.
Household and Income Data from Penn-Jersey Transportation Study, Field
Surveys and Household Interviews, 1960-61.

TABLE 6--Continued

HOUSEHOLDS, AREA, AND INCOME: 1959-61

C - BURLINGTON COUNTY STUDY AREA

| Penn-Jersey Zone | Political Name | Penn-Jersey Household Count | Area Square Miles | Density per Sq. Mi. | Penn-Jersey Estimated Median Annual Income |
|---|---|---|---|---|---|
| 7451 | Delanco B. | 1,175 | 2.16 | 544 | $ 6,606 |
| 7452 | Beverly C. & Edgewater Pk. Twp. | 1,850 | 2.40 | 770 | 5,833 |
| 7461 | Levittown Twp. * | 428 | 5.32 | 81 | 6,725 |
| 7462 | Levittown Twp. | 2,022 | 1.83 | 1,123 | 7,146 |
| 7471 | Burlington C. | 3,650 | 3.06 | 1,193 | 5,105 |
| 7472 | Burlington Twp. * | 520 | 3.00 | 173 | 7,236 |
| 7473 | Burlington Twp. * | 620 | 7.80 | 79 | 5,394 |
| 7474 | Burlington Twp. * | 720 | 4.00 | 180 | 6,178 |
| 7481 | Florence Twp. * | 2,370 | 5.70 | 416 | 5,556 |
| 7482 | Florence Twp. * | 60 | 4.00 | 15 | 9,948 |
| 7483 | Mansfield Twp. * | 170 | 5.20 | 33 | 4,663 |
| 7484 | Mansfield Twp. * | 230 | 6.50 | 35 | 5,819 |
| 7485 | Springfield Twp. * | 120 | 5.40 | 22 | 4,663 |
| 7486 | Springfield Twp. * | 40 | 3.70 | 11 | 5,497 |
| 7491 | Bordentown C. | 1,690 | .92 | 1,837 | 6,022 |
| 7492 | Bordentown Twp. * & Fieldsboro B. | 1,152 | 4.40 | 262 | 6,293 |
| 7493 | Bordentown Twp. * | 1,178 | 4.40 | 268 | 6,307 |
| 7571 | Westampton Twp. * | 100 | 5.00 | 20 | 6,631 |
| 7572 | Westampton Twp. * & Eastampton Twp. * | 460 | 7.30 | 63 | 6,796 |
| 7573 | Hainesport & Lumberton Twp. * | 1,260 | 6.90 | 183 | 5,697 |
| 7574 | Mt. Holly Twp. | 3,830 | 2.91 | 1,316 | 5,640 |
| | Total & Mean Density | 23,645 | 91.90 | 257 | |

* Portion only of municipality

Sources: Area Data from New Jersey Department of Conservation and Economic Development, 1961. In portions of municipalities, estimated by Geography Department, Rutgers, The State University.
Household and Income from Penn-Jersey Transportation Study, Field Surveys & Household Interviews, 1960-61.

TABLE 6--Continued

HOUSEHOLDS, AREA, AND INCOME: 1959-61

D - GLOUCESTER COUNTY STUDY AREA

| Penn-Jersey Zone | Municipality | Penn-Jersey Household Count | Area Square Miles | Density per Sq. Mi. | Penn-Jersey Estimated Median Annual Income |
|---|---|---|---|---|---|
| 7811 | Westville B. | 1,520 | 1.04 | 1,461 | $ 5,717 |
| 7812 | Woodbury City | 3,970 | 2.13 | 1,864 | 6,068 |
| 7813 | Deptford Twp.* | 1,279 | 4.90 | 261 | 5,579 |
| 7821 | Deptford Twp.* & Woodbury Hts. | 2,827 | 2.60 | 1,087 | 6,384 |
| 7822 | Deptford Twp.* & Wenonah B. | 1,159 | 5.50 | 211 | 6,720 |
| 7823 | Deptford Twp.* | 1,795 | 6.60 | 272 | 5,939 |
| 7912 | National Park B. | 910 | .99 | 1,088 | 6,330 |
| 7911 | W. Deptford Twp.* | 1,807 | 5.50 | 328 | 6,357 |
| 7921 | W. Deptford Twp.* | 490 | 6.90 | 71 | 5,441 |
| 7922 | W. Deptford Twp.* | 913 | 3.70 | 247 | 6,448 |
| 7923 | Paulsboro B. | 2,270 | 2.00 | 1,135 | 5,480 |
| | Total & Mean Density | 18,940 | 41.86 | 452 | |

*Portion only of municipality

Sources: Area Data from New Jersey Department of Conservation and Economic Development, 1961. In portions of municipalities, estimated by Geography Department, Rutgers, The State University.
Household and Income from Penn-Jersey Transportation Study, Field Surveys and Household Interviews, 1960-61.

TABLE 7

INVENTORY OF ESTABLISHMENTS:  1962

A - MIDDLE BUCKS COUNTY STUDY AREA

| Municipality | Finance & Insurance | Professional Services | Food Sales | Eating & Drinking | Shopping Goods |
|---|---|---|---|---|---|
| Doylestown B. | 30 | 69 | 10 | 16 | 40 |
| New Hope B. | 7 | 12 | 6 | 16 | 16 |
| Buckingham Twp. | 5 | 10 | 13 | 15 | 6 |
| Solebury Twp. | 1 | 4 | 3 | 9 | 3 |
| Total | 43 | 95 | 32 | 56 | 65 |

| Municipality | Auto Sales | Service Stations | Other Retail | Personal & Repair Services | Total |
|---|---|---|---|---|---|
| Doylestown B. | 5 | 15 | 42 | 53 | 280 |
| New Hope B. | 2 | 1 | 42 | 9 | 111 |
| Buckingham Twp. | 2 | 8 | 38 | 24 | 121 |
| Solebury Twp. | 1 | 3 | 14 | 3 | 41 |
| Total | 10 | 27 | 136 | 89 | 553 |

Source:   Field Survey, Geography Department, Rutgers, The State University, 1962.

TABLE 7--Continued

INVENTORY OF ESTABLISHMENTS: 1962

B - LOWER BUCKS COUNTY STUDY AREA

| Zone Number | Municipality | Finance & Insurance | | Professional Services | | Food Sales | | Eating & Drinking | |
|---|---|---|---|---|---|---|---|---|---|
| | | No. | Sq. Ft. | No. | Sq. Ft. | No. | Sq. Ft. | No. | Sq. Ft. |
| 3841 | Bensalem Twp. * | 8 | 6,550 | 1 | 1,000 | 2 | 1,500 | 13 | 17,650 |
| 3842 | Bensalem Twp. * | - | - | - | - | 1 | 750 | 1 | 1,500 |
| 3843 | Bensalem Twp. * | 1 | 200 | - | - | - | - | - | - |
| 3911 | Bensalem Twp. * | 10 | 11,150 | 9 | 5,600 | 8 | 7,550 | 6 | 8,200 |
| 3912 | Bensalem Twp. * | 6 | 2,450 | - | - | 5 | 5,650 | 5 | 5,500 |
| 3913 | Bensalem Twp. * | 2 | 1,100 | - | - | 4 | 21,100 | - | - |
| 3851 | Langhorne B. | 7 | 6,050 | 16 | 9,700 | 3 | 2,700 | 4 | 3,800 |
| 3852 | Penndel B. & Langhorne Manor | 5 | 5,950 | 6 | 4,500 | 6 | 17,100 | 10 | 13,400 |
| 3853 | Middletown Twp. * | 2 | 350 | - | - | 3 | 2,300 | 3 | 2,400 |
| 3854 | Middletown Twp. * Hulmeville B. | 3 | 1,450 | 3 | 2,500 | 3 | 2,550 | 5 | 5,700 |
| 3855 | Middletown Twp. * | 3 | 2,600 | 2 | 2,000 | 5 | 13,200 | 1 | 1,500 |
| 3856 | Middletown Twp. * | - | - | 11 | 8,100 | 3 | 22,400 | 3 | 3,500 |
| 3857 | Middletown Twp. * | 4 | 1,600 | - | - | - | - | 8 | 10,100 |
| 3861 | Falls Twp. * | 6 | 5,900 | 20 | 12,600 | 4 | 16,500 | 7 | 9,500 |
| 3862 | Falls Twp. * | 5 | 2,050 | 1 | 1,000 | 5 | 11,950 | 3 | 2,350 |
| 3932 | Falls Twp. * | 2 | 1,300 | 11 | 9,500 | 4 | 14,800 | 2 | 3,600 |
| 3933 | Falls Twp. * | - | - | - | - | - | - | - | - |
| 3871 | Morrisville B. | 7 | 8,600 | 9 | 6,100 | 13 | 20,200 | 13 | 14,500 |
| 3921 | Bristol B. | 16 | 27,100 | 33 | 23,100 | 35 | 30,400 | 27 | 19,700 |
| 3922 | Bristol Twp. * | 4 | 1,100 | 4 | 2,100 | 13 | 28,600 | 18 | 19,050 |
| 3923 | Bristol Twp. * | - | - | 7 | 5,700 | 3 | 3,250 | 4 | 3,800 |
| 3924 | Bristol Twp. * | 3 | 1,600 | 1 | 1,000 | 1 | 800 | 2 | 1,600 |
| 3925 | Bristol Twp. * | 2 | 1,300 | - | - | 3 | 3,450 | 1 | 750 |
| 3926 | Bristol Twp. * | 8 | 3,400 | 10 | 7,700 | 11 | 31,600 | 6 | 7,600 |
| 3927 | Bristol Twp. * | 9 | 5,100 | 7 | 4,800 | 2 | 2,100 | 11 | 14,300 |
| 3928 | Bristol Twp. * | 2 | 750 | 19 | 14,800 | 3 | 6,900 | 1 | 2,400 |
| 3931 | Tullytown B. | 6 | 6,900 | 9 | 7,800 | 5 | 25,000 | 4 | 5,600 |
| | Total | 121 | 104,550 | 179 | 129,600 | 145 | 292,350 | 158 | 178,000 |

*Portion only

Source: Field Survey, Geography Department, Rutgers, The State University, 1962.

## TABLE 7--Continued

### INVENTORY OF ESTABLISHMENTS: 1962

### B - LOWER BUCKS COUNTY STUDY AREA

| Shopping Goods | | Auto Sales | | Service Stations | | Other Retail | | Personal & Repair Services | | Total | |
|---|---|---|---|---|---|---|---|---|---|---|---|
| No. | Sq. Ft. | No. | Sq. Ft. | No. | Sq. Ft. | No. | Sq. Ft. | No. | Sq. Ft. | No. | Sq. Ft. |
| 7 | 64,300 | 2 | 3,700 | 16 | 19,650 | 10 | 9,600 | 9 | 11,300 | 68 | 135,250 |
| - | - | 1 | 13,550 | - | - | - | - | 3 | 6,800 | 6 | 22,600 |
| - | - | - | - | 1 | 1,050 | - | - | 2 | 10,700 | 4 | 11,950 |
| 8 | 4,750 | 3 | 3,400 | 3 | 3,600 | 7 | 9,000 | 27 | 25,100 | 81 | 78,350 |
| 6 | 4,600 | 3 | 5,200 | 8 | 8,950 | 9 | 6,250 | 19 | 21,900 | 61 | 60,500 |
| 2 | 1,550 | - | - | 2 | 2,300 | 3 | 2,300 | 3 | 3,700 | 16 | 32,050 |
| 3 | 3,300 | 1 | 4,900 | 1 | 1,050 | 7 | 5,700 | 11 | 8,050 | 53 | 45,250 |
| 9 | 12,550 | - | - | 7 | 8,100 | 7 | 13,250 | 12 | 18,250 | 62 | 93,100 |
| - | - | 1 | 2,400 | 5 | 4,250 | 3 | 3,050 | 1 | 750 | 18 | 15,500 |
| 2 | 850 | 1 | 2,600 | 5 | 5,450 | 3 | 2,300 | 13 | 10,800 | 38 | 34,200 |
| 1 | 2,100 | - | - | 3 | 3,650 | 2 | 3,600 | 8 | 8,700 | 25 | 37,350 |
| 6 | 31,600 | 2 | 16,500 | 1 | 1,650 | 1 | 1,800 | - | - | 27 | 85,550 |
| 4 | 15,200 | 10 | 35,650 | 2 | 1,650 | 5 | 5,700 | 4 | 5,150 | 37 | 75,050 |
| 7 | 57,500 | 2 | 2,400 | 7 | 6,850 | 7 | 12,350 | 11 | 18,650 | 71 | 142,250 |
| 6 | 11,900 | 4 | 28,350 | 7 | 7,950 | 9 | 15,550 | 12 | 11,200 | 52 | 92,300 |
| 5 | 8,100 | 2 | 2,100 | 3 | 2,850 | 4 | 3,300 | 4 | 5,500 | 37 | 51,050 |
| - | - | - | - | - | - | - | - | 3 | 5,600 | 3 | 5,600 |
| 10 | 14,300 | 4 | 28,000 | 5 | 5,200 | 22 | 30,300 | 31 | 44,900 | 114 | 172,100 |
| 27 | 61,400 | 12 | 37,300 | 14 | 14,100 | 48 | 45,800 | 62 | 53,150 | 274 | 312,050 |
| 10 | 9,200 | 3 | 7,150 | 13 | 14,700 | 22 | 27,350 | 1 | 700 | 88 | 109,950 |
| 3 | 5,800 | 2 | 1,450 | 4 | 4,950 | 1 | 900 | 2 | 1,100 | 26 | 26,950 |
| 3 | 154,200 | 1 | 700 | 2 | 1,800 | 3 | 1,000 | 15 | 5,200 | 31 | 167,900 |
| 3 | 4,100 | 2 | 5,400 | 3 | 3,450 | 3 | 3,300 | 2 | 3,600 | 19 | 25,350 |
| 15 | 14,650 | 1 | 3,600 | 7 | 7,400 | 15 | 16,050 | 26 | 42,650 | 99 | 134,650 |
| 9 | 13,500 | 8 | 9,900 | 17 | 17,400 | 9 | 8,100 | 14 | 17,000 | 86 | 92,200 |
| 3 | 3,650 | - | - | 5 | 5,800 | 3 | 4,150 | 3 | 2,050 | 39 | 40,500 |
| 26 | 337,100 | 1 | 4,200 | 2 | 2,900 | 25 | 43,150 | 11 | 14,650 | 89 | 447,300 |
| 175 | 836,200 | 66 | 218,450 | 143 | 156,700 | 228 | 273,850 | 309 | 357,150 | 1,524 | 2,546,850 |

TABLE 7--Continued

INVENTORY OF ESTABLISHMENTS

C - BURLINGTON COUNTY STUDY AREA

| Zone Number | Municipality | Finance & Insurance No. | Sq. Ft. | Professional Services No. | Sq. Ft. | Food Sales No. | Sq. Ft. | Eating & Drinking No. | Sq. Ft. |
|---|---|---|---|---|---|---|---|---|---|
| 7451 | Delanco B. | 3 | 1,550 | 1 | 1,000 | 4 | 1,500 | 3 | 1,550 |
| 7452 | Beverly C. & Edgewater Park Twp. | 12 | 8,000 | 10 | 6,100 | 7 | 11,600 | 7 | 5,220 |
| 7461 | Willingboro Twp.* | 1 | 200 | 10 | 8,300 | 3 | 3,600 | 2 | 1,400 |
| 7462 | Willingboro Twp.* | 5 | 9,800 | 23 | 18,700 | 9 | 47,750 | 2 | 1,950 |
| 7471 | Burlington City | 17 | 13,800 | 40 | 23,200 | 27 | 35,400 | 18 | 18,200 |
| 7472 | Burlington Twp.* | 2 | 4,500 | - | - | 3 | 6,200 | 3 | 1,850 |
| 7473 | Burlington Twp.* | 2 | 3,200 | 1 | 1,000 | 1 | 1,250 | 1 | 600 |
| 7474 | Burlington Twp.* | - | - | - | - | 2 | 800 | 4 | 2,400 |
| 7481 | Florence Twp.* | 13 | 5,550 | 7 | 4,800 | 11 | 7,950 | 29 | 17,800 |
| 7482 | Florence Twp.* | - | - | - | - | - | - | - | - |
| 7483 | Mansfield Twp.* | - | - | - | - | 2 | 400 | 3 | 3,700 |
| 7484 | Mansfield Twp.* | 3 | 1,500 | - | - | 1 | 1,550 | 1 | 1,200 |
| 7485 | Springfield Twp.* | - | - | - | - | 1 | 300 | - | - |
| 7486 | Springfield Twp.* | 1 | 300 | - | - | 11 | 12,850 | 4 | 3,500 |
| 7491 | Bordentown C. | 10 | 4,550 | 16 | 10,750 | 13 | 9,350 | 17 | 21,650 |
| 7492 | Bordentown Twp.* & Fieldsboro B. | 1 | 300 | - | - | 2 | 9,600 | 3 | 2,100 |
| 7493 | Bordentown Twp.* | - | - | - | - | 2 | 1,100 | 7 | 14,650 |
| 7571 | Westampton Twp.* | 1 | 350 | - | - | - | - | - | - |
| 7572 | Westampton Twp.* & Eastampton Twp.* | - | - | 1 | 1,000 | - | - | 2 | 1,900 |
| 7573 | Hainesport & Lumberton Twp.* | 4 | 2,650 | 1 | 1,000 | 5 | 21,300 | 11 | 20,400 |
| 7574 | Mt. Holly Twp. | 36 | 27,100 | 57 | 30,800 | 43 | 83,800 | 16 | 14,890 |
| | Total | 111 | 83,350 | 167 | 108,150 | 147 | 251,300 | 133 | 134,910 |

* Portion Only

TABLE 7--Continued

INVENTORY OF ESTABLISHMENTS

C - BURLINGTON COUNTY STUDY AREA

| Shopping Goods | | Auto Sales | | Service Stations | | Other Retail | | Personal & Repair Services | | Total | |
|---|---|---|---|---|---|---|---|---|---|---|---|
| No. | Sq. Ft. | No. | Sq. Ft. | No. | Sq. Ft. | No. | Sq. Ft. | No. | Sq. Ft. | No. | Sq. Ft. |
| 3 | 900 | - | - | 3 | 3,550 | 4 | 1,600 | 7 | 2,550 | 28 | 14,200 |
| 7 | 6,100 | 1 | 3,000 | 8 | 7,600 | 17 | 19,200 | 24 | 21,750 | 93 | 88,570 |
| 1 | 3,850 | - | - | 3 | 2,150 | 3 | 1,500 | 1 | 1,350 | 24 | 22,350 |
| 8 | 83,800 | - | - | 4 | 4,700 | 3 | 3,550 | 8 | 8,400 | 62 | 78,150 |
| 39 | 94,100 | 2 | 12,500 | 26 | 31,200 | 41 | 38,200 | 81 | 83,400 | 291 | 352,000 |
| 3 | 9,900 | 1 | 3,750 | 6 | 6,700 | 4 | 3,650 | 6 | 9,100 | 28 | 45,650 |
| 2 | 6,000 | - | - | 2 | 1,900 | 2 | 5,400 | 1 | 1,200 | 12 | 20,550 |
| 2 | 16,800 | - | - | - | - | 4 | 2,300 | 2 | 3,200 | 14 | 25,500 |
| 6 | 8,900 | 1 | 2,400 | 10 | 12,300 | 4 | 7,700 | 7 | 19,350 | 88 | 86,750 |
| - | - | - | - | - | - | - | - | - | - | - | - |
| - | - | - | - | 4 | 4,600 | 1 | 100 | 2 | 400 | 12 | 9,200 |
| - | - | - | - | 3 | 3,700 | 1 | 2,500 | 2 | 2,500 | 11 | 12,950 |
| - | - | - | - | 1 | 1,500 | - | - | - | - | 2 | 18,000 |
| 12 | 14,500 | - | - | 2 | 2,100 | 8 | 4,700 | 4 | 2,200 | 42 | 40,150 |
| 21 | 25,100 | 3 | 10,150 | 7 | 7,550 | 3 | 12,650 | 20 | 27,550 | 110 | 129,300 |
| 3 | 6,750 | 2 | 3,100 | 12 | 13,050 | 1 | 100 | 5 | 11,400 | 29 | 46,400 |
| 12 | 148,100 | 2 | 4,600 | 6 | 6,300 | 3 | 650 | 3 | 2,250 | 35 | 177,600 |
| - | - | - | - | - | - | 1 | 350 | - | - | 2 | 700 |
| 1 | 2,100 | 2 | 8,200 | 1 | 1,000 | 1 | 450 | 3 | 2,100 | 11 | 16,750 |
| 7 | 14,300 | 6 | 33,500 | 9 | 11,800 | 10 | 19,550 | 14 | 32,350 | 67 | 156,750 |
| 31 | 41,200 | 12 | 21,350 | 14 | 17,800 | 28 | 23,100 | 45 | 111,600 | 282 | 371,640 |
| 158 | 492,400 | 32 | 102,450 | 121 | 139,500 | 139 | 147,350 | 235 | 342,650 | 1,343 | 1,801,960 |

Source: Field Survey, Geography Department, Rutgers, The State University, 1962.

TABLE 7--Continued

INVENTORY OF ESTABLISHMENTS

D - GLOUCESTER COUNTY STUDY AREA

| Zone Number | Municipality | Finance & Insurance No. Sq. Ft. | | Professional Services No. Sq. Ft. | | Food Sales No. Sq. Ft. | | Eating & Drinking No. Sq. Ft. | |
|---|---|---|---|---|---|---|---|---|---|
| 7811 | Westville B. | 2 | 2,200 | 12 | 9,200 | 6 | 11,350 | 6 | 7,850 |
| 7812 | Woodbury C. | 28 | 22,664 | 40 | 40,000 | 18 | 64,920 | 15 | 11,195 |
| 7813 | Deptford Twp.* | 1 | 1,050 | 2 | 1,500 | 7 | 25,260 | 7 | 8,375 |
| 7821 | Deptford Twp.* & Woodbury Hts. B. | 1 | 1,200 | 2 | 1,500 | 4 | 4,850 | 9 | 29,330 |
| 7822 | Deptford Twp.* & Wenonah B. | 1 | 1,050 | 4 | 2,500 | 5 | 5,600 | 3 | 3,330 |
| 7823 | Deptford Twp.* | 1 | 475 | - | - | 4 | 3,550 | 8 | 9,450 |
| 7912 | National Park B. | - | - | 2 | 2,000 | 3 | 2,730 | 2 | 3,100 |
| 7911 | W. Deptford Twp.* | 1 | 100 | - | - | 3 | 3,825 | 7 | 10,004 |
| 7921 | W. Deptford Twp.* | - | - | - | - | 2 | 4,500 | 4 | 8,975 |
| 7922 | W. Deptford Twp.* | 1 | 1,800 | 6 | 4,600 | 6 | 41,225 | 6 | 6,675 |
| 7923 | Paulsboro B. | 5 | 3,744 | 20 | 16,700 | 12 | 12,220 | 18 | 11,910 |
| | Total | 41 | 34,283 | 88 | 78,000 | 70 | 180,030 | 85 | 110,164 |

* Portion only

Source: Field Survey, Geography Department, Rutgers, The State University, 1962.

TABLE 7--Continued

INVENTORY OF ESTABLISHMENTS

D - GLOUCESTER COUNTY STUDY AREA

| Shopping Goods | | Auto Sales | | Service Stations | | Other Retail | | Personal & Repair Services | | Total | |
|---|---|---|---|---|---|---|---|---|---|---|---|
| No. | Sq. Ft. | No. | Sq. Ft. | No. | Sq. Ft. | No. | Sq. Ft. | No. | Sq. Ft. | No. | Sq. Ft. |
| 8 | 14,450 | – | – | 5 | 5,880 | 4 | 3,575 | 11 | 4,565 | 54 | 59,070 |
| 39 | 61,460 | 8 | 21,893 | 16 | 18,089 | 57 | 67,540 | 52 | 44,679 | 273 | 352,440 |
| 1 | 55,250 | – | – | 9 | 9,290 | 9 | 11,850 | 6 | 2,545 | 42 | 115,120 |
| 1 | 2,100 | 1 | 4,375 | 7 | 7,581 | 4 | 7,850 | 7 | 5,130 | 36 | 63,916 |
| 2 | 1,050 | 1 | 1,500 | 5 | 5,604 | 1 | 1,400 | 3 | 2,025 | 25 | 24,029 |
| 1 | 600 | 2 | 2,400 | 10 | 12,236 | 5 | 6,640 | 6 | 1,900 | 37 | 38,251 |
| – | – | – | – | 2 | 1,176 | 2 | 4,000 | 2 | 525 | 13 | 13,531 |
| 1 | 1,575 | 1 | 4,000 | 5 | 9,328 | 1 | 1,400 | 2 | 1,260 | 21 | 31,492 |
| 1 | 300 | 2 | 3,600 | 3 | 1,850 | 3 | 8,850 | 4 | 12,925 | 19 | 41,000 |
| 10 | 23,950 | – | – | 3 | 3,528 | 4 | 6,750 | 9 | 12,300 | 45 | 100,828 |
| 20 | 34,860 | 2 | 6,525 | 9 | 9,508 | 24 | 16,985 | 18 | 6,019 | 128 | 118,471 |
| 84 | 195,595 | 17 | 44,293 | 74 | 85,070 | 114 | 136,840 | 120 | 93,873 | 693 | 958,148 |

(Zone 7811) with 28. The ratio rises to 1:30 or 1:40 or even as high as 1:50 or 1:60 in the urban places which are less developed commercially and in portions of township where urbanization had begun in 1950 or earlier. The highest ratios occur in new urbanized territory where population growth has been extremely rapid since 1950. Here ratios of establishments to households are often between 1:50 and 1:80. Extreme examples of disproportion are found in parts of Falls and Middletown Townships, where there are over 100 households for every establishment (Zones 3855 and 3932). In non-urban townships with densities of less than 100 households per square miles in the Middle Bucks and Burlington study area the ratios range from 10 (Buckingham) to 60 (Zone 7485, Springfield Township). These are outer metropolitan townships in which farm land use is predominant and small villages or hamlets are still the local service centers. (Compare Zones 7486 and 7482.)

Despite the observed variability there is a positive relationship between the distribution of business establishments and the distribution of households. One way of examining this relationship both aggregately and for categories of central services is by means of regression analysis. However, considerable caution must be exercised in interpreting the statistical results. Certain biases introduced by data classifications as well as certain defects in the data used render questionable any inferential applications of the computed relations. Consequently, a least squares fit represents an average relationship applicable only to the sample data. The coefficient of determination ($r^2$) should be regarded as a measure of the closeness of an observed relation between two variables, useful for descriptive and comparative purposes.

Efforts to relate the distributions of establishments and households in the study area lead to the conclusion that their relationship is not linear but curvilinear and can be described best by the formulation $Y = a X^b$. Figure 16 shows the relationship when the variables are plotted logarithmically with establishments as the dependent variable. Logarithmically the functional relationship is $\log Y = \log a + b \log X$.[5] The coefficient of determination is .45, which means that less than half the variation of log Y is explained by the variation of log X. In terms of the variables, the distribution of households has a

[5]This regression equation has been applied by other geographers to measurement of the concentration of office facilities, employment, and functional units in central places. See Edgar M. Horwood and Ronald R. Boyce, Studies of the Central Business District and Urban Freeway Development, Seattle: University of Washington Press, 1959; also Lorne H. Russwurm, "The Changing Central Business District Retail Sales Mix, 1948-1958," Discussion Paper No. 1, University of Illinois, Department of Geography, 1963; Howard A. Stafford, "The Functional Bases of Small Towns," Economic Geography, Vol. 39, 1963, pp. 165-175.

significant effect on the distribution of business establishments, but the degree of explained variation is less than might be expected.

Extrapolation from the regression indicates that an "expected threshold" for an establishment would exist for 45 households. Actually, in outer Burlington County there is one zone (7482) with no establishment, and the minimum number observed is two establishments in zones where there are 100 and 120 households (zones 7571 and 7485, respectively). There is the likelihood that in two out of three instances as many as nine establishments would be found in a zone with 100 households. However, a maximum number of 42 is observed in Springfield Township (Zone 7486) where there are only 40 households in outer metropolitan Burlington County. The unusual number of small food, dry goods and miscellaneous retail stores exists here in the Columbus Farmers' Market. Few of these shops offer anything but low-priced goods and none have a large volume of trade, being active about three days only in a week.

As an average relationship, about five establishments might be expected in a zone where there are 200 households; 33 establishments in a zone with 1,000 households; and 155 establishments where there are 4,000 households. Bristol, Burlington, Mt. Holly, and Woodbury with between 273 and 291 establishments and from 3,650 to 3,970 households differ from this relationship but the deviation is not statistically significant. The instances where significant deviations exist are the extremes already pointed out; (1) Doylestown, New Hope, Tullytown, and Langhorne, which are all on the plus side, in keeping with their low establishment-household ratios, and (2) the recently urbanized zones in Middletown and Falls townships (zones 3855 and 3932) with exceptionally high ratios, which fall below the limits of expectation.

Much of the unexplained variation in the relationship between the distributions of establishments and households is due to the presence of some extreme cases. Outstanding deviations are expected where rapid population growth has occurred in previously rural townships with the immediate appearance of local service centers, while at the same time old commercial centers persist and develop without commensurate population growth. Present-day modes of transportation, changes in marketing methods and rising income have made some elements of the old hierarchy of services obsolete and inevitably there is a time lag while new business types replace the old ones. Thus, the current distribution of establishments must be viewed as an imperfect reflection of the forces at work today.

The spatial pattern of central services is to be interpreted in the light of two basic factors:

(1) the geographic concentration of demand necessary to provide support for one or more profitable enterprises; and,

TABLE 8

STATISTICAL ANALYSIS OF RELATION BETWEEN

ESTABLISHMENTS AND HOUSEHOLDS

| X<br><br>Households | Y<br><br>Type of<br>Business<br>Establishments | N<br><br>Number of Zones<br>with<br>Establishments | Per Cent of<br>Variance of Log Y<br>Explained by<br>Variance of Log X |
|---|---|---|---|
| Households | All Types | 63 | 44.7 |
| Households | Finance and<br>Insurance<br>Services | 51 | 20.4 |
| Households | Professional<br>Services | 42 | 17.3 |
| Households | Food Stores | 57 | 24.8 |
| Households | Eating and<br>Drinking Places | 57 | 13.4 |
| Households | Shopping Goods | 53 | 6.9 |
| Households | Auto Dealers | 42 | 12.8 |
| Households | Filling Stations | 58 | 36.9 |
| Households | Miscellaneous<br>Retail Stores | 58 | 13.1 |
| Households | Personal and<br>Repair Services | 59 | 21.7 |

Source: Households from U.S. Bureau of the Census and Penn-Jersey
Transportation Study (see Table 6, footnotes).
Establishments from field observations 1962 (see Table 7).

85

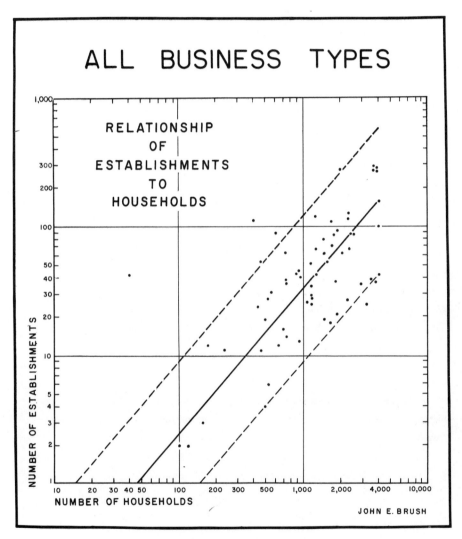

Fig. 16--All Business Types

(2) the distance people are willing to travel in order to satisfy their requirements for a given commodity or service.

Since the threshold[6] of population density and average distance traveled both vary from one type of business to another, a mixed response is to be expected. It has been shown in the previous chapter that during the 19th Century general stores, blacksmiths, wheelwrights, elementary schools, and churches existed in the smallest hamlets. These establishments then had the lowest thresholds and smallest service areas. Specialized retail stores and professional services were located occasionally in large villages and were always to be found in the towns, indicating the higher thresholds and the larger areas of support necessary. It is possible to analyze certain aspects of the new spatial pattern by further analysis of the relationships between each of several types of business and the distribution of households. (See Table 8 and Figs. 17 and 18.)

## Business Types in Relation to Households

Although there are significant differences in the spatial pattern of various business types, no single type has closer relationship to the distribution of households than the aggregate of all types. When the numbers of establishments in each of nine categories[7] are converted to logarithms and treated in relation to the logarithms of households, it is seen (Table 8) that the percentage of variation of establishments (Y) in each business type explained by the variation of households (X) is always lower than where the business types are undifferentiated. Gasoline filling stations show the closest relation to the distribution of households, with 37 per cent of the variation being explained. The poorest relationship is found in shopping goods, for which only seven per cent of the variation is explained. Apparently the spatial pattern of filling stations follows the distribution of population more than any other business type, while that of stores selling clothing, shoes, furniture, and appliances is the least closely related to distribution of population.

The other business types are divided into two groups on the basis of their degree of relationship to households. Food stores, personal and repair services, finance and insurance services, and professional services appear to follow the distribution

---

[6]The concept of threshold has been stated by Brian J. L. Berry and William L. Garrison, "Functional Bases of the Central Place Hierarchy," Economic Geography, Vol. 34, 1958, pp. 145-154, and tested by Arthur Getis, "A Theoretical and Empirical Inquiry into the Spatial Structure of Retail Activities," Unpublished Ph. D. Dissertation, University of Washington, 1961.

[7]The nine business types adhere to the Penn-Jersey classification. See Table 20.

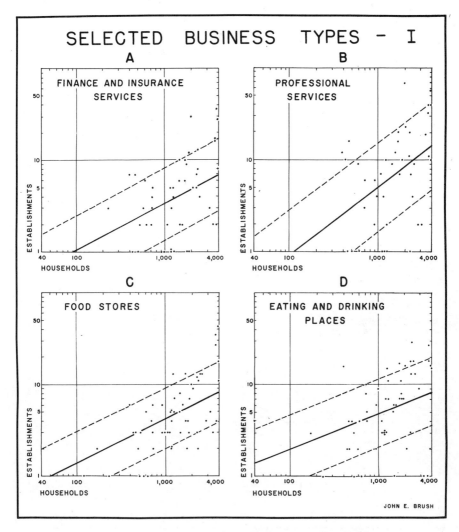

Fig. 17.--Relationships of Establishments to Households:
Selected Business Types - I

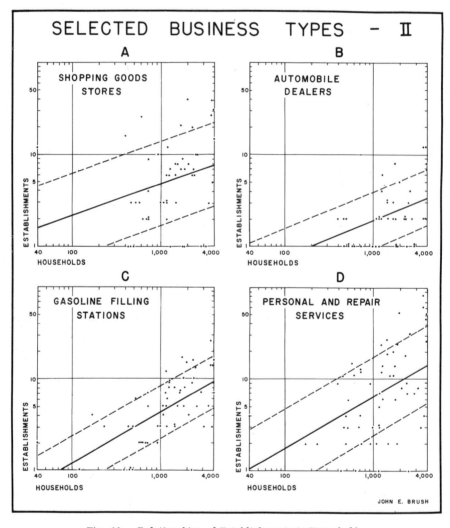

Fig. 18.--Relationships of Establishments to Households:
Selected Business Types - II

of population, although less closely than filling stations. The percentage of explained variance in these business types diminishes from 25 to 22, 20 and 17, respectively. The remaining business types resemble shopping goods in having less relationship to population. Only 13 per cent of the variance in the number of eating and drinking places and in the number of miscellaneous retail stores is related to the number of households. Less than 13 per cent of the variance in number of auto dealers is explained by the variation in number of households. Nevertheless, distribution of establishments in these three categories is not as variable as in the case of shopping goods.

The threshold of entry for one establishment in each of eight business types, extrapolated from the regressions, is seen to be less than 100 households in all categories but two, i.e., professional services and auto dealers. (See Figs. 17 and 18.) Since there is great variability in the occurrence of single establishments, a more meaningful threshold is found when a minimum of two establishments of any type appear in a zone. The observed thresholds of two or more establishments in the five categories, which have been pointed out as having the closest relation to households, are as follows: filling stations-- 40, food stores--170, personal and repair services--170, finance and insurance--230, and professional services--390. (See data, Tables 6 and 7.) The estimated thresholds of entry for two establishments of each of these types are not consistent with the observed thresholds, varying from about 130 for personal and repair services to 350 for finance and insurance services. Extreme variability is observed and calculated for each of the other four categories, the highest thresholds, either observed or calculated for one or two establishments, being for automobile dealers.

In summary it may be stated that the statistical analysis of the relationships between numbers of establishments in various business types and population distribution, shows certain types, especially filling stations, food stores, and personal or repair services, to be more closely in accord with population than other business types, such as auto sales and shopping goods, which are variable in distribution. It appears that observed and calculated thresholds of entry for two or more establishments are consistently low for the first three business types named above. But there is little regularity in the observed and calculated thresholds of entry for the latter types. The evidence permits inferences that the goods and services provided by establishments of the first three types are those demanded most frequently for which people expect to travel short distances and that the last-named types of business are those less frequently required for which people are willing to travel greater distances.

## Relationship of Size and Number of Establishments

Estimates of the area of enclosed floor space devoted to display and storage of goods for sale or to performance of personal and professional services provide a means of measuring the geographical concentration of business. Square footage is a more satisfactory measure of concentration than a simple count of the establishments found in an area. It has the advantage of being determined readily in the field. The authors recognize, of course, that employment and/or dollar volume are more accurate criteria of the relative concentration of business activity. But such data were not accessible to the authors for the purposes of this analysis. Observations were made of the square footage of all establishments existing during 1962 in the Lower Bucks, Burlington, and Gloucester study areas and grouped according to the Penn-Jersey Transportation Study's zones and type-of-business categories. However, estimates of square footage are not available for establishments observed in the Middle Bucks study area.

Consider first the relationship between square footage of enclosed space and the total number of establishments. (See Figure 19.) Here the X axis represents establishments and square footage is the dependent variable. Using a log . log conversion from the raw data (Table 7) and the same regression formula as previously, the relationship is shown to be statistically more significant than any previously considered (Table 9). More than 80 per cent of the variation of log Y is explained by the variation of log X.

The fit of the regression is best where data are between ten establishments, which contain about 9,000 square feet of space on the average, and 60 establishments, which contain about 100,000 square feet. Observations between these limits fall within the range of one standard error of estimate from the regression line. The variation in square footage to be expected in two out of three cases is from 3,500 to 20,000 for ten establishments and from 40,000 to 250,000 for 60 establishments.

However, in zones where there are less than ten establishments the observed deviations are extreme, ranging over 10,000 square feet where two, four, and six establishments exist in Bensalem and Springfield townships and in Westampton Township, where there are two small establishments with only 700 square feet. (See Table 7.) Such cases do not represent more than a few small stores or services, perhaps located in a relict hamlet or dispersed along the roadsides.

On the other hand, deviations from the regression observed at the upper limits are significant. Tullytown (Zone 3931) has 447,300 square feet of enclosed space contained in 89 stores and service establishments. This largest single concentration of commercial square footage in the three study areas is accounted for by the existence of a regional shopping center (Levittown Shop-A-Rama) within the Tullytown Borough

TABLE 9

STATISTICAL ANALYSIS OF RELATION BETWEEN
SQUARE FOOTAGE AND ESTABLISHMENTS

| X<br>Type of<br>Business<br>Establishments | Y<br><br>Square<br>Footage | N<br>Number of Zones<br>with<br>Establishments | Per Cent of<br>Variance of Log Y<br>Explained by<br>Variance of Log X |
|---|---|---|---|
| All Types | Square feet | 59 | 88.6 |
| Finance and<br>Insurance<br>Services | Square feet | 47 | 76.5 |
| Professional<br>Services | Square feet | 38 | 98.0 |
| Food Stores | Square feet | 53 | 65.8 |
| Eating and<br>Drinking Places | Square feet | 53 | 84.5 |
| Shopping Goods<br>Stores | Square feet | 49 | 49.4 |
| Auto Dealers | Square feet | 38 | 54.1 |
| Filling Stations | Square feet | 54 | 94.8 |
| Miscellaneous<br>Retail Stores | Square feet | 54 | 74.0 |
| Personal and<br>Repair Services | Square feet | 55 | 75.2 |

Source: Data from field observations (see Table 7, footnotes).

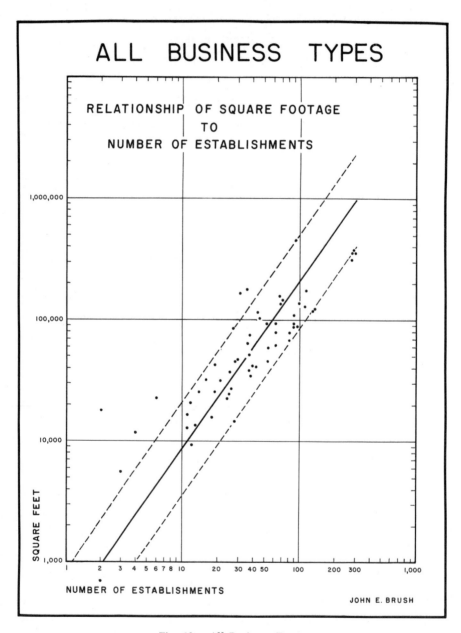

Fig. 19.--All Business Types

boundaries. In square footage terms not one of the old established towns with well-developed central functions is the equal of Tullytown. Bristol, Burlington, Mt. Holly, and Woodbury, which have between 312, 050 and 371, 640 square feet of enclosed space, fall significantly below the nearly 1, 000, 000 square feet to be expected from the regression relationship computed for 290 establishments. Two cases of exceptionally large proportional square footage are observed where 31 and 37 establishments contain 167, 900 and 177, 600 square feet, respectively, in Lower Bucks County (Zone 3924) and Burlington County (Zone 7493). The explanation is that a single large discount store is located near a major highway in each zone, where there is not much other concentrated commercial development. Such zones contain as much or more square footage as the old established urban places of Morrisville, Bordentown, and Paulsboro.

These instances of large deviations reflect the large scale of commercial expansion occurring in new urbanized parts of the metropolitan fringe in contrast to the concentration of relatively small establishments in the old commercial centers. The evidence demonstrates that a planned regional shopping center contains more commercial square footage than a town of 10, 000 or more inhabitants with a business district made up of hundreds of small stores and offices. It is also observed that a single free-standing discount store may so expand the square footage of commercial area in a peripheral township as to equal or exceed the area found in a small town of some 4, 000 to 8, 000 inhabitants.

## Variations in Establishment Size by Business Type

Important differences in size of establishments are found among the several business types (Table 10). The mean square footage per establishment is estimated to be below 1, 000 in finance and insurance services and in professional services, whereas shopping goods, stores, and automobile dealers exceed 3, 000. Food stores with an average of 2, 000 square feet are the only other type of business in which the mean exceeds 1, 200. The typical eating or drinking place, gasoline filling station, and personal or repair service in the study areas is housed in some 1, 100 to 1, 200 square feet of enclosed space (20 to 25 by 50 to 60 feet). However, square footage taken along do not provide a fair comparison of relative sizes of enterprises because much activity may occur in the open air on the premises, e.g., auto dealers and filling stations, or off the premises, in which case the square footage refers to office space only, e.g., insurance agencies, physicians, and lawyers.

As previously noted, dollar value of sales or receipts would provide a more accurate measure of relative size. It is unfortunate that data on sales volume are available only for certain retail trade categories and not in the year when our field work was carried out (Table 10). The definitions of categories followed by the U.S. Census Bureau are not precisely the same as those employed by the Penn-Jersey Transportation Study and adhered to in the authors' analysis, but they do provide an approximation of business volumes per establishment in 1958. Data from the 1958 business census are not compared in detail with the data from our inventory classified by the Penn-Jersey zones and business types because of inconsistencies of categories and uncertainties regarding geographic location of some business establishments reported in the 1958 business census.

The available data on sales per establishment in five kinds of business during 1958 (Table 10) reveal that automotive dealers rank highest in dollar volume, whether calculated per establishment or per square foot of enclosed space. Stores selling clothing, shoes, hardware, and appliances, i.e., shopping goods, do not report a dollar volume commensurate with their physical dimensions and not as much as establishments in the three other types of retail trade for which comparisons are made. Food stores are reported to have the second largest sales volume and stand fairly high in proportion to square footage of enclosed area. Gasoline filling stations and eating or drinking places differ in sales per establishment and per square foot in about the same proportions.

Certain other aspects of the variation in size of establishments are revealed by the graphs (Figures 20 and 21) and by regression analysis. Although the goodness of fit differs among the regressions computed, all relationships are significant. The percentage of variation of square footage (X) explained by the variation in number of establishments (Y) is at least 49 per cent for shopping goods and goes to 95 per cent for filling stations and as high as 98 per cent for professional services. The physical dimensions of shopping goods stores are extremely heterogeneous because small specialty shops are grouped in this category along with clothing or furniture stores and large department stores. There is little difference in variability observed in zones with a large number of establishments as compared to those with small numbers. Gasoline filling stations tend to be much more uniform, wherever they are located, and the increase in number of stations in more densely populated zones is not usually accompanied by much change in average size of stations, because of the standardization of facilities and management units. Professional offices are also of much the same dimensions whether they occur in small or large concentrations, undoubtedly on account of the tendency of professional people to maintain individual enterprises or to go into small partnerships in the study areas.[8]

---

[8]A note of caution on reliability of the data must be given here. Estimates of square feet in office space were usually made in the field by external inspection only. This procedure is thought to create a bias in the data towards uniformity in the case of professional services because these offices often are accommodated in remodelled dwellings, the dimensions of which were assumed to be rooms of ordinary size.

TABLE 10

AVERAGE SIZE OF ESTABLISHMENTS

| Business Type: Field Inventory 1962 | Mean Square Footage per Establishment | Kind of Business: 1958 | Annual Sales: 1958 | |
|---|---|---|---|---|
| | | | Dollars per Establishment | Dollars per Square foot |
| Finance and Insurance Services | 814 | N.A. | -- | -- |
| Professional Services | 728 | N.A. | -- | -- |
| Food Stores | 1,999 | Food Stores | $161,248 | $81 |
| Eating and Drinking Places | 1,125 | Eating and Drinking Places | 42,741 | 38 |
| Shopping Goods Stores | 3,655 | General Merchandise, Apparel, Furniture | 84,834 | 23 |
| Auto Dealers | 3,176 | Automotive Sales | 371,050 | 117 |
| Filling Stations | 1,128 | Gasoline Filling Stations | 67,796 | 60 |
| Other Retail Stores | 1,160 | N.A. | -- | -- |
| Personal and Repair Stores | 1,195 | N.A. | -- | -- |

Sources: Field Survey, Lower Bucks, Burlington and Gloucester Study Areas (see Table 7 B, C, and D).
U.S. Census of Business: 1958, Vol. II, Part 2, Washington, D.C., 1961.
Mean sales are from combined data for Bucks, Burlington, and Gloucester Counties.
N.A. - Not Available.

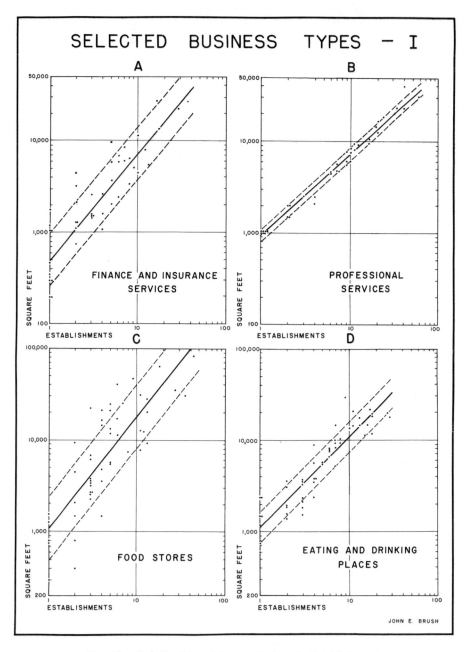

Fig. 20.--Relationships of Square Footage to Establishments
Selected Business Types - I

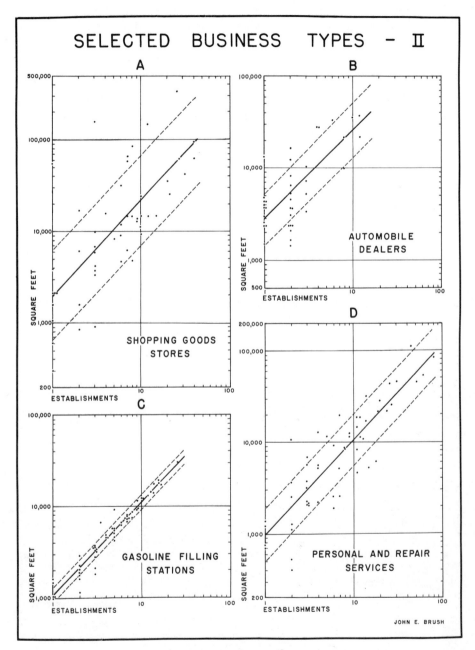

Fig. 21.--Relationships of Square Footage to Establishments
Selected Business Types - II

Food stores and auto sales agencies are heterogeneous, like shopping goods stores. Many small food stores exist, both in hamlets situated in the rural townships and in the old closely-built urban areas, where they depend upon neighborhood trade, whereas modern supermarkets with large stocks of meats, frozen goods, and baked goods are located in the old urban centers along with small stores as well as in the newly-urbanized townships. The mean square footage of finance and insurance services is small, but there are large variations in size which is understandable when it is pointed out that everything from substantial urban banks to small loan offices and insurance agencies, maintained in private homes, are included. Everything from a little home beauty parlor or television repair shop to a large laundry or auto repair garage is included in the category of personal and repair services. Eating and drinking establishments tend to be fairly uniform in size, whatever the concentration of numbers.

### Spatial Relationships of Central Services

The analysis thus far has shown some general and specific relationships between the distribution of households and establishments and between establishments and square footage, but it has indicated nothing about the existence of a spatial ordering of central places. Indeed, it appears that the variables form continua from small to large concentrations of stores and services without discernible size classes or ranks among the territorial units under examination. One could hardly expect the results to be otherwise. More or less continuous variations from small to large centers have been found in previous studies of hierarchies in rural areas. [9] The problem of determining discrete classes among centers has been phrased aptly by Howard E. Bracey, the British geographer, who said in personal correspondence, "...I find it almost impossible to strike grades although quite easy to give a grading,"[10] in his studies of towns in rural England. Subsequently, spatial ordering of three classes of service centers has been demonstrated in southern England as well as in agricultural regions of North America. [11]

---

[9] See Howard A. Stafford, "The Functional Bases of Small Towns," Economic Geography, Vol. 39, 1963, pp. 165-175. The clearest statement of the concept of a continuum rather than a step-like hierarchy of central places is found in Rutledge Vining, "A Description of Certain Spatial Aspects of an Economic System," Economic Development and Cultural Change, Vol. 3, 1955, pp. 147-195.

[10] Letter from Howard E. Bracey, University of Bristol, England, November 16, 1953.

[11] John E. Brush and Howard E. Bracey, "Rural Service Centers in Southwestern Wisconsin and Southern England," Geographical Review, Vol. 45, 1955, pp. 559-569.

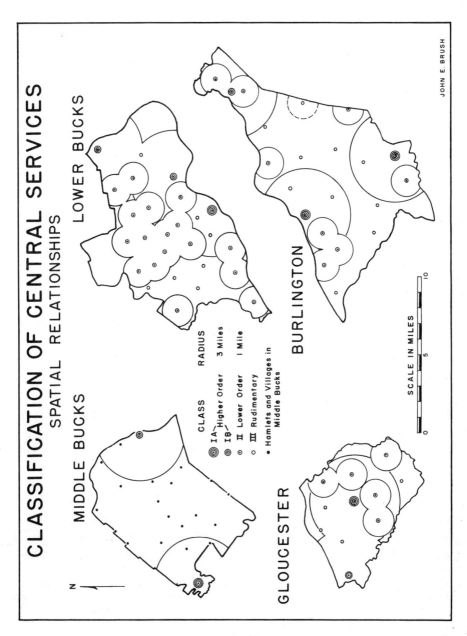

Figure 22.

Recently Berry has offered data to show that spatial order exists in both rural and urban areas.[12]

A spatial ordering of centers according to size is the crux of any classification which may be offered. By cartographic analysis it is possible to demonstrate that there is such an ordering of central places on the metropolitan fringe. When the field inventory data are mapped according to zones, certain spatial relationships become evident. Assuming that the stores and services are grouped near the centroid of each zone, circles are struck which outline proximate areas for zones in each of two size classes. No a priori determinations of size classes or radii are made; they are determined by map experimentation. It becomes clear that the largest concentration of stores and services are located farthest apart and necessarily have larger radii of influence than the lesser concentrations which have smaller radii. A three-mile radius is found suitable to describe proximate areas of zones with larger concentrations of establishments. One mile is satisfactory to describe the zones with smaller concentrations. No arcs are shown for the zones with the smallest concentrations and, for the sake of map legibility, overlapping arcs are eliminated in the larger size classes. While it is known from field work that all establishments are not located at the centroid of any zone and it is to be demonstrated in Chapter IV that not all households which support the establishments found in any given zone are located within its proximate area, one can reasonably assume that most establishments in any zone are within a distance of one mile of the zone centroid[13] and a substantial part of their trade comes from within the proximate area. The resulting map (Figure 22) should not be considered anything more than a schematic representation of service centers and service areas. Yet it is the essential key to the spatial pattern which forms the principal criterion of the classification offered here (Table 11).

In addition to spatial relationships, the varying proportions of the several business types are taken into account. In Class I zones, which inevitably stand out in the study areas as the largest local concentrations of stores and services, the professions and stores dealing in shopping goods and finance and insurance services are relatively more important in the assemblage of establishments than they are elsewhere. On the other hand, the most common business types in zones with low concentrations, designated Class III, are personal and repair services, gasoline filling stations, eating and drinking

---

[12]Brian J. L. Berry and Harold M. Mayer, Comparative Studies of Central Place Systems, Final Report, Geography Branch, U.S. Office of Naval Research, Project 389-126, Contract 2121-18, c. 1962; B. J. L. Berry, Commercial Structure and Commercial Blight, Retail Patterns and Processes in the City of Chicago. Department of Geography, University of Chicago, Research Paper No. 85, 1963.

[13]A circle with a mile radius, centered in a zone of three square miles could be expected to enclose nearly all parts of the zone, the area of the circle being 3.14 square miles according to the formula $\pi r^2$.

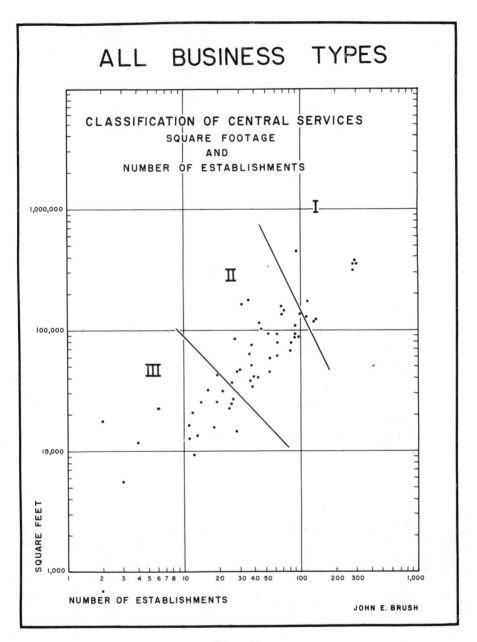

Figure 23.

places, and food stores. There are 17 Class III zones in Lower Bucks County and the two New Jersey study areas. In Middle Bucks County the hamlets and small villages of Buckingham and Solebury townships have rudimentary services roughly corresponding to those in Class III and, if there were Data Collection Zones in these two townships, undoubtedly they would fall into the same classification. A total of 30 zones with intermediate levels of concentration are put in Class II. Professional services, shopping goods, and other retail stores assume more prominence in the typical assemblage of establishments found in Class II.

Class I zones, which are by all criteria at the highest level of central services, have more than 100 business establishments and at least 100,000 square feet of enclosed space devoted to business purposes, or, if there are less than 100 establishments, over 400,000 square feet of enclosed floor area (Figure 23). The four old towns in Group I-A (Table 11) with at least 270 establishments and 300,000 square feet of enclosed area are located at a minimum distance of seven miles from one another (Burlington-Mt. Holly) and six miles from any large city (Woodbury-Camden). The five centers in Group I-B are found to be as little as three and a half miles from any other Class I center (Bristol-Tullytown) or as much as ten or eleven miles from any Class I center. Morrisville is only a mile from downtown Trenton, and Bristol is only two miles from Burlington, but in each instance the intervening Delaware River necessitates use of bridges with consequent costs in tolls and/or delay due to traffic congestion. The median of eleven distances measured between centers of Class I or between Class I centers and Trenton or Camden is six miles.

Turning to zones where the concentration of central services falls at the opposite extreme, it is observed (Figure 23) that they tend to be grouped in belts, situated either in close proximity to Class I centers or far from such higher-order places in the outer metropolitan fringe. These are Class III zones with rudimentary central services, not exceeding 30 establishments and enclosed floor area of less than 45,000 square feet (Figure 24). Many of the stores and sources found in the 17 zones in Class III (Table 11) are dispersed along highways, but nucleations often exist which are the remnants of 19th-Century hamlets and villages. The median distance between centroids of Class III zones is two miles, increasing to as much as three miles in Burlington County. The typical spacing of centers is similar to Middle Bucks County, where the actual location of hamlets and small villages is shown on the map in the absence of Penn-Jersey Data Collection Zones.

Zones in Class II are intermediate concentrations ranging from a minimum of 25 establishments to a maximum of 99 and from about 34,000 square feet of enclosed area to nearly 178,000 square feet (Table 11 and Figure 22). It is the number and variety

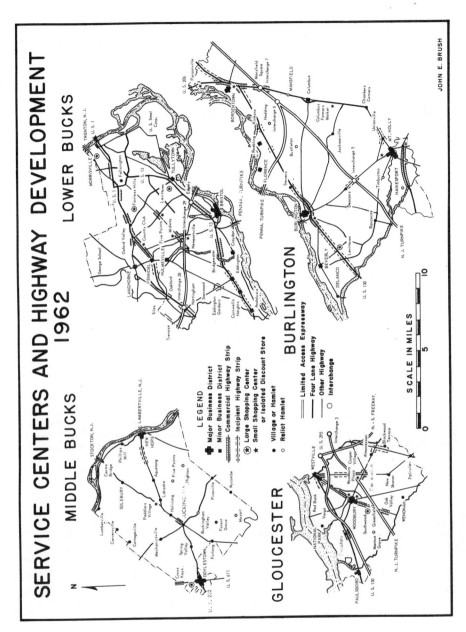

Figure 24.

TABLE 11

CLASSIFICATION OF CENTRAL SERVICES

Class I -- Higher-Order Centers

Group I-A:  Old Urban Places with Highly Developed Services

| Penn-Jersey Zone | Name of Municipality | C. B. D. :  Central Business District<br>S. C. :  Shopping Center |
|---|---|---|
| No Zone | Middle Bucks County<br>Doylestown Borough | C. B. D. and S. C. |
| 3921 | Lower Bucks County<br>Bristol Borough | C. B. D. only |
| 7471<br>7574 | Burlington County<br>Burlington City<br>Mt. Holly Township | C. B. D. only<br>C. B. D. only |
| 7812 | Gloucester County<br>Woodbury City | C. B. D. and S. C. |

| All Establishments | Business Types | Mean Number: Estimated from log Regression for Total of 280 | Range: Variation in Observed Number of Establishments |
|---|---|---|---|
| Mean Number---282 | Personal & Repair<br>Shopping Goods<br>Other Retail | 37<br>36<br>36 | 45 to 81<br>27 to 40<br>28 to 57 |
| Range:  273 to 291 | Professions<br>Eating & Drinking<br>Food | 33<br>22<br>18 | 33 to 37<br>15 to 27<br>10 to 43 |
| Square Footage of Enclosed Area: 312,050 to 371,000 | Finance & Insurance<br>Gasoline<br>Automobiles | 15<br>14<br>4 | 16 to 36<br>14 to 26<br>2 to 12 |

TABLE 11--Continued

CLASSIFICATION OF CENTRAL SERVICES

## Class I -- Higher-Order Centers

Group I-B: Old Urban Places and Small Municipalities with
Developed Services

| Penn-Jersey Zone | Name of Municipality | C. B. D.: Central Business District S. C.: Shopping Center |
|---|---|---|
| No Zone | Middle Bucks County<br>New Hope Borough | C. B. D. only |
| 3871<br>3831 | Lower Bucks County<br>Morrisville Borough<br>Tullytown Borough | C. B. D. and S. C.<br>S. C. only |
| 7491 | Burlington County<br>Bordentown City | C. B. D. and S. C. |
| 7923 | Gloucester County<br>Paulsboro Borough | C. B. D. only |

| All Establishments | Business Types | Mean Number: Estimated from log Regression for Total of 110 | Range: Variation in Observed Number of Establishments |
|---|---|---|---|
| Mean Number---110 | Personal & Repair<br>Other Retail<br>Shopping Goods | 16<br>14<br>12 | 9 to 31<br>4 to 42<br>10 to 26 |
| Range: 89 to 128 | Professions<br>Eating & Drinking<br>Food | 12<br>10<br>9 | 9 to 20<br>4 to 18<br>6 to 13 |
| Square Footage of Enclosed Area: 118,470 to 447,300 | Gasoline<br>Finance & Insurance<br>Automobiles | 8<br>6<br>3 | 1 to 9<br>6 to 10<br>3 to 4 |

TABLE 11--Continued

CLASSIFICATION OF CENTRAL SERVICES

Class II -- Lower-Order Centers

Small City, Borough, or Portion of Township with Commercial Development

| Penn-Jersey Zone | Name of Municipality | Name of Local Settlement or Housing Development | Central Business District, Shopping Center or Highway |
|---|---|---|---|
| | | Lower Bucks County | |
| 3841 | Bensalem Township* | Penn Valley, Trevose, Siles | U. S. Route One, Penna. Turnpike, Interchange 28 |
| 3911 | Bensalem Township* | Andalusia, Cornwells Hts. | U. S. 13 |
| 3912 | Bensalem Township* | Eddington, Bridgewater | U. S. 13 |
| 3851 | Langhorne Borough Langhorne Manor Boro.* Borough* | -- -- | C. B. D. |
| 3852 | Penndel Borough L. Manor Borough* | -- -- | C. B. D. (U. S. 1) |
| 3854 | Middletown Township* Hulmeville Borough | -- -- | -- -- |
| 3855 | Middletown Township* | Levittown | Midway |
| 3856 | Middletown Township* | Levittown | U. S. 1, Country Club S. C. |
| 3857 | Middletown Township* | Oxford Valley, George School | U. S. 1 |
| 3861 | Falls Township* | Fairless Hills | Fairless Hills S. C. U. S. 1 |
| 3862 | Falls Township* | Fairless Hills, Fallsington | U. S. 1 and U. S. 13 |
| 3932 | Falls Township* | Levittown | U. S. 13 |
| 3922 | Bristol Township* | Croydon | U. S. 13 |
| 3924 | Bristol Township* | Newportville | Bargain City |
| 3926 | Bristol Township* | Levittown | Midway, Five Points |
| 3927 | Bristol Township* | Edgely, Levittown | U. S. 13, Penna. Turnpike, Interchange 29 |
| 3928 | Bristol Township* | Levittown | -- |

* Portion only

TABLE 11--Continued

CLASSIFICATION OF CENTRAL SERVICES

Class II -- Lower-Order Centers

Small City, Borough, or Portion of Township with Commercial Development

| Penn-Jersey Zone | Name of Municipality | Name of Local Settlement or Housing Development | Central Business District, Shopping Center or Highway |
|---|---|---|---|
| | | Burlington County | |
| 7452 | Beverly City and Edgewater Park Twp. | -- Del Vue | C. B. D. and U. S. 130 |
| 7462 | Willingboro Twp.* | Levittown | Levittown S. C. U. S. 130 |
| 7472 | Burlington Township* | -- | U. S. 130 |
| 7481 | Florence Township* | Florence & Roebling | C. B. D. |
| 7492 | Bordentown Township* & Fieldsboro Borough | -- | U. S. 130 & 206 N. J. Tpke., Interch. 7 |
| 7493 | Bordentown Township* | Parsonville | U. S. 130, Two Guys |
| 7486 | Springfield Township* | Chambers Corners | U. S. 206, Columbus Farmers Market |
| 7573 | Hainesport Township* & Lumberton Township* | -- | N. J. 38 |
| | | Gloucester County | |
| 7811 | Westville Borough | -- | C. B. D. |
| 7813 | Deptford Township* | Westville Grove | Woodbury Plaza S. C., N. J. 47 |
| 7821 | Deptford Township* & Woodbury Hts. Borough | Oak Valley | -- -- |
| 7823 | Deptford Township* | Gardenville, Cooper Village, Almonesson, Blackwood Terrace, Fairview | N. J. 41 |
| 7922 | West Deptford Township* | Greenfields Cool Spring | Southwood S. C. N. J. 45 |

* Portion only

TABLE 11--Continued

CLASSIFICATION OF CENTRAL SERVICES

Class II - Lower Order Centers

| All Establishments | Business Types | Mean Number: Estimated from log regression for | | Range: Variation in Observed No. of Establishments |
|---|---|---|---|---|
| | | 40 estabs. | 80 estabs. | |
| Mean Number: 54 | Personal & Repair | 6 | 12 | 0 to 24 |
| | Other Retail | 5 | 10 | 0 to 27 |
| | Eating & Drinking | 5 | 8 | 1 to 29 |
| Range: 25 to 99 | Professions | 4 | 9 | 0 to 23 |
| | Shopping Goods | 4 | 9 | 1 to 15 |
| | Food | 4 | 7 | 0 to 13 |
| Square Footage of | Gasoline | 4 | 6 | 1 to 16 |
| Enclosed Area-- | Finance & Insurance | 3 | 5 | 0 to 13 |
| 34,200 to 177,600 | Automobiles | 2 | 2 | 0 to 10 |

Class III -- Rudimentary Service Centers

Small Borough or Portion of Township with Little or
No Commercial Development

| Penn-Jersey Zone | Name of Municipality | Name of Local Settlement or Housing Development | Central Business District, Shopping Center or Highway |
|---|---|---|---|
| | | Lower Bucks County | |
| 3842 | Bensalem Township* | Eddington Gardens, Stanwood | -- |
| 3843 | Bensalem Township* | Bensalem Church | -- |
| 3913 | Bensalem Township* | Ellerslie | -- |
| 3853 | Middletown Township* | Langhorne Terrace Parkland | U. S. 1 |
| 3933 | Falls Township* | Fairless Works Penns Manor | -- |
| 3923 | Bristol Township* | West Bristol, Rockdale | U. S. 13 |
| 3925 | Bristol Township* | Bristol Terrace | U. S. 13 |

* Portion only

TABLE 11--Continued

CLASSIFICATION OF CENTRAL SERVICES

Class III (Continued)

| Penn-Jersey Zone | Name of Municipality | Name of Local Settlement or Housing Development | Central Business District, Shopping Center or Highway |
|---|---|---|---|
| | | Burlington County | |
| 7451 | Delanco Borough | -- | -- |
| 7471 | Willingboro Township* | Levittown & Rancocas | -- |
| 7473 | Burlington Township* | Deacons | County 541 |
| 7474 | Burlington Township* | Stevens | U.S. 130 |
| 7482 | Florence Township* | Bustleton | -- |
| 7483 | Mansfield Township* | Kinkora, Hedding | U.S. 130 |
| 7484 | Mansfield Township | Columbus | U.S. 206 |
| 7485 | Springfield Township* | Jacksonville | -- |
| 7571 | Westampton Township | -- | -- |
| 7572 | Westampton Township* & Eastampton Township* | Timbuctoo, Unionville | N.J. Turnpike Interchange 5 |
| | | Gloucester County | |
| 7822 | Wenonah Borough & Deptford Township | New Sharon | N.J. 47 |
| 7911 | West Deptford Township* | Red Bank, Verga | U.S. 130 |
| 7912 | National Park Borough | -- | -- |
| 7921 | West Deptford Township* | Thorofare, Mantua Grove | U.S. 130 |

* Portion only

| All Establishments | Business Types | Mean Number: Estimated from log regression for | | Range: Variation in Observed Number of Establishments |
|---|---|---|---|---|
| | | 6 estabs. | 15 estabs. | |
| Mean Number: 14 | Personal & Repair | 1 | 3 | 0 to 3 |
| | Gasoline | 1 | 3 | 0 to 10 |
| | Eating & Drinking | 1 | 2 | 0 to 8 |
| | Food | 1 | 2 | 0 to 5 |
| Range: 0 to 28 | Professions | 1 | 1 | 0 to 10 |
| | Other Retail | 1 | 1 | 0 to 5 |
| | Finance & Insur. | 1 | 1 | 0 to 3 |
| Square Footage of | Shopping Goods | 1 | 1 | 0 to 3 |
| Enclosed Area-- 0 to 41,000 | Automobiles | 1 | 1 | 0 to 2 |

of central services which makes Class II different than Class III. Map analysis shows
that the median distance for Class II is two miles, precisely the same as for Class III.
Centroids of Class II zones are typically two to four miles apart, the widest spacing
being observed in Burlington County and the closest in the Lower Bucks study area where
clustering at intervals of less than two miles is common (Figure 22). No Class II centers
appear in Middle Bucks County. Many Class II zones contain shopping centers and commercial strips along major highways. (Compare Figures 24 and 22.) Some doubt is cast
upon the usefulness of mapping centroids and proximate areas where the arrangement of
stores and services is so scattered and disorderly. However, it is clear that the spacing
of identifiable centers of concentration is greater for centers in Class I. The median
distance for Class II is two miles. The maximum distances between centroids of Class
II zones, where no Class I zones intervene, is seven miles. The minimum distance observed is less than a mile, not differing essentially from Class III.

The results of the foregoing analysis are as follows:

TABLE 12

SPACING OF CLASS I, II, AND III ZONES

| Class of Zones | Median Distance (miles) | Range (miles) | Number of Measurements |
|---|---|---|---|
| I | 6 | 1 to 11 | 11 |
| II | 2 | 0.7 to 7 | 54 |
| III | 2 | 1 to 3.5 | 55 |

Class I differs from the others both in spatial pattern and function, while the
two lower classes are alike in spacing, but distinguished by degree of development. Class
II zones are the most dynamic and least well ordered portions of the metropolitan fringe.
Further examination of the geographic context of Class II zones and comparison with both
higher and lower levels of the hierarchy shows that these zones comprise nearly all the
areas of recent urban development, the median household density being about 400 per
square mile. (See Table 13.) Some zones, especially those located in Lower Bucks
County, exceed 1,000 households per square mile. When it is pointed out that the median
area of Class II zones is 2.8 square miles in which the median household count is about
1,500, the trade potential of such areas for establishment of shopping centers and growth
of highway strips is obvious. Their attractiveness is enhanced by the relatively high
income of the population, the median reported being $6,250 per household. Median in-
come rises well above this figure in certain zones, some of which are Class III zones
(Figure 25). But it is clear that the concentration of income is much higher per square
mile in Class II than generally in Class III zones.

111

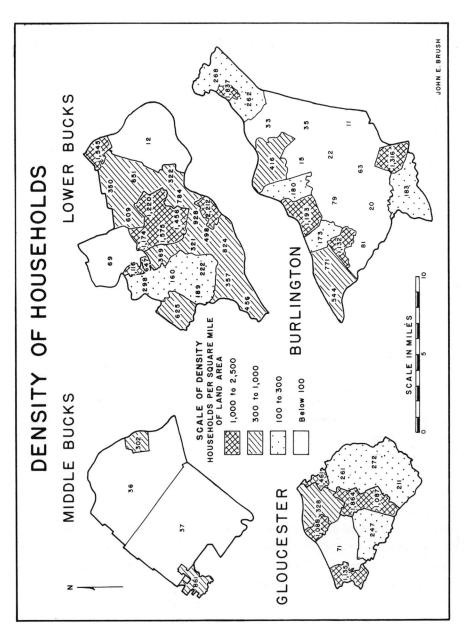

Figure 25.

Typical geographic situations most favorable for commercial development in Class II zones are: (a) adjacent to well developed towns of Class I A where major highways and secondary roads bring together the maximum numbers of consumers, and (b) in areas of large housing developments, where both household densities and incomes are high. Zones adjacent to Burlington, Mt. Holly, and Woodbury represent situations of the first type, where the consumers from one or more sectors of the town's trading territory now find many goods and services offered at readily accessible highway locations. Prime examples of Class II zones in situations of the second type are in the Levittown (Zones 3855, 3856, 3932, 3926, 3927, 3928) and Fairless Hills (Zones 3861, 3862) housing tracts of Lower Bucks County and Levittown in Burlington County, New Jersey (7462). Here the local thresholds for many goods and services are reached at a distance of three to five miles from any Class I A center.

TABLE 13

AREA, HOUSEHOLDS, AND INCOME IN CLASS I, II, AND III ZONES

| Class of Zones | Median Zone Area (Sq. Mi.) | Median Household Density (per sq. mi.) | Median Annual Household Income |
|---|---|---|---|
| I | 1.9 | 1,430 | 5,830 |
| II | 2.8 | 436 | 6,250 |
| III | 4.0 | 160 | 6,180 |

Class III zones cannot support such concentrations of stores and services, although household income levels are nearly as high as in Class II zones and commonly there have been recent population increases. The areas of these zones are generally larger than for the higher classes while household densities are much lower. Thus, there is insufficient geographic concentration of demand to approach the threshold of entry for many kinds of goods and services. Filling stations, small food stores, eating and drinking places, and simple personal services are found in relect hamlets and villages or on the highways, and the inhabitants remain dependent upon other places for all but these rudimentary goods and services. The least urban parts of the Burlington study area typify this situation, where household densities are well below 100 per square mile, and most of the land is being farmed. Buckingham and Solebury townships also typify this situation. Here shopping trips of five to ten miles are necessary, but there is little traffic congestion to impede consumers en route to town. It seems unlikely that the market equilibrium will shift without sharp increases of population in Class III zones.

Class I zones comprise the places with small areas and lowest income levels. Population increases have occurred recently in all but three places (Bristol, Bordentown, and New Hope) and generally the population increases are less in relative terms than in

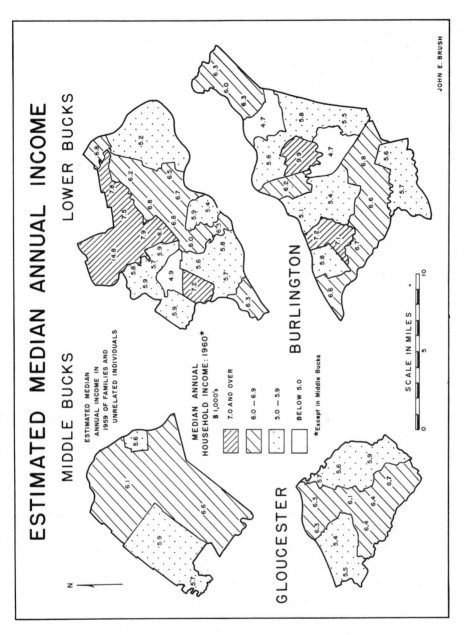

Figure 26.

the lower classes. Yet most of the Class I zones have household densities high enough to bring about the highest concentration of income per square mile, almost twice as high as in Class II zones, taking the median figures as the basis of calculation. As already pointed out, these zones contain the most intensive commercial development, and those in Class I A have the traditional role of central places for a wider radius than any other places in the study areas. No Class II zone as yet has grown to be the equal of the variety and intensity of development in any Class I zone. To a large degree Class I centers retain their primacy in professional services and a variety of personal, financial, and repair services, although beset with problems of traffic congestion and small or inefficient and obsolete establishments.

CHAPTER IV

ANALYSIS OF CONSUMER TRIPS

The objective of this chapter is to gain some understanding of geographical patterns of trips made by consumers living in the vicinity of the central places which have been described and classified in the foregoing chapter. Attention is drawn to evidence of travel gradients, reflecting the influence of one or more centers upon the patterns of consumer trips. Finally, an attempt is made to develop a simple model to approximate the observed patterns of consumer travel. The mathematical expression is a stochastic transformation of the gravity model.

## Dominance of the Automobile

At the outset it should be emphasized that almost all local travel analyzed in each of the four study areas is accomplished by means of privately-owned automobiles. The 1960 census data for Bucks, Burlington , and Gloucester counties indicate that at least one automobile is available in 88 to 93 per cent of all households. Data for certain townships in which a 20 per cent sample of households was taken in 1960 show that the percentage of households with one or more cars available varies from 96 to 98 per cent in much of Lower Bucks County. (See Table 14.) In some census tracts in Bristol Township, which lie partly or wholly within the Levittown housing areas, the percentage of households with automobiles rises to 99. Between one-quarter and one-third of the households here have two cars available, while generally throughout the three counties one-fifth of the households have two cars available. As a rule, about two-thirds of the households have one automobile only.

It can be postulated on the basis of limited evidence that the percentages of households with one or more automobiles are somewhat less in the older, more densely occupied municipalities within the study areas. In the City of Philadelphia the percentage of all households with autos drops to 56 and the percentage with one auto only is 48.[1] The Penn-Jersey Transportation Study in analyzing data for all parts of the region with the

---

[1]U. S. Census of Population and Housing: 1960. Census Tracts. Final Report PHC (1)-116, Washington, D. C.: 1962. Table H-2, p. 417.

115

116

Cordon Line reports that, when population reaches a density of 4,000 persons per quarter square mile, automobile ownership falls to less than one per household.[2] Bristol Borough, Tullytown, Bordentown Borough, Burlington Borough, Mt. Holly, and Woodbury, are municipalities mentioned in the Penn-Jersey News where less than one car is owned per household. However, virtually every sample household included in the Penn-Jersey travel data analyzed in the following pages reports at least one car owned and in one of every three or four households two cars are owned. (See Table 15.)

Table 14

AUTOMOBILES AVAILABLE: 1960

| County or Municipality | Per Cent of Households | | | |
|---|---|---|---|---|
| | Automobiles Available | | | No Automobile Available |
| | One | Two | Three or more | |
| Bucks County | 61.4 | 28.5 | 3.6 | 6.5 |
| Bristol Township | 71.5 | 22.2 | 1.9 | 4.4 |
| Falls Township | 67.6 | 26.5 | 3.6 | 2.3 |
| Middletown Township | 57.3 | 35.9 | 2.7 | 4.1 |
| Burlington County | 64.3 | 22.0 | 2.7 | 11.3 |
| Gloucester County | 63.3 | 20.9 | 3.2 | 12.6 |

Source: U.S. Census of Population and Housing: 1960. Census Tracts. Final Report PHC (1)-116 (Philadelphia, Pa. - N.J.). Washington, D.C., 1962. Table H-2, pp. 417-418.

Furthermore, the vehicles are used a great deal. The Penn-Jersey data show a mean of 930 to 1,600 trips a day per 100 households. Trips tend to occur in multiples of two. The minimum is one outbound trip paired with a return trip home the same day, although some are linked in a series of intermediate destinations. It is evident that the modal frequency is six trips per day in the Burlington and Gloucester study areas. (See Figure 27.)

Not only are private automobiles generally available to residents of the study areas, but they are used more frequently for shopping and personal business than for journeys to work. The Penn-Jersey Transportation Study reports that in the region as a whole, automobiles are used for 88 per cent of trips for personal business purposes.[3] Automobiles are used for 68 per cent of trips to work, as compared to 32 per cent for

[2]Penn-Jersey News, Vol. 2, No. 3, 1962, (June-July).

[3]Penn-Jersey News, Vol. 2, No. 4, 1962, (August-September).

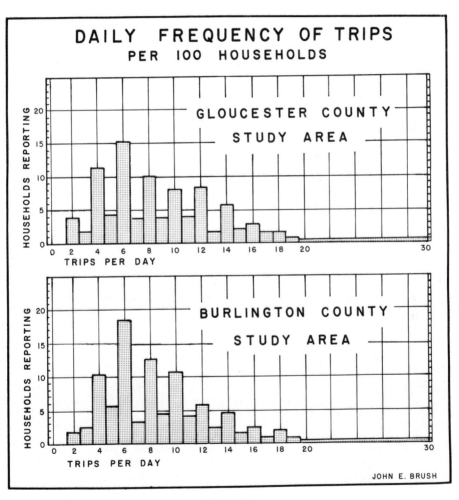

Figure 27.

the various modes of mass transportation. The highest dependence on autos among major trip purposes reported in the Penn-Jersey Study is for social and recreational activities being used for 91 per cent of all trips in this category. Of course, the above percentages are based on data for the area within the Cordon Line, including the cities of Philadelphia, Camden, and Trenton, where mass transportation is more prevalent than in the outer fringes. In the study areas it appears that automobiles are used for 97 to 98 per cent of all trips, originating from home. This conclusion is based on the data for origins of daily person trips in the areas of the Penn-Jersey Study located within the Cordon Line in Bucks, Burlington, and Gloucester counties.[4] Local travel in the Middle Bucks Study Area may be presumed to be even more dependent upon privately-owned automobiles because of its outlying location, moderately high income level and low population density.

The conclusion that residents of the study areas depend almost exclusively upon private automobiles for shopping is born out by the special survey of weekly food buying in and near Woodbury conducted during 1962.[5] Of the 354 householders interviewed in a sample of nearly 4,000 households in the City of Woodbury, only 19 persons reported that they walked to grocery stores, while two used taxicabs, and three traveled by bus. Thus, in this long-established, compact urban community with public transportation available and average ownership of less than one car per household, more than 93 per cent of the food shoppers used private cars and only five per cent were pedestrians.

Table 15

AUTOMOBILE OWNERSHIP AND TRIP FREQUENCY: 1960-61

| Penn-Jersey Data Collection Zones in Study Area | Mean Number per 100 Households | |
|---|---|---|
| | Automobiles Owned | Trips per Day |
| Lower Bucks County | 137 | 1,062 |
| Burlington County | 135 | 931 |
| Gloucester County | 128 | 1,002 |

Source: Penn-Jersey Transportation Study, Household Interviews, 1960-61.

[4] Penn-Jersey News, Vol. 2, No. 7, 1963, (December-January).

[5] James A. Perry, "The Shopping Center and Its Effect on Consumer Food Shopping Patterns; Woodbury, N. J., 1962," Unpublished Report, Department of Geography, Rutgers University, New Brunswick, N. J., 1963.

Food Shopping Patterns in Bucks County

In Bucks County there is an abundance of geographical data on food shopping. The County Planning Commission supervises the local census conducted in each municipality every third year for purposes of tax assessment and school enrollment. Among the several questions asked of a householder is one phrased as follows: "Where do you go for weekly food shopping?" Interviewers are instructed to obtain specific answers as to store name and location. The data so obtained are compiled by the Planning Commission in such a manner as to make it possible to locate each household on cadastral maps and thus to convert the data to cartographic form. In certain municipalities of Middle and Lower Bucks County, where responses to this question are in excess of 90 per cent of all households, it is useful to analyze weekly food shopping patterns. By striking concentric arcs of circles around destinations most frequently reported and taking counts of households depending on stores at these destinations, the influence of various centers can be observed. In this way relationships between distances and distribution of households can be measured in representative areas of the outer and inner metropolitan fringes.

Data from Buckingham and Solebury townships in Middle Bucks County are representative of the outer metropolitan fringe, where population density is comparatively low and geographical patterns of shopping are simple. No large food stores exist within these two townships, so it is relatively easy to analyze external travel towards Doylestown destinations on the one hand and towards New Hope, or the two nearby New Jersey destinations of Lambertville and Stockton, on the other hand. (See Table 16 and Figure 28.) Clearly there is a diminution of influence, as expressed in the density of households dependent on a given center, as the distance from that center increases. Doylestown has more extensive influence than New Hope, combined with the two nearby New Jersey centers, as is evident from the fact that the boundary of relative predominance of Doylestown extends seven miles, as compared to three miles for the latter places. The preponderance of Doylestown is related to the greater size and number of food stores there and reflects New Hope's tendency to cater to tourists rather than to serve the regular needs of local householders. The relatively minor influence of small neighborhood stores in the villages and hamlets, situated at three to five miles from either Doylestown or New Hope is evident. The incidence of households reporting trips to stores located in other places is greatest beyond three miles from Doylestown or New Hope, although the density of such households and their relative importance is low except in the outskirts of Doylestown. It is significant to note that, whereas the intensity of influence measured in terms of household density, bears an inverse relation to distance from Doylestown and the other local centers, the total number of households reporting dependence on these centers reaches the maximum at distances of between two and four

Table 16

DENSITY OF HOUSEHOLDS REPORTING FOOD SHOPPING

BUCKINGHAM AND SOLEBURY TOWNSHIPS, BUCKS COUNTY

| Distance from Doylestown or Cross Keys (miles) | Food Store Location | | | | | |
|---|---|---|---|---|---|---|
| | Doylestown and Cross Keys | | Local Villages and Hamlets | | Other Places | |
| | House-holds | Density per sq. mi. | House-holds | Density per sq. mi. | House-holds | Density per sq. mi. |
| Within 1 | 17 | 177 | 1 | 1 | 2 | 21 |
| 1 - 2 | 108 | 51 | 0 | - | 7 | 3 |
| 2 - 3 | 206 | 57 | 8 | 3 | 8 | 2 |
| 3 - 4 | 208 | 38 | 24 | 8 | 19 | 3 |
| 4 - 5 | 179 | 25 | 18 | 6 | 19 | 3 |
| 5 - 6 | 133 | 15 | 7 | 2 | 19 | 2 |
| 6 - 7 | 163 | 16 | N. D. | - | N. D. | - |
| 7 - 8 | 96 | 8 | N. D. | - | N. D. | - |
| 8 - 9 | 34 | 3 | N. D. | - | N. D. | - |
| 9 - 10 | 24 | 2 | N. D. | - | N. D. | - |

| Distance from Lambertville or Stockton (miles) | Food Store Location | | | | | |
|---|---|---|---|---|---|---|
| | New Hope, Lambert-ville, N. J., and Stockton, N. J. | | Local Villages and Hamlets | | Other Places | |
| | House-holds | Density per sq. mi. | House-holds | Density per sq. mi. | House-holds | Density per sq. mi. |
| Within 1 | 36 | 80 | 4 | 1 | 3 | 7 |
| 1 - 2 | 155 | 34 | 0 | - | 9 | 2 |
| 2 - 3 | 139 | 19 | 20 | 3 | 10 | 1 |
| 3 - 4 | 73 | 7 | 18 | 8 | 13 | 1 |
| 4 - 5 | 36 | 3 | 7 | 6 | 8 | 1 |
| 5 - 6 | 12 | 1 | 7 | 2 | 2 | 1 |
| 6 - 7 | 4 | 1 | N. D. | - | N. D. | - |
| 7 - 8 | 1 | 1 | N. D. | - | N. D. | - |

Source:  Triennial Census, Bucks County Planning Commission, 1961

N. D. = Not Determined

121

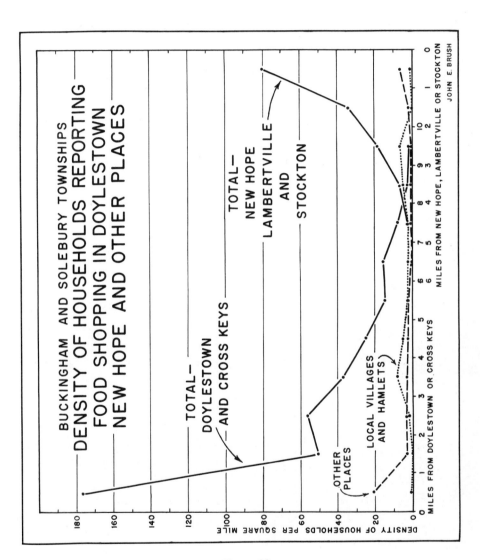

Figure 28.

Table 17

PERCENTAGE DISTRIBUTION OF FOOD SHOPPING REPORTED BY HOUSEHOLDS
BUCKINGHAM AND SOLEBURY TOWNSHIPS, BUCKS COUNTY

| Distance from Doylestown or Cross Keys (miles) | Total House-holds | Food Store Location | | | | | | | | | |
|---|---|---|---|---|---|---|---|---|---|---|---|
| | | Doylestown Shopping Center | | Other Doylestown | | Cross Keys | | Local Villages & Hamlets | | Other Places | |
| | | House-holds | Per Cent | House-holds | Per Cent | House-holds | Per Cent | House-holds | Per Cent | House-holds | Per Cent |
| Within 1 | 20 | 8 | 40 | 2 | 10 | 7 | 35 | 1 | 5 | 2 | 10 |
| 1 - 2 | 115 | 67 | 58 | 27 | 23 | 14 | 12 | 0 | - | 7 | 6 |
| 2 - 3 | 222 | 158 | 71 | 42 | 19 | 6 | 3 | 8 | 4 | 8 | 4 |
| 3 - 4 | 251 | 147 | 58 | 41 | 16 | 20 | 8 | 24 | 10 | 19 | 8 |
| 4 - 5 | 216 | 146 | 67 | 20 | 9 | 13 | 6 | 18 | 8 | 19 | 9 |
| 5 - 6 | 159 | 105 | 66 | 19 | 12 | 9 | 6 | 7 | 4 | 19 | 12 |

| Distance from Lambertville, N. J. or Stockton, N.J. (miles) | Total House-holds | Food Store Location | | | | | | | | | |
|---|---|---|---|---|---|---|---|---|---|---|---|
| | | New Hope | | Lambertville, N. J. | | Stockton, N. J. | | Local Villages & Hamlets | | Other Places | |
| | | House-holds | Per Cent | House-holds | Per Cent | House-holds | Per Cent | House-holds | Per Cent | House-holds | Per Cent |
| Within 1 | 43 | 9 | 21 | 14 | 32 | 13 | 30 | 4 | 9 | 3 | 7 |
| 1 - 2 | 164 | 75 | 46 | 71 | 43 | 9 | 5 | 0 | - | 9 | 5 |
| 2 - 3 | 169 | 76 | 45 | 56 | 33 | 7 | 4 | 20 | 12 | 10 | 6 |
| 3 - 4 | 104 | 29 | 28 | 42 | 40 | 2 | 2 | 18 | 17 | 13 | 12 |
| 4 - 5 | 51 | 14 | 27 | 21 | 41 | 1 | 2 | 7 | 14 | 8 | 16 |
| 5 - 6 | 21 | 4 | 19 | 8 | 38 | 0 | - | 7 | 33 | 2 | 9 |

Source:  Triennial Census, Bucks County Planning Commission, 1961.

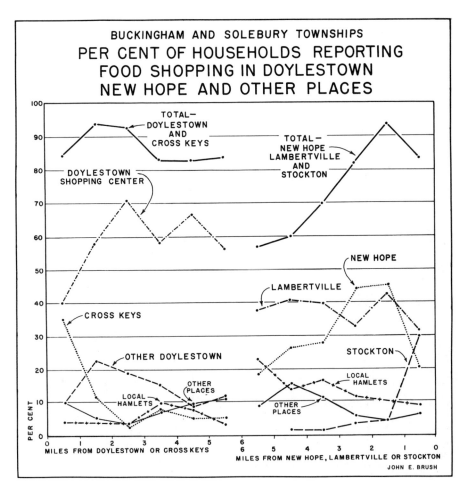

Figure 29.

Table 18

DENSITY OF HOUSEHOLDS REPORTING FOOD SHOPPING

MIDDLETOWN TOWNSHIP, BUCKS COUNTY

| Distance from Midway (miles) | Food Store Location | | | |
|---|---|---|---|---|
| | Midway | | Five Points, Country Club and Other Places | |
| | Households | Density/Sq. Mi. | Households | Density/Sq. Mi. |
| Within .25 | 2 | N. D. | 0 | 0 |
| .25 - .50 | 57 | 1,046 | 8 | 147 |
| .50 - .75 | 94 | 930 | 34 | 336 |
| .75 - 1.00 | 126 | 565 | 63 | 282 |
| 1.00 - 1.25 | 37 | 112 | 54 | 163 |
| 1.25 - 1.50 | 107 | 306 | N. D. | - |
| 1.50 - 1.75 | 79 | 209 | N. D. | - |
| 1.75 - 2.00 | 17 | 68 | N. D. | - |
| 2.00 - 2.25 | 3 | N. D. | N. D. | - |

| Distance from Five Points (miles) | Food Store Location | | | |
|---|---|---|---|---|
| | Five Points | | Midway, Country Club and Other Places | |
| | Households | Density/Sq. Mi. | Households | Density/Sq. Mi. |
| Within .25 | N. A. | - | N. A. | - |
| .25 - .50 | 35 | 1,048 | 9 | 269 |
| .50 - .75 | 142 | 1,013 | 42 | 300 |
| .75 - 1.00 | 155 | 736 | 75 | 356 |
| 1.00 - 1.25 | 84 | 429 | 84 | 429 |
| 1.25 - 1.50 | 24 | 82 | N. D. | - |
| 1.50 - 1.75 | 38 | 78 | N. D. | - |
| 1.75 - 2.00 | 18 | 41 | N. D. | - |
| 2.00 - 2.25 | 2 | N. D. | N. D. | - |

| Distance from Country Club (miles) | Food Store Location | | | |
|---|---|---|---|---|
| | Country Club | | Midway, Five Points and Other Places | |
| | Households | Density/Sq. Mi. | Households | Density/Sq. Mi. |
| Within .25 | 124 | 1,549 | 20 | 250 |
| .25 - .50 | 276 | 1,452 | 29 | 152 |
| .50 - .75 | 163 | 594 | 120 | 437 |
| .75 - 1.00 | 283 | 628 | 232 | 514 |
| 1.00 - 1.25 | 95 | 310 | 48 | 157 |
| 1.25 - 1.50 | 131 | 429 | N. D. | - |
| 1.50 - 1.75 | 99 | 235 | N. D. | - |
| 1.75 - 2.00 | 17 | 119 | N. D. | - |
| 2.00 - 2.25 | 5 | N. D. | N. D. | - |

Source: Triennial Census, Bucks County Planning Commission, 1962.

N.A. = Not Available

N.D. = Not Determined

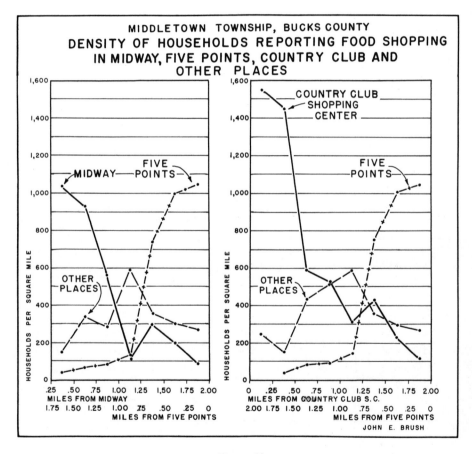

Figure 30.

Table 19

PERCENTAGE DISTRIBUTION OF FOOD SHOPPING REPORTED BY HOUSEHOLDS
MIDDLETOWN TOWNSHIP, BUCKS COUNTY

| Distance From Midway (miles) | Total Households | Food Store Location | | | |
|---|---|---|---|---|---|
| | | Midway | | Five Points, Country Club and Other Places | |
| | | Households | Per Cent | Households | Per Cent |
| Within .25 | 2 | N.D. | N.D. | 0 | 0 |
| .25 - .50 | 65 | 57 | 88 | 8 | 12 |
| .50 - .75 | 128 | 94 | 73 | 34 | 27 |
| .75 - 1.00 | 189 | 126 | 67 | 63 | 33 |
| 1.00 - 1.25 | 91 | 37 | 41 | 54 | 59 |

| Distance from Five Points (miles) | Total Households | Food Store Location | | | |
|---|---|---|---|---|---|
| | | Five Points | | Midway, Country Club and Other Places | |
| | | Households | Per Cent | Households | Per Cent |
| Within .25 | N.A. | N.A. | - | N.A. | - |
| .25 - .50 | 44 | 35 | 79 | 9 | 20 |
| .50 - .75 | 184 | 142 | 77 | 42 | 23 |
| .75 - 1.00 | 230 | 155 | 67 | 75 | 33 |
| 1.00 - 1.25 | 168 | 84 | 50 | 84 | 50 |

| Distance from Country Club (miles) | Total Households | Food Store Location | | | |
|---|---|---|---|---|---|
| | | Country Club | | Midway, Five Points and Other Places | |
| | | Households | Per Cent | Households | Per Cent |
| Within .25 | 144 | 124 | 86 | 20 | 14 |
| .25 - .50 | 305 | 276 | 90 | 29 | 10 |
| .50 - .75 | 283 | 163 | 58 | 120 | 42 |
| .75 - 1.00 | 471 | 238 | 51 | 232 | 49 |
| 1.00 - 1.25 | 143 | 95 | 66 | 48 | 34 |

Source: Triennial Census, Bucks County Planning Commission, 1962.

N.D. = Not Determined

N.A. = Not Available

127

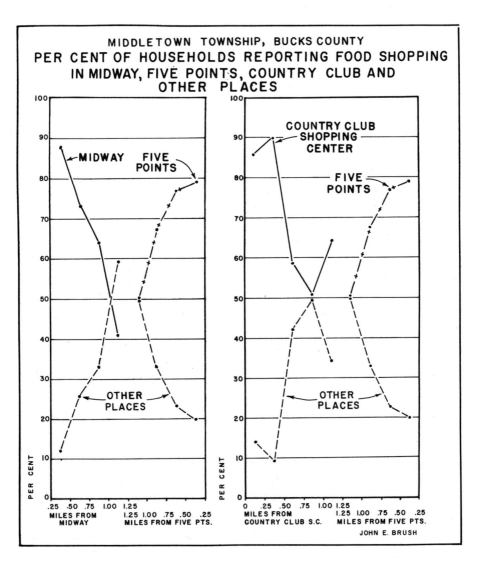

Figure 31.

128

miles due to the progressively larger areas enclosed by successive arcs.

Percentage distribution patterns (Table 17 and Figure 29) show some interesting relationships. The highest proportions of households reporting food shopping in
Doylestown and Cross Keys, or in New Hope, Lambertville, and Stockton combined,
occurs between the second and third or fourth mile arcs. Beyond the third mile the percentage of households dependent on Doylestown is well sustained, due mainly to the
attraction of stores in the shopping center. The relative influence of New Hope, combined
with the two nearby places in New Jersey, declines markedly after the third mile. Beyond
three miles the attraction of Lambertville's food stores (which enjoy the advantage of
location in New Jersey where there is no food sales tax in contrast to Pennsylvania) is
larger than New Hope's food stores. Thus, the analysis of the relative influence of the
local centers upon consumers living in this area of dispersed households show that in
some instances attraction may be sustained or increased as distance increases. In sum,
the data from Middle Bucks County support the anticipated geographical relationships
between relative sizes of centers, distances and consumer interaction, although there are
certain exceptions for special reasons food shoppers are repelled or attracted.

Turning to the data from Middletown Township in Lower Bucks County, it is
clear that the distance to food stores also has a pronounced impact on consumer behavior.
The data pertain to a section of the township (Penn-Jersey Zones 3855 and 3856, Figure
15) in Levittown, where household densities and family income levels are high. (See
Figures 25 and 26.) Private auto ownership is virtually universal in such a residential
area and possibly as many as a third of the families have two or more cars. Several
modern supermarkets are available at Midway, Five Points, and the Country Club
Shopping Center on U. S. Route One, all within two miles of the households. It might be
supposed that here, if anywhere on the metropolitan fringe, the personal mobility and
apparently random trips of many individuals would diminish the intensity of travel
gradients.

Yet consumer behavior en masse seems very much in accordance with the
basic principle of centrality, i.e., that people generally go to the nearest store. (See
Table 18 and Figure 30.) Initial densities of households dependent upon stores located
at each of the three centers are much higher than in Middle Bucks, a feature which is to
be accounted for by the lack of data on food shopping within Doylestown Borough and the
low density of housing on the fringe of the Borough. In contrast there is close spacing
of dwellings in Levittown, averaging from 1,000 to 1,600 households per square mile.
Furthermore, the distribution of households in highly uniform in Levittown, whereas
there is an irregular scattering of houses in Buckingham and Solebury Townships and
the mean density is generally less than 40 per square mile. These facts account for the

low slope of the density gradient of households dependent upon Doylestown food stores. But density gradients in Lower Bucks decline sharply as distance increases from any given destination because of the relatively rapid diminution of households dependent on stores in that location, not because of decrease in the density of households representing potential customers. The density gradients of households dependent upon food stores in any one of the three locations in Lower Bucks fall off sharply within the first mile. Between each pair of destinations there is clearly a boundary of relative dominance about a mile and a quarter from each destination. The density of households reporting food shopping at other places is considerably higher than in Middle Bucks County and it reaches its maximum in the interstitial areas near the bounds of predominant influence from any one of the three local destinations.

Certain points of similarity and some significant differences are to be drawn from further comparison of food shopping patterns in the two Bucks County study areas. Generalized forms of the geographical relationships are derived for this purpose. (See Tables 20 and 21 and Figure 32.) The gradient for Doylestown is adjusted here to show a probable household density of 775 per square mile within the Borough limits up to a .75 mile radius, assuming that 90 per cent of the households in 1960 are dependent upon food stores located within the Borough. This is a reasonable assumption, attested by the Woodbury food shopping survey.[6] The adjusted Doylestown gradient is taken to be representative of relationships to be expected in the outer metropolitan fringe where strong centrality exists around an isolated town. The density gradient in Middletown Township is a mean of the three gradients described above, taken to represent the relationships to be expected wherever there are new shopping centers of both of planned and unplanned types in close juxtaposition to extensive tracts of new housing with a density of 1,000 dwelling units or more per square mile. The probable number of households which might depend upon these centers for food shopping is estimated on the basis of these densities, assuming that the attraction of the stores extends equally in all directions from any center. The following relationships are observed:

1. The pronounced density gradients found around food stores, whether they are located in the inner or the outer metropolitan fringes, accords with the general rule of an inverse relationship between distance and the density of consumers.

2. Around Doylestown the gradient is initially lower because of the lower density of households in the outer metropolitan fringe.

3. The absolute number of households reporting food shopping at a given destination may reach maxima in rings which are some distance removed from the

---

[6]James A. Perry, Op. cit.

Table 20

FOOD SHOPPING IN DOYLESTOWN AND CROSS KEYS
ESTIMATED DENSITY AND NUMBER OF HOUSEHOLDS

| Distance from Destination (Miles) | Household Density (per sq. mi.) | Number of Households within Assumed Area of Successive Arcs | Cumulative Total of Households |
|---|---|---|---|
| Within  .75* | 775* | 1,369 | 1,369 |
| .75 to 1.00 | 177 | 242 | 1,611 |
| 1.00 to 2.00 | 51 | 480 | 2,091 |
| 2.00 to 3.00 | 56 | 879 | 2,970 |
| 3.00 to 4.00 | 38 | 835 | 3,805 |
| 4.00 to 5.00 | 25 | 706 | 4,511 |
| 5.00 to 6.00 | 15 | 518 | 5,029 |
| 6.00 to 7.00 | 16 | 652 | 5,681 |
| 7.00 to 8.00 | 8 | 377 | 6,058 |
| 8.00 to 9.00 | 3 | 160 | 6,218 |
| 9.00 to 10.00 | 2 | 120 | 6,338 |

Source: Triennial Census, Bucks County Planning Commission, 1961;
U. S. Census of Population and Housing: 1960. Census Tracts.
Final Report PHC (1)-116. Washington, D. C., 1962.

Household density is that observed in Buckingham and
Solebury Townships food shopping in Doylestown, Doylestown
Shopping Center and Cross Keys. (See Table 16.)

Assumed areas of successive arcs are increments calculated to lie between complete circles with radii determined by
the distances from destination.

* In Doylestown Borough it is assumed that 90 per cent of the
households, 861 per square mile based on the 1960 census,
are dependent upon food stores located in the Borough.

Table 21


FOOD SHOPPING IN SELECTED AREAS OF
MIDDLETOWN TOWNSHIP
ESTIMATED DENSITY AND NUMBER OF HOUSEHOLDS


| Distance from Destination (Miles) | Household Density (per sq. mi.) | Number of Households within Assumed Area of Successive Arcs | Cumulative Total of Households |
|---|---|---|---|
| Within .25 | 1,549 | 304 | 304 |
| .25 to .50 | 1,326 | 781 | 1,085 |
| .50 to .75 | 876 | 859 | 1,944 |
| .75 to 1.00 | 691 | 950 | 2,894 |
| 1.00 to 1.25 | 372 | 657 | 3,551 |
| 1.25 to 1.50 | 272 | 587 | 4,138 |
| 1.50 to 1.75 | 138 | 214 | 4,352 |
| 1.75 to 2.00 | 76 | 216 | 4,568 |

Source: Triennial Census, Bucks County Planning Commission, 1962.

Household Density is the mean of densities observed for households reporting food shopping in Midway, Five Points, and Country Club Shopping Center. (See Table 18.)

Assumed areas of successive arcs are increments calculated between complete circles with radii determined by distances from destination.

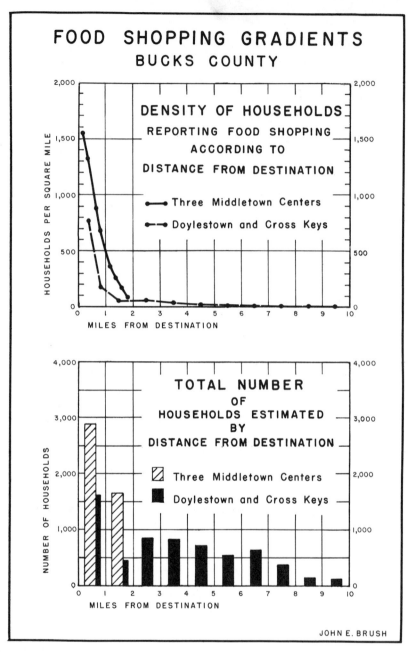

Figure 32.

destination simply because of the areal properties of circles. For example, in Middletown Township only 304 dependent households are estimated to be within the first quarter of a mile, while 950 are between .75 and 1.00 mile. Thereafter, the number of households declines. The maximum number of households dependent on stores in or adjacent to Doylestown undoubtedly lies within the Borough where household density is much above Buckingham Township. However, a secondary maximum is estimated to lie in the ring between two and three miles distant, where the density has fallen to about 50 per square mile. The estimated numbers of households dependent on Doylestown remain high up to a radius of seven miles, although household densities decline to only 15 or 16 per square mile, because there are large areas enclosed between successive arcs.

4. On account of these geometric relationships of concentric rings and the higher general density of households in the inner metropolitan fringe, i.e., Middletown Township, about 4,500 dependent households are estimated to be within a radius of two miles, or some 12.5 square miles, as compared to approximately an equal number of households lying within a five-mile radius, or about 28 square miles, in the outer fringe in and around Doylestown.

5. In sparsely-settled areas dependent upon the food stores of an isolated outer metropolitan center, i.e., Doylestown, the median distance travelled by consumers is over two miles for food shopping as compared to a median distance less than one mile in the more densely-settled inner fringe of Middletown Township, where shopping centers are located about two miles apart.

6. Food shopping of consumers living in the area around an isolated center in the outer metropolitan fringe is more completely dominated by stores located in the center, there being no substantial competition from stores in other locations within a five-mile radius; whereas in the inner fringe the attraction of stores in any one center became diffused and mingled with stores in other centers beyond a one-mile radius. These relationships are suggested by the percentage distribution of households reporting various food shopping destinations within the first mile and a quarter from the centers in Middletown Township and the first five miles from Doylestown and New Hope, or the two nearby places in New Jersey. (Compare Figures 29 and 31.)

### All Personal Business and Shopping Trips

The sample data for all types of personal business and shopping trips, from the Penn-Jersey Transportation Study, are useful in gaining fuller understanding of consumer travel patterns. These household interviews yield data which are representative of an average working day (Monday through Friday) during the period from June 1960 to January 1961. Trips made for other purposes, such as work, school, social and recreational activities, are excluded from the present analysis. The data under analysis pertain to about four per cent of households in Lower Bucks County and about ten per cent in Burlington and Gloucester counties, expanded to estimate the whole number of trips. (See Table 24, footnote.) The personal business and shopping trips are tabulated by Penn-Jersey Zones grouped by purpose into nine categories (Table 22) according to trip origin (Table 23). It must be pointed out that, while the 8,560 trips relate only to households located within the Cordon Line in the three study areas, all do not originate at home. Some of the trips are linked in series with trips for purposes other than personal business or shopping. However, the zone of origin tabulated hereafter in this report is the location of the home zone of the household involved.

Conclusions regarding frequencies of trips for various purposes are drawn from a summary of data for the study areas (Table 24). Food and shopping goods always rank first and second, respectively, together comprising over half to nearly two-thirds of all trips for personal business and shopping. Professional services and finance rank next, although much below the first two categories. Trips for gasoline or automobiles and for eating or drinking have little importance in the pattern of consumer travel on an average week day. The categories of miscellaneous retail and personal or repair services, each of which has an important collective role, include trips for a large variety of goods and services. The frequency of trips reported for all the above purposes runs between 250 and 275 per 100 households (Table 24). Return trips after accomplishing personal business or shopping purposes are excluded in our analysis. Hence, approximately double these numbers of trips actually are generated, comprising about half of the mean of about 1,000 trips per 100 households, occurring on an average week day.(See Table 15.)

Analysis of destinations of personal business and shopping trips, tabulated according to location of trip ending, reveals the influences exerted on consumer travel. (See Table 25.) It should be noted that trips originating from households outside the limits of the study areas are omitted, while trips relating to households in the study areas are included, whether or not the destinations were outside. The omission of trips originating outside has the effect of diminishing the apparent influence of establishments located in the study areas, especially in zones with developed central services which are located on the peripheries of the study areas, e.g., Morrisville, Mt. Holly, Bordentown, and Paulsboro. Inclusion of data on all trips, regardless of place of ending, shows that some-what over 20 per cent of the local consumers seek satisfaction of their consumer requirements outside the study areas.

The complexity of consumer travel to various destinations is illustrated by a series of zones situated along U. S. Highway #13 in Lower Bucks County (Figure 33). At the bottom of the graph are vertical lines and bars, representing the number and square

135

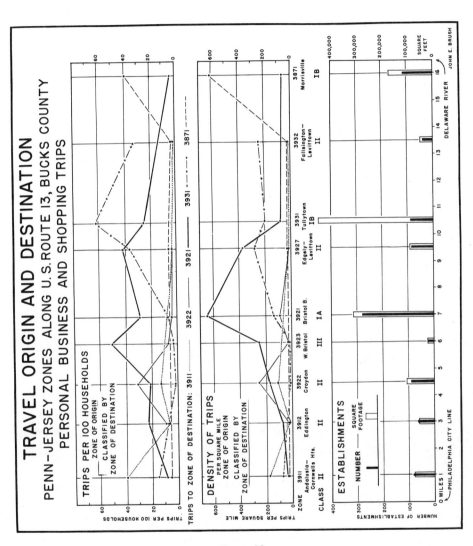

Figure 33.

footage of enclosed space. These data were obtained in field observation. The Penn-Jersey Zone numbers and local names of settlements appear above the bars, together with the functional class according to the hierarchical orders of central services as analyzed in the preceding chapter. Extending in two horizontal series are the travel gradients, expressed on the basis of density of trips reported per square mile and as a ratio per 100 households. The intersecting gradients illustrate the influences exerted on consumers by several of the destinations accessible to consumers living along a main highway in a portion of the inner metropolitan fringe with old business districts in developed urban places (Bristol Borough and Morrisville), a regional shopping center (Tullytown) and typical smaller centers situated near railroads and along highways in the urbanized townships of Bensalem, Bristol, and Falls.

In a broad sense these gradients illustrate how multiple service areas can be intermingled in urban territory while at the same time the principle of centrality is not negated. The strong position of Bristol Borough, the only Class IA zone of the series, is shown by extension of its influence to all zones up to a distance of 7 to 9 miles and its preponderant influence within a radius of two or three miles. The peak density of trips originating within the Borough is 6,500 per square mile, a feature closely related to the high density of households. The ratio of trips per 100 households within Bristol Borough is only 300, however, as compared to 400 to 450 in adjacent portions of Bristol Township. This phenomenon suggests that establishments in Bristol have relatively less attraction for consumers living in the Borough than for consumers coming from adjacent zones outside the Borough limits. However, the authors suspect that it may be explained to some degree by underreporting of pedestrian trips for short distances within the Borough. This anomaly, which is also found in Morrisville and elsewhere in the older compact urban places in the study areas, could be due to sampling variability. The reverse relationship is observed in Tullytown, where household density and hence trip density is much lower while the ratio of trips exceeds 600 per 100 households. Tullytown's locally dominant influence as a Class IB center reflecting the role of the shopping center (Levittown Shop-A-Rama) extends in a northward direction some three miles in the Levittown housing tracts of Falls Township, but is not extended powerfully in the direction of Bristol, although it does penetrate into nearly all zones along U. S. Route 13. There is evidence that two Class II zones, i.e., Anadalusia-Cornwell Heights (Zone 3911) and Croydon (3922), also have fairly wide radii of influence which are locally stronger than only Bristol in Bensalem Township. Zone 3923, part of Bristol Township, is in Class III with only rudimentary services. Gradients of attraction to this zone and also zones 3912 and 3932 are not shown because they have slight impact upon consumer travel. Thus, one sees in this illustration how consumer interaction develops in a two-order hierarchy on

Table 22

TYPE OF TRIP PURPOSE
(Trip End Land Use Categories)
PENN-JERSEY TRANSPORTATION STUDY

| Group | General Category and Description | |
|---|---|---|
| 15 | **Finance, Insurance and Real Estate** | |
| | Banks and Savings Banks | Operative Builders |
| | Combinations of these with law office or business services | Real Estate Brokers, Agents and Operators |
| | Holding and Investment Firms | Security Brokers and Dealers |
| | Insurance Carriers and Agents | |
| | Loan Brokers and Business Credit Institutions | Small Loan Companies |
| | | Title Companies |
| 16 | **Professional Services** | |
| | Medical and dental offices, and related specialist services and laboratories | |
| | Law offices | |
| 20 | **Food Sales** | |
| | Bakeries    Delicatessen    Meat | |
| | Candy    Fruit and Vegetables    Supermarket | |
| | Dairy    Grocery | |
| 21 | **Eating and Drinking Places** | |
| | Bars    Night Clubs | |
| | Lunch Counters    Restaurants | |
| 22 | **Shopping Goods Stores** | |
| | Apparel and accessories (men's, women's, and children's) | Mail order houses |
| | Custom Tailors | Misc. Gen'l. Mdse. Stores |
| | Department Stores | Radio, television, and music |
| | Furniture, furnishings, and appliances | Shoes |
| | Furs | Variety Stores (dime) |
| | Haberdashery | Yarn, sewing machine, and patterns |
| 23 | **Auto Sales** | |
| | House trailer sales | New and used cars, including service and repair |

138

Table **22**

TYPE OF TRIP PURPOSE
(Continued)

| Group | General Category and Description | |
|---|---|---|
| 24 | Gasoline Stations  Service stations | |
| 25 | Other Retail Sales | |
| | Air craft, marine, and misc. auto parts and accessory dealers | Heating and plumbing equipment |
| | Antiques | Jewelry |
| | Books and stationery | Liquor |
| | Cigar | Paint |
| | Drug | Retail stores not elsewhere classified |
| | Electrical Supply | Sporting Goods |
| | Farm and garden supplies | Tire, battery, and auto accessories |
| | Florists | Vending machines |
| | Hardware and farm equipment | |
| 26 | Personal and Repair Services | |
| | Beauty and Barber Shops | Photographic studios |
| | Electrical repair shops | Pressing, altering and garment repair |
| | Laundry and cleaning pick-up | Shoe repair and hat cleaning shops |
| | Misc. repair shops for consumer goods | Steam baths, massage, etc. |
| | Pawn brokers | Watch and jewelry repair |
| | Undertakers | |
| | Upholstery shops | |

Source: Penn-Jersey Transportation Study, Coding Manual (mimeographed), 1961, pp. 20, 21, 22.

the metropolitan fringe.

## Geographic Patterns of Trips

When all personal business and shopping trips to destinations located within the three study areas are mapped the geographic pattern of consumer interaction is clarified. (See Table 26 and Figures 34, 35, and 36.) With few exceptions the maps show trips ending in Penn-Jersey Study zones, which are in Class I or Class II according to the central services existing in 1962. Since the areas of the zones are fairly uniform, each map can be regarded as a crude approximation of the density of consumer trips to a given zone. The boundary of relative predominance of a zone can be determined by examination of the trip data according to zones of origin. It is assumed that the area in which consumer travel to establishments located in a given Class I or Class II zone is dominant will include those zones which generate more trips to the given zone than to any other zone (Figure 34). While such areas can be discerned in and around all Class I zones and many Class II zones, there are always additional consumer trips from zones outside the area of relative dominance. Thus, the service area of a given zone normally is much more extensive than the area in which it is dominant. Of course, sampling variability may be large where small numbers are involved so that the maps should be interpreted as suggestive rather than definitive.

The first map of consumer trips (Figure 34) shows that distinct areas of dominance exist in and around each Class I zone. Group IA zones, consisting of the four largest urban places (Bristol Borough, Burlington City, Mt. Holly, and Woodbury), exert the strongest influence. Woodbury dominates the Gloucester study area everywhere except in Paulsboro. Mt. Holly would appear to have a similar area of dominance, but its area is truncated by the Cordon Line on the south and east, which is the boundary of the Burlington County study area. The radii of both the Woodbury and the Mt. Holly areas are at least three miles and in open country as much as five miles. The influence of Burlington City also extends five miles or so, but its location on the Delaware River makes it eccentric with respect to its service area. Bristol is not only off center with its area projecting westward in Bristol and Bensalem townships, but it is reduced to the north in the Levittown development tracts where the local shopping centers and highway strips have more influence.

Group IB zones show less extensive areas of dominance and have radii seldom exceeding three miles. Paulsboro's influence does not predominate much beyond its own municipal bounds towards Woodbury, but it undoubtedly draws consumers from Greenwich Township on the west and East Greenwich Township on the south, outside the Gloucester study area. In Bucks County Tullytown with its large shopping center has extensive influence in Bristol and Middletown townships but dominates only to the north in the Levittown

Table 23
TRIP ORIGINS

A – LOWER BUCKS COUNTY STUDY AREA

| Zone Number | Municipality | Type of Trip Purpose | | | | | | | | | Total Trips by Zone |
|---|---|---|---|---|---|---|---|---|---|---|---|
| | | 15 | 16 | 20 | 21 | 22 | 23 | 24 | 25 | 26 | |
| 3841 | Bensalem Twp.* | – | 15 | 60 | 3 | 24 | – | 3 | 13 | 20 | 138 |
| 3842 | Bensalem Twp.* | – | – | 21 | 3 | 52 | – | – | 3 | – | 79 |
| 3843 | Bensalem Twp.* | 10 | – | 16 | – | 31 | – | – | 11 | 10 | 78 |
| 3911 | Bensalem Twp.* | 36 | 20 | 75 | 14 | 42 | – | 10 | 14 | 31 | 242 |
| 3912 | Bensalem Twp.* | 25 | 5 | 53 | 6 | 39 | – | – | 3 | 10 | 136 |
| 3913 | Bensalem Twp.* | 5 | 5 | 33 | 3 | 16 | – | – | 6 | – | 68 |
| 3851 | Langhorne B. | – | – | 13 | – | 26 | – | – | – | – | 39 |
| 3852 | Penndel B. & Langhorne Manor B. | – | 5 | 10 | – | 13 | – | – | – | – | 28 |
| 3853 | Middletown Twp.* | 21 | 5 | 18 | 6 | 39 | – | 8 | 5 | 5 | 107 |
| 3854 | Middletown Twp.* & Hulmeville B. | – | – | 20 | 6 | 19 | – | – | 3 | – | 42 |
| 3855 | Middletown Twp.* | 20 | 77 | 109 | 21 | 116 | 18 | 3 | 42 | 10 | 416 |
| 3856 | Middletown Twp.* | 15 | 25 | 89 | 6 | 80 | – | – | 19 | 21 | 255 |
| 3857 | Middletown Twp.* | – | – | 11 | 3 | 3 | – | – | 6 | 21 | 49 |
| 3861 | Falls Twp.* | 16 | 26 | 68 | – | 74 | – | 13 | 13 | 20 | 230 |
| 3862 | Falls Twp.* | 10 | 15 | 27 | 6 | 11 | – | 3 | 11 | 10 | 93 |
| 3932 | Falls Twp.* | 67 | 78 | 108 | 6 | 155 | 5 | 8 | 60 | 36 | 523 |
| 3933 | Falls Twp.* | – | – | 3 | – | – | – | – | – | – | 3 |
| 3871 | Morrisville | 16 | 36 | 60 | – | 67 | – | 3 | 24 | – | 206 |
| 3921 | Bristol B. | 10 | 30 | 61 | 8 | 47 | – | 3 | 8 | 21 | 188 |
| 3922 | Bristol Twp.* | 16 | 47 | 89 | 3 | 56 | – | 3 | 26 | 37 | 277 |
| 3923 | Bristol Twp.* | 10 | – | 42 | 11 | 61 | – | – | – | 21 | 145 |
| 3924 | Bristol Twp.* | 10 | – | 8 | 3 | 16 | – | – | 6 | – | 43 |
| 3925 | Bristol Twp.* | 16 | 16 | 64 | 5 | 26 | – | – | 29 | 16 | 172 |
| 3926 | Bristol Twp.* | 20 | 57 | 127 | 11 | 74 | 14 | 3 | 23 | 5 | 334 |
| 3927 | Bristol Twp.* | – | 36 | 70 | 12 | 71 | – | – | 10 | 31 | 230 |
| 3928 | Bristol Twp.* | 36 | 42 | 122 | – | 122 | 3 | 6 | 13 | 25 | 369 |
| 3931 | Tullytown B. | 5 | 10 | 13 | 5 | 5 | – | – | 8 | – | 46 |
| | Total | 364 | 550 | 1,390 | 135 | 1,285 | 40 | 66 | 356 | 350 | 4,536 |

*Portion only     Source:  Penn-Jersey Transportation Study, Household Interviews, 1960–61.

Table 23 (Continued)

TRIP ORIGINS

B - BURLINGTON COUNTY STUDY AREA

| Zone Number | Municipality | Type of Trip Purpose | | | | | | | | | Total Trips by Zone |
|---|---|---|---|---|---|---|---|---|---|---|---|
| | | 15 | 16 | 20 | 21 | 22 | 23 | 24 | 25 | 26 | |
| 7451 | Delanco B. | 2 | 4 | 14 | 1 | 11 | – | – | – | 4 | 36 |
| 7452 | Beverly C. & Edgewater Pk. Twp. | 14 | 8 | 27 | 2 | 22 | – | – | 9 | 8 | 90 |
| 7461 | Levittown Twp.* | – | 8 | 15 | 1 | 2 | – | – | 2 | 2 | 30 |
| 7462 | Levittown Twp.* | 8 | 6 | 32 | 8 | 30 | 1 | – | 13 | 4 | 102 |
| 7471 | Burlington C. | 20 | 20 | 116 | 7 | 40 | 3 | 2 | 30 | 28 | 266 |
| 7472 | Burlington Twp.* | 12 | 10 | 30 | 2 | 7 | 1 | – | 4 | 12 | 78 |
| 7473 | Burlington Twp.* | 14 | 18 | 35 | 3 | 9 | – | – | 14 | 22 | 115 |
| 7474 | Burlington Twp.* | 2 | 16 | 28 | 1 | 13 | 2 | – | 14 | 4 | 80 |
| 7481 | Florence Twp.* | 18 | 34 | 81 | 7 | 59 | 2 | 5 | 26 | 20 | 252 |
| 7482 | Florence Twp.* | – | – | 2 | – | – | – | – | – | – | 2 |
| 7483 | Mansfield Twp.* | 2 | – | 17 | 1 | 4 | 1 | – | – | – | 25 |
| 7484 | Mansfield Twp.* | 10 | 14 | 12 | 1 | 3 | – | 3 | 2 | 2 | 47 |
| 7485 | Springfield Twp.* | 2 | 6 | 14 | – | 9 | – | – | 3 | 2 | 36 |
| 7486 | Springfield Twp.* | – | – | 5 | – | – | – | – | 3 | – | 8 |
| 7491 | Bordentown C. | 16 | 28 | 47 | 2 | 41 | 5 | 3 | 6 | 12 | 160 |
| 7492 | Bordentown Twp.* & Fieldsboro B. | 8 | 10 | 13 | 1 | 18 | – | – | 7 | 12 | 69 |
| 7493 | Bordentown Twp.* | 14 | 18 | 47 | 3 | 17 | 4 | 1 | 9 | 4 | 117 |
| 7571 | Westampton* | 2 | 6 | 4 | 1 | 1 | – | – | 5 | – | 19 |
| 7572 | Westampton Twp.* & Eastampton Twp.* | 6 | 4 | 15 | 2 | 10 | – | – | 9 | – | 46 |
| 7573 | Hainesport & Lumberton Twp.* | 12 | 16 | 57 | 2 | 23 | 2 | 1 | 15 | 16 | 144 |
| 7574 | Mt. Holly Twp.* | 46 | 34 | 126 | 13 | 70 | 2 | – | 37 | 34 | 362 |
| | Total | 208 | 260 | 737 | 58 | 389 | 23 | 15 | 208 | 186 | 2,084 |

Source: Penn-Jersey Transportation Study, Household Interviews, 1960–61.

*Portion only

Table 23 (Continued)

TRIP ORIGINS

C – GLOUCESTER COUNTY STUDY AREA

| Zone Number | Municipality | Type of Trip Purpose | | | | | | | | | Total Trips by Zone |
|---|---|---|---|---|---|---|---|---|---|---|---|
| | | 15 | 16 | 20 | 21 | 22 | 23 | 24 | 25 | 26 | |
| 7811 | Westville B. | 6 | 20 | 36 | 4 | 43 | - | - | 7 | 10 | 126 |
| 7812 | Woodbury C. | 70 | 44 | 111 | 7 | 82 | 4 | 3 | 31 | 22 | 374 |
| 7813 | Deptford Twp.* | 12 | 10 | 42 | 11 | 12 | - | 1 | 6 | 14 | 108 |
| 7821 | Deptford Twp.* & Woodbury Hts. B. | 40 | 36 | 69 | 6 | 104 | - | 8 | 23 | 36 | 322 |
| 7822 | Deptford Twp.* & Wenonah B. | 6 | 12 | 52 | 5 | 40 | - | - | 10 | 18 | 143 |
| 7823 | Deptford Twp.* | 28 | 22 | 57 | 2 | 39 | - | - | 11 | 12 | 171 |
| 7912 | National Park B. | 14 | 20 | 26 | 1 | 22 | - | - | 5 | 8 | 96 |
| 7911 | W. Deptford Twp.* | 46 | 22 | 77 | 10 | 43 | - | 5 | 15 | 18 | 236 |
| 7921 | W. Deptford Twp.* | 8 | 8 | 5 | - | 14 | - | 1 | - | - | 36 |
| 7922 | W. Deptford Twp.* | 8 | 16 | 36 | 15 | 39 | 6 | 2 | 7 | 10 | 139 |
| 7923 | Paulsboro B. | 24 | 24 | 46 | 6 | 36 | 4 | - | 23 | 26 | 189 |
| | Total | 262 | 234 | 557 | 67 | 474 | 14 | 20 | 138 | 174 | 1,940 |

* Portion only

Source: Penn-Jersey Transportation Study, Household Interviews, 1960-61.

Table 24

PERSONAL BUSINESS AND SHOPPING TRIPS
TYPE OF TRIP PURPOSE AND NUMBER PER 100 HOUSEHOLDS

| Type of Trip Purpose* | Study Areas | | | | | | Total | |
|---|---|---|---|---|---|---|---|---|
| | Lower Bucks County | | Burlington County | | Gloucester County | | | |
| | Number | Per Cent | Number | Per Cent | Number | Per Cent | Number | Per Cent |
| 15 | 364 | 8.2 | 208 | 10.0 | 262 | 13.5 | 834 | 9.7 |
| 16 | 550 | 12.1 | 260 | 12.5 | 234 | 12.1 | 1,044 | 12.2 |
| 20 | 1,390 | 30.6 | 737 | 35.4 | 557 | 28.7 | 2,684 | 31.4 |
| 21 | 135 | 3.0 | 58 | 2.8 | 67 | 3.5 | 260 | 3.0 |
| 22 | 1,285 | 28.3 | 389 | 18.7 | 474 | 24.4 | 2,148 | 25.1 |
| 23 | 40 | 0.9 | 23 | 1.1 | 14 | 0.7 | 77 | 0.9 |
| 24 | 66 | 1.5 | 15 | 0.7 | 20 | 1.0 | 101 | 1.2 |
| 25 | 256 | 7.8 | 208 | 10.0 | 138 | 7.1 | 702 | 8.2 |
| 26 | 350 | 7.7 | 186 | 8.9 | 174 | 9.0 | 710 | 8.3 |
| Total | 4,536 | 100.0 | 2,084 | 100.0 | 1,940 | 100.0 | 8,560 | 100.0 |
| House-holds Sampled | 1,795 | | 807 | | 708 | | 3,310 | |
| Trips per 100 House-holds | 252 | | 258 | | 274 | | 258 | |

Source: Penn-Jersey Transportation Study, Households Interviews, 1960-61. Trips
are estimated from 10 per cent sample, except in Bucks County where 4 per
cent sample is expanded by a factor of 2.5.

*Please refer to Table 22.

144

Table 25
TRIP DESTINATIONS

A - LOWER BUCKS COUNTY STUDY AREA

| Zone Number | Municipality | Types of Trip Purpose | | | | | | | | | Total Trips by Zone |
|---|---|---|---|---|---|---|---|---|---|---|---|
| | | 15 | 16 | 20 | 21 | 22 | 23 | 24 | 25 | 26 | |
| 3841 | Bensalem Twp.* | – | – | 5 | 3 | 39 | – | 3 | 13 | – | 63 |
| 3842 | Bensalem Twp.* | – | – | 9 | – | 5 | – | – | – | – | 14 |
| 3843 | Bensalem Twp.* | – | – | 13 | – | – | – | – | – | – | 13 |
| 3911 | Bensalem Twp.* | 10 | 5 | 72 | 3 | – | – | 10 | 3 | 16 | 119 |
| 3912 | Bensalem Twp.* | – | – | 10 | 11 | 3 | – | – | 6 | 5 | 35 |
| 3913 | Bensalem Twp.* | – | – | 9 | – | – | – | – | – | – | 9 |
| 3851 | Langhorne B. | 16 | 10 | 18 | – | 3 | – | – | 5 | 5 | 57 |
| 3852 | Penndel B. & Langhorne Manor B. | – | 21 | 40 | 3 | – | – | – | 3 | – | 67 |
| 3853 | Middletown Twp.* | – | – | 8 | – | – | – | – | – | – | 8 |
| 3854 | Middletown Twp.* & Hulmeville B. | – | – | 5 | – | – | – | – | – | – | 5 |
| 3855 | Middletown Twp.* | 31 | 36 | 91 | 3 | 221 | 3 | 3 | 49 | 20 | 457 |
| 3856 | Middletown Twp.* | 20 | 10 | 49 | – | 49 | 8 | – | 19 | 16 | 171 |
| 3857 | Middletown Twp.* | – | – | 5 | 3 | 3 | 3 | – | – | 21 | 35 |
| 3861 | Falls Twp.* | 26 | 25 | 80 | – | 77 | – | 10 | 21 | 10 | 249 |
| 3862 | Falls Twp.* | – | – | 34 | 5 | 68 | – | 3 | – | – | 110 |
| 3932 | Falls Twp.* | – | 67 | 79 | – | – | – | 5 | 10 | 10 | 171 |
| 3933 | Falls Twp.* | – | – | – | – | 3 | – | – | – | – | 3 |
| 3871 | Morrisville | 26 | 26 | 71 | 11 | 45 | 5 | 6 | 19 | 5 | 214 |
| 3921 | Bristol B. | 82 | 93 | 162 | – | 118 | 10 | – | 53 | 109 | 627 |
| 3922 | Bristol Twp.* | 5 | 21 | 69 | 12 | – | 3 | 3 | 13 | 16 | 142 |
| 3923 | Bristol Twp.* | – | – | 5 | – | 3 | – | – | – | – | 8 |
| 3924 | Bristol Twp.* | – | – | 22 | – | 126 | – | – | 3 | – | 151 |

Table 25(Continued)
TRIP DESTINATIONS

A – LOWER BUCKS COUNTY STUDY AREA (Continued)

| Zone Number | Municipality | Types of Trip Purpose | | | | | | | | | Total Trips by Zone |
|---|---|---|---|---|---|---|---|---|---|---|---|
| | | 15 | 16 | 20 | 21 | 23 | 23 | 24 | 25 | 26 | |
| 3925 | Bristol Twp.* | - | 10 | 11 | 10 | - | - | 3 | - | - | 34 |
| 3926 | Bristol Twp.* | 5 | 10 | 131 | 3 | 19 | - | 3 | 29 | 10 | 210 |
| 3927 | Bristol Twp.* | 5 | - | 13 | 16 | - | - | 3 | 11 | - | 48 |
| 3928 | Bristol Twp.* | - | 52 | 16 | 8 | 26 | - | 3 | 13 | 15 | 133 |
| 3931 | Tullytown B. | 57 | 21 | 233 | - | 185 | - | 3 | 36 | 26 | 561 |
| | Destinations Outside Study Area | | | | | | | | | | |
| - | Camden City | - | - | - | 3 | - | - | - | - | - | 3 |
| - | Phila. Center City | 31 | 20 | - | 6 | 44 | - | - | 3 | - | 104 |
| - | Other Philadelphia | 45 | 57 | 57 | 20 | 118 | - | - | 14 | 56 | 367 |
| - | Adjacent Zone | - | - | 34 | - | 5 | - | - | - | 10 | 49 |
| - | Non-Adjacent Zone | 5 | 15 | 21 | 12 | 43 | 8 | 8 | 14 | 5 | 126 |
| - | Outside Cordon Line | - | 10 | 8 | - | 5 | - | - | - | - | 23 |
| - | Trenton City | - | 41 | 10 | 3 | 77 | - | - | 19 | - | 150 |
| | Total | 364 | 550 | 1,380 | 135 | 1,285 | 40 | 66 | 356 | 350 | 4,536 |

*Portion only

Source: Penn-Jersey Transportation Study, Household Interviews, 1960-61.

Table 25 (Continued)
TRIP DESTINATIONS

B – BURLINGTON COUNTY STUDY AREA

| Zone Number | Municipality | Types of Trip Purpose | | | | | | | | | Total Trips by Zone |
|---|---|---|---|---|---|---|---|---|---|---|---|
| | | 15 | 16 | 20 | 21 | 22 | 23 | 24 | 25 | 26 | |
| 7451 | Delanco B. | - | 4 | 1 | - | - | - | - | - | - | 5 |
| 7452 | Beverly C. Edgewater Pk. Twp. | 10 | 4 | 11 | - | 4 | - | - | 6 | 18 | 53 |
| 7461 | Levittown Twp.* | 2 | 4 | 15 | 4 | 5 | - | - | 1 | - | 31 |
| 7462 | Levittown Twp.* | 4 | 2 | 42 | 2 | 16 | - | - | 11 | 2 | 79 |
| 7471 | Burlington C. | 42 | 56 | 228 | 8 | 80 | 6 | 2 | 64 | 58 | 544 |
| 7472 | Burlington Twp.* | 6 | 4 | 24 | 3 | - | 1 | - | 1 | - | 39 |
| 7473 | Burlington Twp.** | - | - | 4 | 1 | 2 | - | - | 2 | - | 9 |
| 7474 | Burlington Twp.* | - | - | 9 | 1 | - | - | - | - | - | 10 |
| 7481 | Florence Twp.* | 18 | 12 | 14 | 3 | 3 | - | 7 | 16 | 12 | 85 |
| 7482 | Florence Twp.* | - | - | - | - | - | - | - | - | - | - |
| 7483 | Mansfield Twp.* | - | - | - | - | - | - | - | - | - | - |
| 7484 | Mansfield Twp.* | 4 | - | 13 | 1 | 12 | - | - | 3 | - | 33 |
| 7485 | Springfield Twp.* | - | - | - | - | - | - | - | - | - | - |
| 7486 | Springfield Twp.* | - | - | 1 | - | - | - | - | - | - | 1 |
| 7491 | Bordentown C. | 30 | 16 | 22 | 2 | 15 | 8 | 2 | 18 | 16 | 129 |
| 7492 | Bordentown Twp.* & Fieldsboro B. | - | - | 90 | 3 | 7 | - | 2 | - | - | 102 |
| 7493 | Bordentown Twp. | - | - | 2 | - | 43 | 1 | 1 | - | - | 47 |
| 7571 | Westampton* | - | - | 1 | 1 | - | - | - | - | - | 2 |

## Table 25 (Continued)
## TRIP DESTINATIONS

### B – BURLINGTON COUNTY STUDY AREA

| Zone Number | Municipality | Types of Trip Purpose | | | | | | | | | Total Trips by Zone |
|---|---|---|---|---|---|---|---|---|---|---|---|
| | | 15 | 16 | 20 | 21 | 22 | 23 | 24 | 25 | 26 | |
| 7572 | Westampton Twp.* & Eastampton Twp.* | - | 6 | 1 | 3 | - | - | - | - | 4 | 14 |
| 7573 | Hainesport & Lumberton Twp.* | 2 | - | 43 | 1 | - | 3 | 1 | 6 | - | 56 |
| 7574 | Mt. Holly Twp. | 62 | 30 | 135 | 4 | 38 | - | - | 47 | 32 | 348 |
| | Destinations Outside Study Area | | | | | | | | | | |
| - | Camden City | 4 | 4 | 2 | - | 16 | - | - | 2 | - | 28 |
| - | Phila. Center City | - | 12 | 2 | 5 | 23 | - | - | - | - | 42 |
| - | Other Philadelphia | - | - | - | 2 | 2 | - | - | - | 2 | 6 |
| - | Adjacent Zone | 6 | 20 | 30 | 6 | 30 | 2 | - | 8 | 10 | 112 |
| - | Non-Adjacent Zone | 4 | 24 | 40 | 6 | 13 | 1 | - | 1 | 14 | 103 |
| - | Outside Cordon Line | - | 10 | 6 | 1 | 10 | 1 | - | 11 | 4 | 43 |
| - | Trenton | 14 | 52 | 1 | 1 | 70 | - | - | 11 | 14 | 163 |
| | Total | 208 | 260 | 737 | 58 | 389 | 23 | 15 | 208 | 186 | 2,084 |

*Portion only

Source: Penn-Jersey Transportation Study, Household Interviews, 1960-61.

Table 25 (Continued)
TRIP DESTINATIONS

## C - GLOUCESTER COUNTY STUDY AREA

| Zone Number | Municipality | Types of Trip Purpose | | | | | | | | | Total Trips by Zone |
|---|---|---|---|---|---|---|---|---|---|---|---|
| | | 15 | 16 | 20 | 21 | 22 | 23 | 24 | 25 | 26 | |
| 7811 | Westville B. | 16 | 8 | 25 | 5 | 2 | – | 3 | – | 6 | 65 |
| 7812 | Woodbury C. | 156 | 88 | 304 | 12 | 98 | 6 | 5 | 69 | 72 | 810 |
| 7513 | Deptford Twp. * | 6 | 2 | 25 | 2 | 88 | – | – | 8 | 6 | 137 |
| 7821 | Deptford Twp. * & Woodbury Hts. | 10 | 4 | 22 | – | 64 | – | 4 | 4 | 10 | 118 |
| 7822 | Deptford Twp. * & Wenonah B. | – | 18 | 10 | 3 | 1 | – | – | – | 2 | 34 |
| 7823 | Deptford Twp. * | – | 6 | 7 | 1 | – | – | – | 1 | – | 15 |
| 7912 | National Park B. | – | – | 12 | – | 1 | – | – | 3 | 2 | 18 |
| 7911 | W. Deptford Twp. * | – | – | 9 | 6 | – | – | 1 | – | – | 16 |
| 7921 | W. Deptford Twp. * | 4 | – | 5 | 3 | 1 | – | – | 3 | – | 16 |
| 7922 | W. Deptford Twp. * | 4 | – | 18 | 5 | 36 | 2 | 2 | 1 | 8 | 76 |
| 7923 | Paulsboro B. | 10 | 14 | 34 | 3 | 13 | 2 | – | 17 | 14 | 107 |
| | **Destinations Outside Study Area** | | | | | | | | | | |
| | Camden City | 8 | 26 | 2 | 1 | 58 | – | 3 | 3 | 6 | 107 |
| | Phila. Center City | – | 12 | 1 | 2 | 41 | – | – | 3 | 6 | 65 |
| | Other Philadelphia | 4 | 12 | 1 | 4 | 7 | – | – | 1 | 10 | 39 |
| | Adjacent Zone | 34 | 24 | 58 | 7 | 19 | 2 | – | 14 | 6 | 164 |
| | Non-Adjacent Zone | 8 | 20 | 24 | 13 | 36 | 2 | 2 | 10 | 26 | 141 |
| | Outside Cordon Line | 2 | – | – | – | 9 | – | – | 1 | – | 12 |
| | **Total** | 262 | 234 | 557 | 67 | 474 | 14 | 20 | 138 | 174 | 1,940 |

*Portion only

Source: Penn-Jersey Transportation Study, Household Interviews, 1960–61.

Table 26

TRIP ORIGINS AND DESTINATIONS

A - LOWER BUCKS COUNTY STUDY AREA

| Zone of Origin | Municipality | Zone of Destination | | | | | | | | |
|---|---|---|---|---|---|---|---|---|---|---|
| | | 3841 | 3842 | 3843 | 3911 | 3912 | 3913 | 3851 | 3852 | 3853 |
| 3841 | Bensalem Twp.* | 18 | 3 | – | – | – | – | 13 | 3 | – |
| 3842 | Bensalem Twp.* | 21 | – | 5 | 5 | 3 | – | – | – | – |
| 3843 | Bensalem Twp.* | 21 | – | 5 | – | – | – | – | – | 5 |
| 3911 | Bensalem Twp.* | 3 | – | – | 57 | 10 | – | – | 3 | – |
| 3912 | Bensalem Twp.* | – | 8 | – | 10 | 6 | 3 | – | – | – |
| 3913 | Bensalem Twp.* | – | – | 3 | 5 | 3 | 3 | – | 3 | – |
| 3851 | Langhorne B. | – | – | – | – | – | – | 3 | 5 | – |
| 3852 | Penndel B. & Langhorne Manor B. | – | – | – | – | – | – | – | 5 | – |
| 3853 | Middletown Twp.* | – | – | – | – | – | – | 31 | 18 | 3 |
| 3854 | Middletown Twp.* & Hulmeville B. | – | 3 | – | – | – | – | – | 3 | – |
| 3855 | Middletown Twp.* | – | – | – | – | – | – | – | 16 | – |
| 3856 | Middletown Twp.* | – | – | – | – | – | – | 5 | – | – |
| 3857 | Middletown Twp.* | – | – | – | – | – | – | 5 | 3 | – |
| 3861 | Falls Twp.* | – | – | – | – | – | – | – | 8 | – |
| 3862 | Falls Twp.* | – | – | – | – | – | – | – | – | – |
| 3932 | Falls Twp.* | – | – | – | 5 | – | – | – | – | – |
| 3933 | Falls Twp.* | – | – | – | – | – | – | – | – | – |
| 3871 | Morrisville | – | – | – | – | – | – | – | – | – |
| 3921 | Bristol B. | – | – | – | – | – | 3 | – | – | – |
| 3922 | Bristol Twp.* | – | – | – | 32 | 10 | – | – | – | – |
| 3923 | Bristol Twp.* | – | – | – | – | – | – | – | – | – |
| 3924 | Bristol Twp.* | – | – | – | – | 3 | – | – | – | – |
| 3925 | Bristol Twp.* | – | – | – | – | – | – | – | – | – |
| 3926 | Bristol Twp.* | – | – | – | – | – | – | – | – | – |
| 3927 | Bristol Twp.* | – | – | – | 5 | – | – | – | – | – |
| 3928 | Bristol Twp.* | – | – | – | – | – | – | – | – | – |
| 3931 | Tullytown B. | – | – | – | – | – | – | – | – | – |
| | Total | 63 | 14 | 13 | 119 | 35 | 9 | 57 | 67 | 8 |

*Portion only

Source: Penn-Jersey Transportation Study, Household Interviews, 1960-61.

Table 26 (Continued)

TRIP ORIGINS AND DESTINATIONS

A - LOWER BUCKS COUNTY STUDY AREA

| Zone of Origin | Zone of Destination | | | | | | | | | | | | |
|---|---|---|---|---|---|---|---|---|---|---|---|---|---|
| | 3854 | 3855 | 3856 | 3857 | 3861 | 3862 | 3932 | 3933 | 3871 | 3921 | 3922 | 3923 | 3924 |
| 3841 | – | 3 | 5 | – | – | – | – | – | 5 | 18 | – | – | – |
| 3842 | – | 3 | – | – | – | – | – | – | – | – | 8 | – | 10 |
| 3843 | – | – | – | – | – | – | – | – | – | 13 | 3 | – | 5 |
| 3911 | – | 5 | – | – | – | – | – | – | 10 | 13 | – | – | – |
| 3912 | – | 5 | – | – | – | – | – | – | – | 31 | 13 | – | – |
| 3913 | – | – | – | – | – | – | – | – | – | 34 | 3 | – | – |
| 3851 | – | 5 | 3 | 5 | – | – | – | – | 5 | 5 | – | – | – |
| 3852 | – | – | 5 | 3 | – | 5 | – | – | – | – | – | – | – |
| 3853 | – | 10 | 13 | – | – | 5 | – | – | – | – | – | – | – |
| 3854 | – | – | – | – | – | 8 | – | – | – | 8 | – | – | 6 |
| 3855 | 5 | 98 | 52 | – | 24 | 10 | 15 | – | 11 | 10 | 8 | – | 16 |
| 3856 | – | 34 | 67 | – | 11 | 5 | – | – | 5 | 3 | – | – | 16 |
| 3857 | – | – | – | 24 | – | – | – | – | 3 | – | – | – | – |
| 3861 | – | 31 | – | – | 106 | 14 | 5 | 3 | 5 | – | – | – | – |
| 3862 | – | 5 | – | – | 23 | 3 | 8 | – | 37 | – | – | – | – |
| 3932 | – | 78 | 13 | – | 50 | 34 | 64 | – | 9 | – | – | – | – |
| 3933 | – | – | – | – | – | – | – | – | 3 | – | – | – | – |
| 3871 | – | – | – | – | 3 | 8 | – | – | 100 | 10 | – | – | 5 |
| 3921 | – | 5 | – | – | – | – | – | – | – | 107 | 15 | – | 3 |
| 3922 | – | 8 | – | – | – | – | 5 | – | – | 53 | 77 | – | 16 |
| 3923 | – | 29 | – | – | 3 | – | 3 | – | – | 55 | 6 | 8 | 18 |
| 3924 | – | 8 | – | – | – | – | – | – | – | 26 | – | – | 3 |
| 3925 | – | 5 | 3 | – | 3 | – | – | – | 5 | 95 | 11 | – | 8 |
| 3926 | – | 63 | – | – | 10 | – | 21 | – | 3 | 38 | 6 | – | 26 |
| 3927 | – | 13 | – | – | 3 | – | 13 | – | 8 | 83 | 5 | – | 8 |
| 3928 | – | 44 | 10 | 3 | 13 | 10 | 37 | – | 5 | 10 | – | – | 8 |
| 3931 | – | 5 | – | – | – | – | – | – | – | 15 | – | – | – |
| Total | 5 | 457 | 171 | 35 | 249 | 110 | 171 | 3 | 214 | 627 | 142 | 8 | 151 |

Table **26** (Continued)

TRIP ORIGINS AND DESTINATIONS

A - LOWER BUCKS COUNTY STUDY AREA

| Zone of Origin | Zone of Destination | | | | | Study Area Total | Outside Study Area | | |
|---|---|---|---|---|---|---|---|---|---|
| | 3925 | 3926 | 3927 | 3928 | 3931 | | Trenton City | Philadelphia Center City | Other Philadelphia |
| 3841 | – | – | – | – | – | 68 | – | – | 42 |
| 3842 | – | – | – | – | 5 | 60 | – | 5 | 6 |
| 3843 | – | – | – | – | – | 52 | – | – | 18 |
| 3911 | – | – | – | – | 23 | 124 | 23 | 42 | 65 |
| 3912 | – | 3 | 5 | – | – | 84 | – | 5 | 63 |
| 3913 | – | – | – | – | – | 54 | – | – | 19 |
| 3851 | – | – | – | – | – | 31 | – | 5 | – |
| 3852 | – | – | – | – | – | 18 | – | – | – |
| 3853 | – | – | – | – | – | 80 | 5 | 8 | 8 |
| 3854 | 3 | 3 | – | – | 3 | 37 | – | – | 25 |
| 3855 | – | 47 | 3 | 28 | 31 | 374 | 5 | – | 16 |
| 3856 | – | 10 | 5 | 8 | 41 | 210 | – | 13 | 5 |
| 3857 | – | – | – | – | – | 35 | – | 3 | 13 |
| 3861 | – | – | – | 6 | 13 | 191 | 10 | – | – |
| 3862 | – | – | – | – | 11 | 87 | 3 | – | – |
| 3932 | – | 21 | – | 21 | 123 | 416 | 4 | 13 | 19 |
| 3933 | – | – | – | – | – | 3 | – | – | – |
| 3871 | – | – | – | – | – | 126 | 19 | – | – |
| 3921 | 21 | 3 | 3 | – | 23 | 183 | 24 | 10 | – |
| 3922 | – | 21 | – | – | 5 | 227 | – | – | 3 |
| 3923 | 5 | – | – | 8 | 5 | 140 | 3 | – | 13 |
| 3924 | – | 13 | – | – | – | 53 | – | – | – |
| 3925 | 5 | – | 8 | 8 | 8 | 159 | – | – | – |
| 3926 | – | 50 | – | 13 | 49 | 279 | 13 | – | 39 |
| 3927 | – | 8 | 13 | – | 62 | 221 | – | – | – |
| 3928 | – | 21 | 6 | 36 | 122 | 325 | 21 | – | 14 |
| 3931 | – | 10 | 5 | 5 | 37 | 77 | – | – | – |
| Total | 34 | 210 | 48 | 133 | 561 | 3,714 | 150 | 104 | 367 |

Table 26 (Continued)

TRIP ORIGINS AND DESTINATIONS

B - BURLINGTON COUNTY STUDY AREA

| Zone of Origin | Municipality | Zone of Destination | | | | | | | | | | | |
|---|---|---|---|---|---|---|---|---|---|---|---|---|---|
| | | 7451 | 7452 | 7461 | 7462 | 7471 | 7472 | 7473 | 7474 | 7481 | 7482 | 7483 | 7484 |
| 7451 | Delanco B. | 1 | – | 1 | 4 | 4 | – | – | – | – | – | – | – |
| 7452 | Beverly C. & Edgewater Pk. Twp. | – | 26 | 8 | 1 | 29 | 1 | – | – | – | – | – | 2 |
| 7461 | Willingboro Twp.* | – | 2 | – | 11 | 8 | 1 | – | – | – | – | – | – |
| 7462 | Willingboro Twp.* | – | – | 9 | 30 | 32 | 8 | 1 | – | – | – | – | – |
| 7471 | Burlington C. | – | 5 | – | 9 | 192 | 18 | 2 | – | – | – | – | 2 |
| 7472 | Burlington Twp.* | – | 6 | 1 | 1 | 54 | 3 | – | – | – | – | – | – |
| 7473 | Burlington Twp. | – | 14 | – | 7 | 65 | – | 1 | – | – | – | – | 2 |
| 7474 | Burlington Twp. | – | – | 1 | 3 | 38 | 7 | 1 | 3 | 4 | – | – | 1 |
| 7481 | Florence Twp.* | 4 | – | 2 | 4 | 57 | 1 | – | 4 | 65 | – | – | 4 |
| 7482 | Florence Twp.* | – | – | 4 | – | 2 | – | – | – | – | – | – | – |
| 7483 | Mansfield Twp.* | – | – | – | – | 2 | – | – | – | 1 | – | – | 2 |
| 7484 | Mansfield Twp.* | – | – | – | – | 5 | – | – | – | 8 | – | – | 8 |
| 7485 | Springfield Twp.* | – | – | – | – | 17 | – | – | 2 | – | – | – | 1 |
| 7486 | Springfield Twp.* | – | – | – | – | – | – | – | – | 2 | – | – | – |
| 7491 | Bordentown C. | – | – | – | 2 | 2 | – | – | 1 | 5 | – | – | 3 |
| 7492 | Bordentown Twp.* & Fieldsboro B. | – | – | – | – | – | – | – | – | – | – | – | – |
| 7493 | Bordentown Twp.* | – | – | – | – | 2 | – | – | – | – | – | – | 1 |
| 7571 | Westampton* | – | – | 1 | – | 11 | – | – | – | – | – | – | – |
| 7572 | Westampton Twp.* & Eastampton Twp.* | – | – | – | 1 | 1 | – | – | – | – | – | – | – |
| 7573 | Hainesport & Lumberton Twp.* | – | – | 2 | 4 | 5 | – | – | – | – | – | – | 2 |
| 7574 | Mt. Holly Twp. | – | – | 2 | 2 | 18 | – | 4 | – | – | – | – | 5 |
| | Total | 5 | 53 | 31 | 79 | 544 | 39 | 9 | 10 | 85 | 0 | 0 | 33 |

*Portion only

Source: Penn-Jersey Transportation Study, Household Interviews, 1960-61.

Table **26**(Continued)

TRIP ORIGINS AND DESTINATIONS

B - BURLINGTON COUNTY STUDY AREA

| Zone of Origin | Zone of Destination | | | | | | | | | Study Area Total | Outside Study Area | | | |
|---|---|---|---|---|---|---|---|---|---|---|---|---|---|---|
| | 7485 | 7486 | 7491 | 7492 | 7493 | 7571 | 7572 | 7573 | 7574 | | Phila. CBD | Other Phila. | Camden | Trenton |
| 7451 | - | - | - | - | - | - | - | - | - | 10 | - | 2 | 6 | - |
| 7452 | - | - | 6 | - | - | - | - | - | - | 13 | 1 | 1 | - | 2 |
| 7461 | - | - | - | - | - | - | - | - | - | 23 | - | - | - | - |
| 7462 | - | - | - | - | - | - | - | - | - | 80 | 4 | - | 5 | - |
| 7471 | - | - | - | - | 3 | - | 6 | - | 8 | 245 | 1 | - | 1 | 2 |
| 7472 | - | - | - | - | 2 | - | 1 | 1 | 2 | 71 | 2 | - | 2 | 3 |
| 7473 | - | - | 2 | - | 2 | - | - | - | 9 | 101 | 1 | - | 2 | 1 |
| 7474 | - | - | - | - | 2 | - | - | - | 3 | 63 | - | - | - | 6 |
| 7481 | - | - | 11 | 24 | 5 | - | - | - | - | 181 | 8 | - | - | 45 |
| 7482 | - | - | - | - | - | - | - | - | - | 6 | - | - | - | - |
| 7483 | - | - | 3 | 13 | - | - | - | - | - | 21 | - | - | - | 1 |
| 7484 | - | 1 | 4 | 4 | 1 | - | - | - | 3 | 34 | - | - | - | 13 |
| 7485 | - | - | - | - | - | - | - | - | 9 | 29 | - | - | - | - |
| 7486 | - | - | - | - | - | - | - | - | 6 | 8 | - | - | - | 1 |
| 7491 | - | - | 49 | 26 | 17 | - | - | - | - | 105 | - | - | - | 44 |
| 7492 | - | - | 21 | 13 | 3 | - | - | - | - | 37 | - | - | - | 21 |
| 7493 | - | - | 28 | 17 | 7 | - | - | - | - | 55 | - | 1 | - | 14 |
| 7571 | - | - | - | - | - | - | - | - | - | 12 | - | - | - | - |
| 7572 | - | - | - | - | - | - | 1 | 2 | 38 | 43 | - | - | 1 | 1 |
| 7573 | - | - | 2 | - | 1 | - | - | 22 | 61 | 99 | 4 | - | 4 | 3 |
| 7574 | - | - | 3 | 5 | 4 | 2 | 6 | 31 | 209 | 291 | 21 | 2 | 7 | 6 |
| Total | 0 | 1 | 129 | 102 | 47 | 2 | 14 | 56 | 348 | 1,587 | 42 | 6 | 28 | 163 |

Table 26 (Continued)

TRIP ORIGINS AND DESTINATIONS

C - GLOUCESTER COUNTY STUDY AREA

| Zone of Origin | Municipality | Zone of Destination | | | | | | |
|---|---|---|---|---|---|---|---|---|
| | | 7811 | 7812 | 7813 | 7821 | 7822 | 7823 | 7912 |
| 7811 | Westville B. | 19 | 30 | 8 | 2 | – | – | – |
| 7812 | Woodbury C. | 12 | 217 | 23 | 10 | 3 | 4 | – |
| 7813 | Deptford Twp. * | 14 | 33 | 24 | 2 | 4 | – | – |
| 7821 | Deptford Twp. * & Woodbury Hts. B. | – | 119 | 22 | 59 | 6 | 1 | 1 |
| 7822 | Deptford Twp. * & Wenonah B. | 1 | 53 | 6 | 9 | 13 | – | – |
| 7823 | Deptford Twp. * | 4 | 52 | 25 | 3 | 4 | 9 | – |
| 7912 | National Park B. | 2 | 57 | 4 | 3 | – | – | 12 |
| 7911 | W. Deptford Twp. * | 10 | 131 | 8 | 12 | – | – | 4 |
| 7921 | W. Deptford Twp. * | – | 14 | 2 | – | 4 | – | 1 |
| 7922 | W. Deptford Twp. * | – | 71 | 9 | 8 | – | 1 | – |
| 7923 | Paulsboro B. | 3 | 33 | 6 | 10 | – | – | – |
| | Total | 65 | 810 | 137 | 118 | 34 | 15 | 18 |

*Portion only

Source: Penn-Jersey Transportation Study, Household Interviews, 1960-61.

Table **26**  (Continued)

TRIP ORIGINS AND DESTINATIONS

C - GLOUCESTER COUNTY STUDY AREA

| Zone of Origin | Zone of Destination | | | | Study Area Total | Outside Study Area | | | |
|---|---|---|---|---|---|---|---|---|---|
| | 7911 | 7921 | 7922 | 7923 | | Philadelphia CBD | Other Philadelphia | Camden City | Trenton City |
| 7811 | – | 1 | – | – | 60 | 7 | 1 | 22 | – |
| 7812 | 2 | 3 | 25 | 5 | 304 | 14 | – | 16 | – |
| 7813 | 5 | – | 1 | 1 | 84 | 4 | 7 | 2 | 3 |
| 7821 | – | – | 18 | 3 | 229 | 18 | 8 | 20 | – |
| 7822 | – | – | – | 1 | 83 | 8 | 7 | 9 | – |
| 7823 | – | 3 | 1 | – | 101 | 5 | – | 11 | – |
| 7912 | 1 | – | 3 | 1 | 83 | 1 | 2 | 4 | – |
| 7911 | 8 | 1 | 8 | – | 182 | 3 | 7 | – | – |
| 7921 | – | – | 1 | 10 | 32 | – | – | 19 | – |
| 7922 | – | 4 | 18 | 6 | 117 | 2 | 1 | 3 | – |
| 7923 | – | 4 | 1 | 80 | 137 | 3 | 6 | 1 | – |
| Total | 16 | 16 | 76 | 107 | 1,412 | 65 | 39 | 107 | 3 |

156

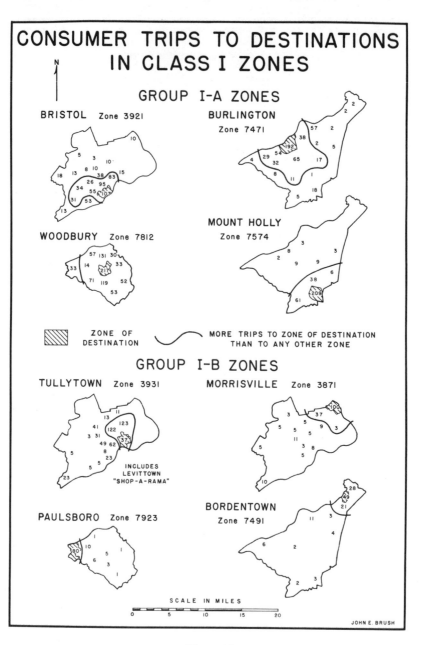

Figure 34.

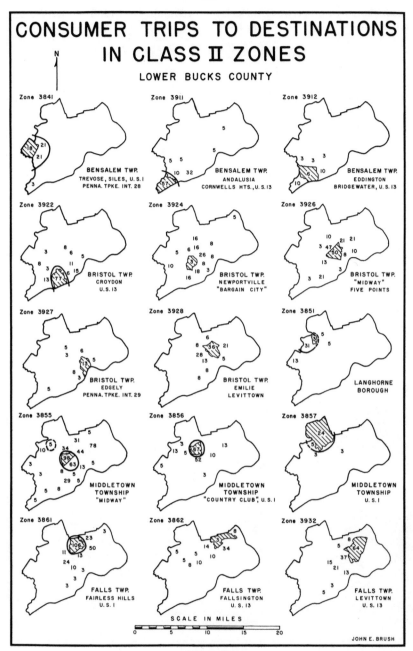

Figure 35.

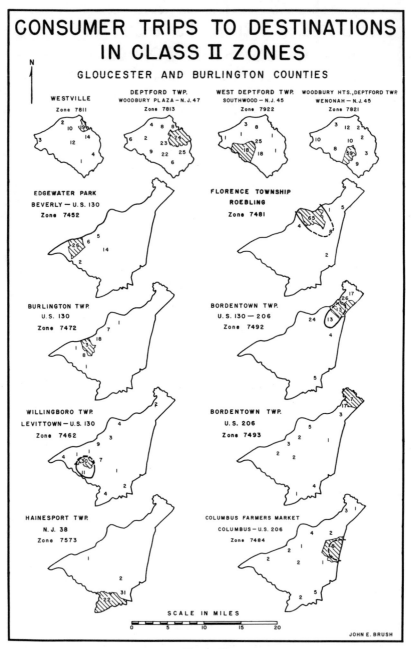

Figure 36.

housing tracts. Morrisville, Bucks County, and Bordentown, Burlington County, have weak but extensive influence, and their respective areas of dominance are restricted to zones in adjacent townships. The evidence leads to the conclusion that the primacy of Class IA zones is being maintained, although one Class IB zone (3931), Tullytown, exerts a powerful influence, because it contains a regional shopping center offering varied goods and services, i.e., the Levittown Shop-A-Rama.

Consumer travel patterns in and around Class II zones indicate considerable local influence but if there is any area of dominance it is usually very restricted and rarely extends beyond the zone itself (Figures 35 and 36). In the Gloucester study area Class II services attract consumers from nearly all parts of the study area, but are never dominant. In Burlington County, there are four zones (7462, 7481, 7484, and 7492) sufficiently powerful to show local dominance or near dominance, as indicated by the broken lines on the map. Three of these areas lie between three and five miles from any Class I center, while the fourth (7492) in Bordentown Township is an important highway strip along U.S. 130-206. In the Lower Bucks study area, where unplanned highway strips and small- to medium-sized shopping centers are concentrated in zones, there are a total of seven such zones with local areas of dominance. (Compare Figures 24 and 36.) Such Class II zones in Bucks County are situated at least three miles from any Class I zone and sometimes as much as 8 or 10 miles. Thus, lower-order service centers (Class II) exhibit subsidiary relationships to the higher-order centers (Class I). If a Class II zone lies adjacent to a Class I zone, it tends to be dominated by it, although it has a distinct influence on consumer behavior. When there is a distance of three miles or more, separating a zone with lower-order services from a high-order zone, then it is likely that the number of trips with local destinations will exceed the number of trips with destinations in the more distant higher-order center.

### Consumer Trips in Relation to Central Services

Analysis of the distribution of trips by purposes in relation to central service classification in the zone of destination reveals certain details of consumer behavior (Table 27). In the first place, it should be noted that Class I and Class II zones together attract three quarters of all trips reported, almost equally divided between the two classes. Class I zones attract a high proportion of trips to finance, insurance, and real estate establishments and are above average in auto sales, miscellaneous retail and personal or repair services. Class II zones are high in shopping goods and gasoline. There is very little difference in the percentage of trips for food shopping and professional services between Class I and Class II destinations. Among the few trips to Class III zones, these two categories together with eating and drinking are relatively most important. When trip-end destinations lie outside the study areas, eating and drinking, auto sales and

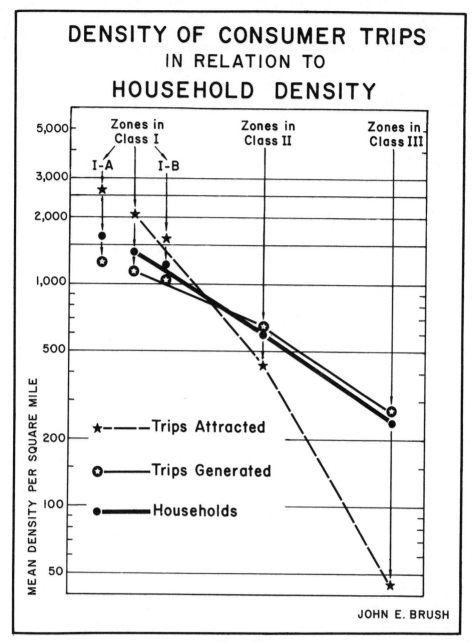

Figure 37.

Table 27

DISTRIBUTION OF PERSONAL BUSINESS AND SHOPPING TRIPS BY CLASSES I, II, III,
OR OTHER DESTINATIONS AND TYPE OF TRIP PURPOSES

| Type of Trip* Purpose | Trips Ending in Study Areas | | | | | | Philadelphia, ** Trenton, & Camden | | All Other Areas | |
|---|---|---|---|---|---|---|---|---|---|---|
| | Class I Zones | | Class II Zones | | Class III Zones | | | | | |
| | Number | Per Cent | Number | Per Cent | Number | Per Cent | Number | Per Cent | Number | Per Cent |
| 15 | 465 | 13.9 | 198 | 6.3 | 6 | 2.4 | 57 | 8.6 | 108 | 9.1 |
| 16 | 344 | 10.3 | 299 | 9.6 | 42 | 17.1 | 167 | 25.2 | 192 | 16.2 |
| 20 | 1,189 | 35.6 | 1,075 | 34.4 | 123 | 50.2 | 18 | 2.7 | 279 | 23.5 |
| 21 | 40 | 1.2 | 96 | 3.1 | 32 | 13.1 | 21 | 3.2 | 71 | 6.0 |
| 22 | 592 | 17.7 | 909 | 29.1 | 21 | 8.6 | 329 | 49.7 | 297 | 25.1 |
| 23 | 37 | 1.1 | 24 | 0.8 | -- | -- | -- | -- | 16 | 1.4 |
| 24 | 18 | 0.5 | 66 | 2.1 | 4 | 1.6 | 3 | 0.5 | 10 | 0.8 |
| 25 | 323 | 9.7 | 255 | 8.2 | 9 | 3.7 | 41 | 6.2 | 74 | 6.2 |
| 26 | 332 | 9.9 | 206 | 6.6 | 8 | 3.3 | 26 | 3.9 | 138 | 11.6 |
| Total | 3,340 | 100.0 | 3,128 | 100.0 | 245 | 100.0 | 662 | 100.0 | 1,185 | 100.0 |

Source: Penn-Jersey Transportation Study, Household Interviews, 1960-61. Data for 10 per cent sample, except in Bucks County where 4 per cent sample is expanded by a factor of 2.5.

* Please see Table 22.
** Philadelphia Center City only.

personal or repair services are usually high in percentage terms. Trips to Philadelphia Center City, Trenton, or Camden, show the most extreme concentration in shopping goods and professional services.

In order to discern the general influence of population distribution and central services upon consumer travel, the zone data on origin and destination of trips are grouped according to the classification of central services and converted into density terms. (See Table 28.) If the household density is taken as a basic parameter, conforming closely to a straight line on a semi-logarithmic scale, (Figure 37) the gradients of trips generated and attracted are seen as variables with positive or negative relationships to the household gradient.

First, it is evident that the means of all three classes of zones fall readily into rank from highest to lowest and, second, that there are net movements of consumers from zones of the two lower classes to Class I, i.e., to the higher-order centers with well developed services. Class I zones attract nearly twice as many consumer trips as they generate, while the two lower orders generate more trips than are attracted to them. It is clear that Class I-B zones occupy a ranking intermediate between Class I-A and Class II, attracting three trips for every two generated while Class I-A zones attract more than twice as many trips as they generate. Class II zones, comprising the small cities or boroughs and the portions of townships with commercial development, attract about two trips for every three trips generated. The most pronounced negative relationship of about five trips generated for every one attracted occurs in Class III zones where there are few rudimentary services.

It is also evident that trip generation is closely linked to household density, although in Class I zones the ratio of trips generated to households is much below the

Table 28

DENSITY OF HOUSEHOLDS AND CONSUMER TRIPS
ACCORDING TO CLASSIFICATION OF CENTRAL SERVICES

| Classification of Central Services (P-J Zones) | Mean Area (Sq. Mi.) | Mean Density per Square Mile | | |
|---|---|---|---|---|
| | | Households | Trips Attracted | Trips Generated |
| I – Higher Order | 2.02 | 1,430 | 2,108 | 1,148 |
| I-A | 2.43 | 1,646 | 2,645 | 1,255 |
| I-B | 1.61 | 1,215 | 1,564 | 1,045 |
| II – Lower Order | 3.43 | 604 | 429 | 634 |
| III – Rudimentary | 4.78 | 242 | 44 | 261 |

Source: Penn-Jersey Transportation Study, Field Survey and Households Interviews, 1960-61. Trip data from sample of households is expanded to represent all households. See Table 25.

ratio near 1:1 prevailing in the two lower classes of zones. Consumer trip frequency per household is about seventy-five per cent as great in Class I as in Class II or Class III zones. This low ratio may be due to a combination of factors among which are the lower income level, lower percentage of families owning automobiles and possibly under-reporting of pedestrian trips in Class I zones. The same relationships are also shown, if household and trip data are separated for zones in Class I-A and Class I-B. (See Table 28.)

Table 29

DENSITY OF ESTABLISHMENTS AND RATIOS OF TRIPS ATTRACTED
ACCORDING TO CLASSIFICATION OF CENTRAL SERVICES

| Classification of Central Services (P-J Zones) | Mean Density per Square Mile | | Trips Attracted per Establishment |
|---|---|---|---|
| | Number of Establishments | Square Feet (1,000's) | |
| I - Higher Order | 96 | 139.6 | 22 |
| I-A | 115 | 142.8 | 23 |
| I-B | 71 | 134.7 | 22 |
| II - Lower Order | 16 | 24.9 | 27 |
| III - Rudimentary | 3 | 3.9 | 13 |

Source: Data on establishments from Rutgers field survey, 1962; trip ratios from Penn-Jersey Transportation Study, Household Interviews, 1960-61.

Comparison of ratios of trips attracted and the number and size of establishments, converted to the unit area basis, show some interesting relationships. (See Table 29.) Class II zones exhibit the highest proportions of trips attracted per establishment, although in a one square mile area Class I zones contain six times as many establishments and attract five times as many consumers as Class II zones. The trip ratio per establishment for Class I zones is not significantly altered by separation of the data into Class I-A and Class I-B. Class III zones, which rank lowest in density and size of establishments also rank the lowest in terms of trip attraction. Attraction of consumers, as should be expected, conforms more closely to the density of retail stores and services than to the density of households.

A Probability Analysis of Consumer Trips

Having both classified service centers and described the observable pattern of consumer trips associated with them, additional insight into spatial interaction in the Penjerdel region can be gained by attempting to provide some estimates of expected patterns of consumer's spatial behavior. Such is the concern of this portion of the report. Specifically, given some limited knowledge of the functional structure of the service centers and of the observed pattern of consumer movements among them, the objective is to generate theoretical patterns of consumer movements that are statistically related to the observed ones. To attempt this, some elementary notions of probability theory will be used in an effort to replicate certain of the travel patterns sampled by the Penn-Jersey Transportation Study.

Efforts to analyze consumer movements are neither new nor unique and consequently there exists a substantial literature which can be drawn upon. Among the factors that have been frequently mentioned as affecting the spatial patterns of consumer behavior, travel costs have probably received principal consideration. Clearly, a consumer's travel behavior is influenced by the expense, in time and effort as well as actual monetary units, that he perceives to be involved in selecting among various service centers offering the goods and services desired. These anticipated costs of travelling, the time and effort involved in preparing for and actually making the trip, are regarded as exerting a force that brings a contraction in distances travelled to satisfy consumer needs.

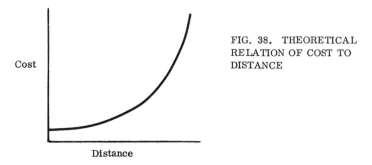

Cost

Distance

FIG. 38. THEORETICAL RELATION OF COST TO DISTANCE

From Figure 38 it can be seen that in the abstract case there are certain fixed costs associated with the preparation for the trip, and that trip costs, as perceived by the consumer, initially rise slowly with incremental increases in distance until, at some point, they rise steeply. The sharp incremental increase with distance reflects the existence of opportunity cost. The consumer has only so much time to devote to any number of activities during a given time period. Consequently if he devotes more time to one activity at the expense of others, the costs of the opportunities that are foregone rise significantly to act as a check against additional time losses. [7]

---

[7] For a more detailed discussion see; David Huff, "Ecological Characteristics of Human Behavior," Papers of the Regional Science Association, 7, 1961, pp. 19-28.

The impact of travel costs upon consumer spatial behavior theoretically works to constrict movement to those service centers situated within minimal radii of travel from the point of origin. In the Penjerdel region, there exists a general tendency for such minimization of consumer trips, as can be inferred from the observed trip patterns. However, the constriction is by no means a perfect one. In the aggregated travel data there is evident a significant consumer movement beyond the travel distances where the greatest volume of trips has terminated.

Empirical evidence in other studies suggest that a large number of consumer shopping decisions are made under conditions of uncertainty.[8] The consumer does not know in advance whether a particular retail unit in a service center will definitely satisfy a specified purchase desire. However, the evidence does suggest that the consumer has some a priori knowledge of the likelihood or probability that various sources might satisfy his shopping demands. This probability is based largely on the number of selections of the kind the consumer desires and believes are offered by each of the various locational sources. Presumably the greater the number of selections offered by each locational source the greater is the consumer's expectation that his shopping trip will be successful. Consequently it might be expected that consumers will show a willingness to travel greater distances for any good or service as the number of offerings increase at the various sources.

In Figure 39 the impact of available offerings is shown in abstract graphic form. It appears that up to some threshold level, the consumer shows a willingness, as the number of offerings of a particular product increases, to incur an increase in his expenditure in the expectation of realizing the greater satisfaction he perceives will be gained from increases in item offerings. In terms of spatial behavior these expectations

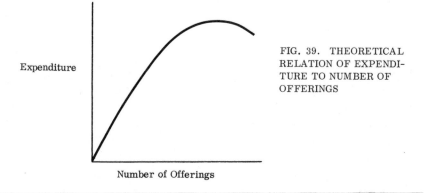

Expenditure

Number of Offerings

FIG. 39. THEORETICAL RELATION OF EXPENDITURE TO NUMBER OF OFFERINGS

---

[8]Cf. William Baumal and Edward Ide, "Variety in Retailing," Management Science, 3, October 1956.

of greater satisfaction tend to extend the radii of trip distances the consumer is willing to consider in seeking to fulfill his needs for goods and services.

As has been indicated earlier, sample results from the Penn-Jersey Transportation Study suggest that consumer travel in the Penjerdel area consists in aggregate of a very large number of short trips with progressively fewer trips reported as distances of travel increase. This pattern can be graphically generalized in the nature of a distribution displaying a regular and steady decline in the number of trips recorded with each increase in travel distance. (Figure 40.) A trip length frequency distribution of this type is not unique to the Penjerdel area. In transportation studies involving Chicago, Detroit, and Pittsburgh similar distributions were reported.

In attempting to give meaning to the above distribution, planners have suggested, at a primitive level of generalization, that it appears to be the result of two somewhat contradictory forces. One of these is travel costs. These costs occur because there is a "friction" component of space that can be overcome only by expending energy for travel. The effect of this frictional component of space is to restrict travel distances in the interest of limiting travel costs. The term cost is broadly conceived and recognizes there are costs in energy, in work, and in requiring the use of resources that might be employed otherwise.

Travel not only involves costs for it is associated as well with rewards arising from the satisfaction of fulfilling a need for various goods and services. These rewards are in part associated with different levels of item and, consequently, satisfaction offerings, as mentioned earlier. Such components of consumer expenditures are a second general force; one that can exert pressure to lengthen a shopping trip. The conditional qualification of this force is important to note as its actual effect will depend largely on the spatial distribution of available offerings in relation to the point or zone of origin.

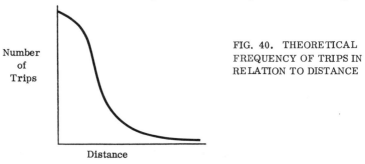

FIG. 40. THEORETICAL FREQUENCY OF TRIPS IN RELATION TO DISTANCE

Attributing observed patterns of travel to a tendency to economize pitted against the attraction of rewards arising from higher levels of probable satisfaction suggests that consumer spatial behavior represents a particular balance or equilibrium between the two forces at a point in time and over a particular arrangement of urban activities or land uses. At a high level of abstraction then, consumer travel can be conceived as representing the resolution of two competing tendencies. However, such a verbal description is not only a simplification of reality but is inadequate for purposes of replicating actual travel patterns. A more precise statement is necessary; one that is operational. To introduce greater precision into the analysis, the following paragraphs will develop a mathematical description of the preceding notions.

It should be noted that the proposed formulation is based on the premise that individual consumer trips defy prediction but that aggregate trips, involving large numbers of purchasers, are subject to probability analysis. However, for illustrative purposes the descriptive algorithm can be easily illustrated by considering an individual trip. It is assumed that in making a trip the consumer seeks to keep it as short as possible in order to avoid higher costs than are necessary. On the other hand, the trip has a definite reason for being made, namely some requirement of the consumer for which a satisfaction is sought. The more selective this requirement the greater the probability of incurring more travel time, and consequently greater cost, in seeking satisfaction.

For purposes of illustration, assume that the consumer seeks a rather common commodity, e.g., one associated with a relatively low level of selectivity because it is sold by a large number of retail units within the consumer's shopping area. It can be established by measurement how many destinations in the region are places that sell this commodity. Assume that it is one out of every 50 retail units. This means that the consumer's chance of finding a randomly chosen destination to be satisfactory in meeting his needs is 1/50. Assuming this person is economical and wishes to travel no further than necessary, he will choose the nearest suitable destination. There is a 1/50 chance that the nearest one will be satisfactory, i.e., sell the product he desires. If this destination isn't satisfactory then the next nearest center is considered, and so on until the closest satisfactory point is found.

The elimination process involved in the preceding example can be described mathematically. The closest possible destination, or first point considered, has a $1/n$ probability of satisfying the consumer. Expressing this value as p, the chance that the consumer will terminate his search at the first point is p and the chance he would not is $1-p$. The chance of finding the next nearest destination point suitable would again be p. However, there is the possibility that the first point has been chosen, eliminating the next closest center from consideration. Thus in the elimination process the chance of a consumer stopping at the second center is less than p. Precisely stated, the chance of the second center being selected is the chance that the first center is not satisfactory, $1-p$, multiplied by the chance of the second center being satisfactory, p. It follows then that the chance of a third center being selected is the chance of rejection of the first two,

$(1-p)^2$, multiplied by the chance of selection of the third, p.

      To generalize, the probability of a specified trip stopping at any randomly chosen destination point may be designated as p. This value is a reflection of the degree of special purpose of the trip. The probability of a trip terminating at a particular destination point will depend not only on the degree of trip specialization or p value, but upon how many other points, x, lie closer to the trip's point of origin. Thus, the chance of a trip's destination being a particular center j is equal to the probability of previously ordered i centers (i=1, 2,.., j-1) being rejected, or $(1-p)^x$, multiplied by p, the probability of the jth center being satisfactory.

      Stated in such elementary terms, the preceding algorithm provides a simple description of consumer spatial behavior. As has been noted, however, the problem of interest is to generate trip destination expectations for aggregate groupings of consumer movements. Fortunately, the algorithm can be modified to consider zones or cluster of destinations rather than individual ones. Again the basic premise is the preference to minimize total travel investment subject to the condition that each cluster of destinations has a stated probability of being accepted, if it is considered. The consumer cannot necessarily go to the nearest destination and stop; if it is unsatisfactory in meeting his demands, he must consider the next nearest and so on until a zone has a level of offerings acceptable to him.

      The probability that a trip will terminate within some cluster of destination points is equal to the probability that this cluster contains an acceptable destination times the probability that an acceptable destination closer to the origin of the trip has not been found. As the latter two probabilities may vary from point to point, the problem must be stated in terms of limitingly small quantities:

$$dq = (1-q)pdx \qquad (1)$$

Where q is the probability a trip has terminated within a cluster x lying closer to the point of origin in order of consideration, and p is the probability density of destination acceptability at the point of consideration.

      If p is constant, the solution of (1) is:

$$q = 1-ke^{-px} \qquad \text{(k is the constant of integration)} \qquad (2)$$

However, k = 1 since q must be zero when x is zero, so:

$$q = 1-e^{-px} \qquad (3)$$

      The expected interchange from zone i to zone j is simply the volume of trip origins at zone i multiplied by the probability of a trip terminating in j, or more precisely:

$$x_{ij} = x_i \left( e^{-px} - e^{-p(x + xj)} \right) \qquad (4)$$

      It is reasonable to extend the formulation by assuming that, although p is constant for each trip, different trips have different p's. This supposition gives rise to the more general equation:

$$x_{ij} = \int_{p\ min}^{p\ max} \left(e^{-px} - e^{-p(x\ xj)}\right) Z_i dp \qquad (5)$$

where: $Z_i = \dfrac{dx_i}{dp}$

It might be argued that the destinations are also distributed in their affinities. Possibly this is the case. Conceptually it might be handled by construing x and xj as some functions of p. However, it is not clear how the computation of equation (5) can be realized in practice without far more knowledge of consumer spatial behavior than is now available in the Philadelphia metropolitan fringe. But equation (4) can be adjusted to approximate (5) by clustering trips into groups with the entries in each group being determined by the same probability density of destination acceptability.

Having advanced a conceptualization of consumer spatial behavior and having stated it in elementary probability terms, it is now possible to proceed with the computation of a series of values of expected consumer trips. Before doing this, however, some general statements from the preceding paragraphs must be translated into operational form.

Some method is necessary to describe the order of search a consumer would use in deciding on his destinations. This is crucial in describing x. Distance, time, and travel costs have been most frequently suggested to establish nearness of a cluster of destinations to a zone of origin. Clearly they are not the same. Distance by itself cannot take into account varying travel speeds nor areas of substantial congestion. In this respect it probably is not a true measure of the weighting the consumer uses in evaluating alternative possible destinations. Measures of time overcome many of the difficulties inherent in distance measurements. Perhaps travel costs would be the preferred measure especially in view of the hypothesis that the theoretical p value of a trip represents some balancing of travel costs, in their broadest sense, against probable rewards or satisfactions. The difficulty with travel costs, however, is that at the present state of knowledge they are difficult to establish and measure. For this reason it was decided to use mean travel time as the most useful measurement for ordering clusters of destinations with respect to each zone of origin. The estimates of travel time were based on information provided by the Penn-Jersey Transportation Study and on field measurements made by the research assistants for this project.

With x described operationally it is possible to measure the characteristics of the p values. Knowing the order of destination clusters from each zone of consumer origin, probability values can be assigned indicating the likelihood of consumer satisfaction at each successive cluster. For each trip type there is a different ordering of the p values from each zone of origin. Assuming different p values, reflecting levels of consumer selectivity, there are also different sets of p values identifiable with each zone of origin. The functional structures of the destination clusters, upon which the p values are based, have been described in the earlier chapters and need not be repeated in this section.

In computing expected consumer trip patterns in the Penn-Jersey area the decision was made to use the smallest county study area, Gloucester, as a test case. In addition, to avoid difficulties inherent in small sample sizes it seemed advisable to limit consideration of different trip types to the five groups of (a) foodstuffs, (b) shopping goods, (c) finance and insurance, (d) professional services, and (e) personal and repair services. The results of the application of the probability formulation to these five groups of trips having zones of origin and destination in Gloucester County are presented in Table 26.

For the sample area of Gloucester County, the number of trips listed in Table 30 are elements of the theoretical frequencies of consumer movements that are expected to occur according to the probability rules of the algorithm. To test the significance of the results, it is necessary to determine whether the observed frequencies of consumer movements, as presented in Table 31, differ significantly from the expected frequencies. A measure of the discrepancy existing between observed and expected frequencies is probided by the statistic $x^2$.

In applying the $x^2$ statistic, we are in essence testing the null hypothesis that there is no significant difference between the actual and theoretical frequencies. If under this hypothesis the computed values of $x^2$ are greater than some specified fiducial values, we conclude that the observed frequencies differ significantly from the expected frequencies and consequently reject the null hypothesis at the corresponding level of significance. The critical fiducial values are those at the .05 and .01 significance levels.

Applying the $x^2$ test of significance to the five groups of trips that have zones of origin and destination in Gloucester County, we can accept the null hypothesis for three of the theoretical frequencies. Among the five groups, the divergence between the expected and actual consumer movements is least for food shopping trips. Clearly, of all shopping trips, the expected trip frequency for purchases of food and related commodities most closely approximates the actual patterns of consumer spatial behavior. There is less than one chance out of a hundred that the differences between the actual and predicted patterns could not be due to chance or sampling variation. The theoretical patterns of trips that are made for purposes of financial and insurance matters and for personal and repair services also correspond reasonably well to actual patterns of spatial interaction. The computed values for these groupings permit us to accept the null hypothesis at the .05 level of significance.

171

Table 30

EXPECTED TRIP DISTRIBUTION

GLOUCESTER COUNTY STUDY AREA

| Zone of Destination | Number of Trips | | | | |
|---|---|---|---|---|---|
| | Food | Finance & Insurance | Personal & Repair Services | Professional Services | Shopping Goods |
| 7811 | 21.2 | 6.1 | 6.1 | 9.6 | 9.9 |
| 7812 | 310.5 | 88.4 | 42.0 | 59.0 | 114.7 |
| 7813 | 26.8 | 2.6 | 2.3 | 3.8 | 106.1 |
| 7821 | 18.4 | 2.3 | 8.2 | 4.2 | 90.2 |
| 7822 | 16.2 | 2.0 | 2.8 | 15.2 | 3.5 |
| 7823 | 14.5 | 1.8 | 1.6 | 1.8 | 2.1 |
| 7912 | 10.6 | – | .5 | 1.4 | 1.0 |
| 7911 | 16.6 | – | .9 | 1.8 | 3.6 |
| 7921 | 7.8 | 3.0 | .3 | 1.0 | 2.6 |
| 7922 | 18.9 | 3.9 | 5.9 | 2.3 | 43.7 |
| 7923 | 32.2 | 9.4 | 9.7 | 11.8 | 20.2 |

Source: Computation by Author.

For the remaining groups of trips that are made for purchases of a diverse number of shopping goods and for professional services we cannot accept the null hypothesis at the critical values of $x^2$ .95 and $x^2$ .99. A comparison of the actual and expected frequencies of trips for these goods and services reveals a consistent tendency to overestimate the latter. On the basis of the number of establishments providing satisfaction for shopping goods and professional services, we would expect more consumer trips to terminate in each zone of the study area. This divergence might suggest some weakness in the conceptualization of the algorithm. However, as we have seen, the algorithm does generate expected trip distributions that are significant for three categories. Furthermore, it is difficult to suggest theoretical grounds on which we can argue that the same probabilistic notions that proved successful in dealing with trip frequencies for food purchases, financial and insurance needs, and personal and repair services, should not be relevant to consumer movements for shopping goods and professional services. A more likely explanation for the significant divergence is to be found in the consideration of the sample study area as a closed system. Because of a lack of information, we have ignored trips that terminate in zones outside of Gloucester County. It will be recalled from the description of consumer movements presented earlier in this chapter that more than 20 per cent of the consumers sampled seek satisfaction of their require-

Table 31

OBSERVED TRIP DISTRIBUTION

GLOUCESTER COUNTY STUDY AREA

| Zone of Destination | Number of Trips | | | | |
|---|---|---|---|---|---|
| | Food | Finance & Insurance | Personal & Repair Services | Professional Services | Shopping Goods |
| 7811 | 25 | 8 | 3 | 4 | 2 |
| 7812 | 304 | 78 | 36 | 44 | 98 |
| 7813 | 25 | 3 | 3 | 1 | 88 |
| 7821 | 22 | 5 | 5 | 2 | 64 |
| 7822 | 10 | – | 1 | 9 | 1 |
| 7823 | 7 | – | – | 3 | – |
| 7912 | 9 | – | – | – | – |
| 7911 | 12 | – | 1 | – | 1 |
| 7921 | 5 | 2 | – | – | 1 |
| 7922 | 18 | 2 | 4 | – | 36 |
| 7923 | 34 | 5 | 7 | 7 | 13 |

Source: Penn–Jersey Transportation Study.  (See Table 25–C.)

ments outside of the study areas. Of the trips made to other sections of the Penjerdel Region the greatest number are made for shopping goods and professional services. Actual consumer travel patterns show a marked tendency to seek satisfaction for these goods and services in the central business districts of Philadelphia, Trenton, and Camden. The omission of this feature of trip frequencies by consumers living in the sample study area has the effect of overestimating the attracting power of centers offering satisfaction for shopping goods and professional services within the limits of Gloucester County. It might also be noted that the trip types for which there exists significant identity between actual and theoretical frequencies are those for which the central business districts of major centers outside of the study area are not frequent zones of destination. If it were possible to include the attraction of Philadelphia, Trenton, and Camden in our analysis, it is quite likely that a closer correspondence would be obtained between the actual and expected trip frequencies.

CHAPTER V

CONCLUSIONS

In the preceding pages the authors have traced the origin and evolution of service centers and analyzed the current patterns of development. The results provide a basis for answering the fundamental questions outlined in the introductory chapter. (See pp. 12-15.)

First, we find that service centers and service areas on the metropolitan fringe are identifiable, both in terms of geographical groupings of establishments in an hierarchical spatial pattern and in terms of service areas based on consumer travel gradients. Service centers of three functional grades, or orders, and service areas associated with the two of these orders have been mapped in the study areas. (See Class I and Class II centers and areas as shown in Figure 41.) We do not find it is possible to distinguish clearly in all cases between the local service areas of lower-order centers (Class II). In many cases the lower-order centers are evidently dominated by the influence of adjacent higher-order centers and lie within their service areas. The service areas associated with centers of the lowest order (Class III) are not clearly distinguishable as a rule and such centers are generally located within the service areas of the centers of the two higher orders (Class I or Class II). We find a few instances where the travel gradients of inhabitants of these areas show dependence upon centers in adjacent areas due to special circumstances. (Note arrows Figure 41, Middle Bucks and Burlington counties.) It is evident either that our data are inadequate or that the existing establishments in centers at the time of our study and reported consumer behavior do not fully reflect factors now at work. Some time lag should be expected in the transition between the shifts in population and the locational pattern of business establishments.

Second, the authors find contrary trends in the development of centers and expansion of service areas of the inner and outer parts of the metropolitan fringe. It appears that on the inner fringe the growth of population creates sufficient geographic concentration of consumers to support both the old developed towns (Class I-A centers)

173

174

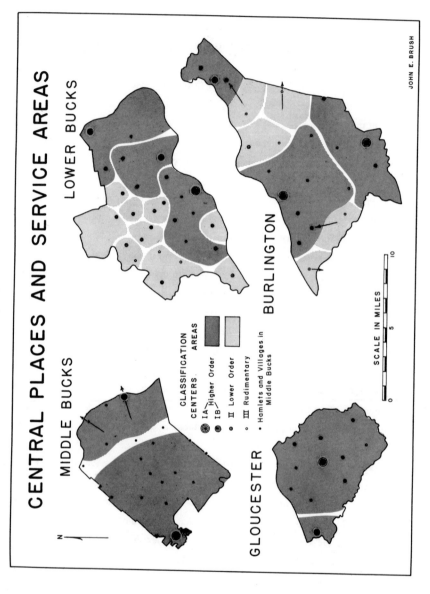

Figure 41

CENTRAL PLACES AND SERVICE AREAS

LOWER BUCKS

BURLINGTON

MIDDLE BUCKS

GLOUCESTER

CLASSIFICATION
CENTERS. AREAS
IA Higher Order
IB
II Lower Order
III Rudimentary
Hamlets and Villages in
Middle Bucks

SCALE IN MILES
0      5      10

JOHN E. BRUSH

and new regional shopping centers or smaller developing towns (Class I-B centers). On the outer metropolitan fringe, however, growth tends to concentrate at a few developed towns (Class I-A) and the many small villages or hamlets (Class III centers) survive as a rudimentary, now relict, order of central places. There is a lower order of central places (Class II) which seems viable in the inner metropolitan fringe where moderately high density of population exists and day-to-day needs of consumers are satisfied at stores and service establishments located in small shopping centers and along the local highways. Therefore, we observe a proliferation of new centers and the splitting of service areas formerly dependent on the old developed towns located in the inner metropolitan fringe. On the outer fringe, we find expansion of the radii of influence of the few developed towns, decline of the smaller towns and stagnation of the old rural villages and hamlets, unless there should be peculiar attractions due to their rustic qualities and special efforts to cater to recreational demands of consumers coming from a much wider territory, i. e. , Middle Bucks County.

In general, these spatial arrangements appear to provide some empirical support to the Isardian scheme referred to in the introductory chapter. This support is limited to the spatial pattern, however, as no attempt has been made to probe the underlying economic theory. We interpret the spatial patterns of service centers and consumer trips on the metropolitan fringe of Philadelphia in terms of a progression from the open countryside, where establishments grouped in a few places supply the needs of widely dispersed consumers, to the closely occupied urban areas, where higher concentrations of consumers support establishments grouped in a close spatial pattern. Within the city still a more complex ordering of centers and service areas is to be found in areas of highest consumer concentration. The apparent chaos and random behavior postulated by Gottmann and Weber is not supported by our studies. We do not expect the outlying towns and small cities of the Philadelphia metropolitan region to lose their identity or their influence to be superceded.

In conclusion, we offer a brief summation of the whole sequence of central-place development observed in the study areas and assess the trend towards local integration in community-of-interest areas.

## Origin and Evolution of Centers

In the rural areas of the Philadelphia region, cities and towns always have had a role as market places. During the seventeenth and eighteenth centuries when subsistence agriculture prevailed and transportation was primitive, rural people rarely could visit any center of trade and services. Burlington, Philadelphia and Bristol were created in the initial stage of settlement during the seventeenth century to serve as centers of government and commerce. But only Philadelphia gained enough concentration of population to become an <u>urban</u> place before the end of the eighteenth century. The city was clearly the first and foremost regional commercial center and always exerted influence throughout the region. Burlington and Bristol were small villages, occupying subsidiary roles with comparatively restricted influence. In the eighteenth century there was insufficient concentration of demand to support the development of many agglomerated centers of rural territory. Small inns and taverns, located at crossroads or near bridges and mill dams, served as centers of communication and social contact.

Transportation improvements began about 1800, at first on the main routes of travel under turnpike companies and later under canal and railroad companies. In the beginning there seemed to be little impact on farmers, but by the middle of the nineteenth century local public roads were being improved for horse-drawn wheeled vehicles and the cheapening of transport costs gave access to larger market areas. In the first half of the nineteenth century farm population was growing and agricultural production was increasing. These circumstances combined with the gains in per capita rural income and the shift from self-sufficiency to a commercial economy meant there was demand sufficient to support numerous local centers of trade in the rural hinterland of Philadelphia.

A more or less regular pattern of central places developed in rural territory with groupings of stores and service establishments, commensurate with travel limitations of rural people. Hamlets and small villages, located at two-to three-mile intervals throughout the countryside, brought general retail stores and rudimentary services within reach of every rural household. This was the limit of most frequent, perhaps daily, travel. The specialized retail stores and various types of personal and professional establishments were concentrated in large villages and small towns, located at intervals of at least five or six miles where they could have larger radii of consumer attraction and would be accessible through less frequent, most commonly weekly, trips for the majority of rural families. In each of these higher-order centers there drew up a distinct concentration of business establishments along the main street and clustered around the business district were the schools, churches and other public or quasi-public services which would thereby gain not only the maximum accessibility for the scattered rural population but now also for the rapidly growing town population. Rural people residing farther away than two or three miles from town (about one hour travel time in a wagon or buggy) had to depend largely upon the stores and schools or churches located in the nearest village or hamlet.

By the late nineteenth century and early twentieth century agricultural population was declining almost everywhere in rural portions of the region, while new employment opportunities in the region were confined mainly to Philadelphia and the satellite cities of Camden and Trenton. There were, of course, suburban residential extensions along the rail and trolley lines in rural territory. But in the rural hinterlands demand for goods and services increased sufficiently to support the continued growth of only a few higher-order centers, which could be considered urban places. The shift to automobile transportation after the 1920's and subsequent paving of local roads tended to increase the influence of these rural-based towns, while the many hamlets and small villages went into stagnation and decline. Rural households had now become dependent upon the outlying country towns for consumer goods, but most urban amenities remained restricted to the residents of small compact areas in these country towns or near the large cities. Urban consumers now had many opportunities for satisfaction of their demands for goods and services from establishments located both in central business districts at the major transport nodes of these large cities and in secondary centers developing at the local transportation nodes within the closely built-up urban areas.

## Growth of New Centers

By the middle of the twentieth century the mobility of employment and residence associated with the automobile age had set the stage for massive urban expansion. Indeed, the preference for single-family dwellings on relatively large lots or "country estates" has reversed the population trends of a hundred years, so that old urban areas have become stable or declining in population and income, while the urban fringes and so-called rural areas are experiencing increases of population and income. Under such circumstances it would be surprising if there were not severe strains upon existing centers and rapid growth of new centers in response to rising consumer demand.

The authors observe the following sequence of development since 1950:

Initially the geographical concentration of business activity is increased in the higher-order centers, i.e., the well-developed towns of Class I-A, because population growth tends to occur in or adjacent to existing urban areas. Traffic continues to converge towards the central business district from all parts of the service area which may have a radius of as much as ten miles for weekly, and often daily, shopping trips. Some small neighborhood stores and service establishments may survive in relict hamlets and villages located within the town's service area. (See Figure 42.) If population growth is relatively slow and diffused, the business entrepreneurs may be able to expand the scale of their operations and increase the variety of goods and services sufficiently to satisfy rising consumer demands. But unless there is some forethought and coordinated planning of traffic movement, construction of adequate facilities for parking and enlargement of the total square footage of enclosed flood space, the second stage will begin. Doylestown is still in this initial stage of development and maintains its role as the center of trade and services in Middle Bucks County. But Cross Keys just north of Doylestown along U. S. Route 611 shows features of the second stage, which probably will be made inevitable, if there is more rapid rate of population growth around Doylestown.

In the second stage the geographical concentration of consumers, severe traffic congestion and/or inadequacies of parking facilities reduce the accessibility of establishments in the old business district. Entrepreneurs seek new sites on highways at the margins of town, where customers driving into town will find it convenient to stop and at the same time townspeople will come out to shop. In time new lower-order centers (Class II) are so formed which have secondary areas of influence, generally lying within the areas tributary to the parent town. (See Figure 43.) In this stage there is not yet sufficient concentration of population in the outlying parts of the town's service area to stimulate development of new centers, although Class II villages may continue to serve local demand beyond three miles from any large town and small towns of Class I-B may flourish beyond a distance of five or six miles. Eventually there may be planned expansion of shopping and service facilities on the marginal highways within or near the municipal limits of the parent Class I town, while relative if not absolute decline of trade occurs in its old business district. Mt. Holly and Woodbury are well advanced into this second stage, while Bristol is suffering more severe distress due to the decline of its business district in competition to development along U. S. Route 13: Bristol has suffered the loss of outlying portions of its service area to the north and northeast where rapid urban expansion has occurred, bringing phenomena which characterize the next stage of change.

It is here in Lower Bucks County in the townships of Bristol, Falls and Middletown that the third stage of metropolitan expansion is observed, where large-scale housing construction enterprises (Levittown and Fairless Hills) brought sudden increases of population and consumer demand during the 1950's. The incipient phase of similar rapid development existed in Willingboro Township, Burlington County, at the time of field survey in the early 1960's. It so happens that in both counties the major new housing tracts and shopping facilities are situated three miles or more from either Bristol or Burlington. In such circumstances, two patterns of development are observed.

(1) concentration of new business establishments in a single regional shopping center, as at the Levittown Shop-A-Rama in Tullytown Borough and as projected at the Willingboro Plaza, Burlington County at the time of surveys; and

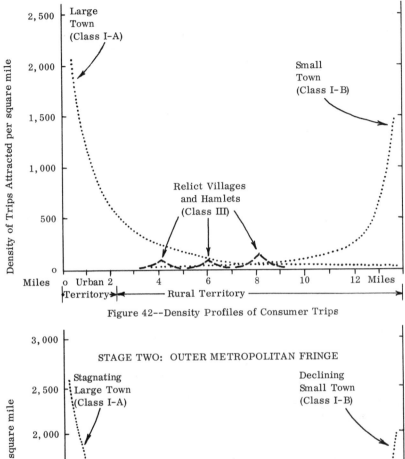

STAGE ONE: OUTER METROPOLITAN FRINGE

Figure 42--Density Profiles of Consumer Trips

STAGE TWO: OUTER METROPOLITAN FRINGE

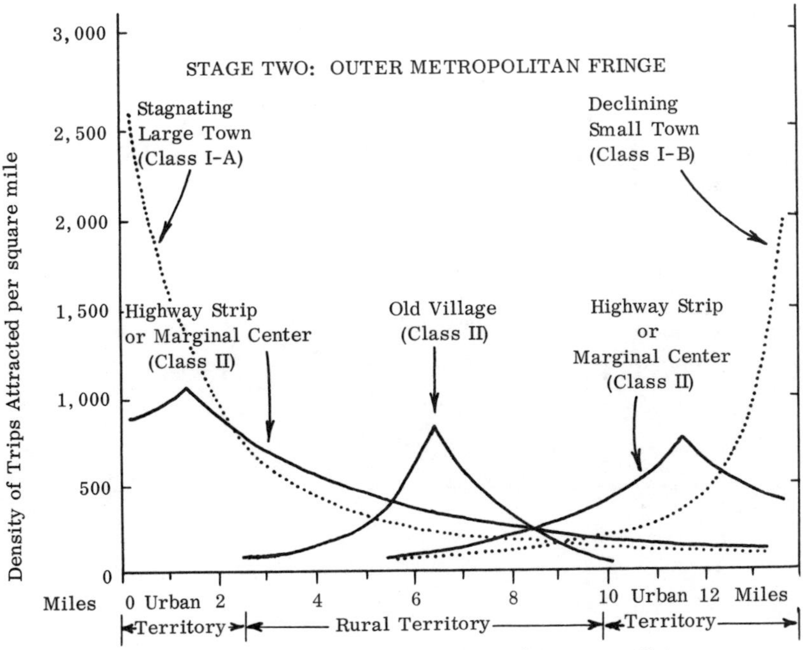

Figure 43--Density Profiles of Consumer Trips

180

(2) diffusion of establishments in several small shopping centers and unplanned
highway strips, as in the townships of Bristols, Falls and Middletown, where some of
the stores and services are located in small or medium-sized shopping centers such as
the Fairless Hills and Country Club Centers, and others stand along the highway, i.e.,
U. S. Route One, Midway, Five Points and Newportville-Fallsington Road.

These different geographical patterns of consumer interaction may be visualized
in relation to nearby towns of Class I-A and Class I-B which formerly served households
in the area. (See Figure 44.) In the first instance, there is a distinct area of dominant
influence extending to consumers located two or three miles from the regional shopping

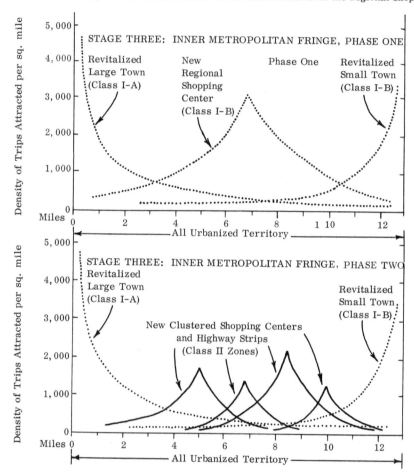

Figure 44--Density Profiles of Consumer Trips

center such as Tullytown which has attained Class IB status.  In the second instance, where no major concentrations of business establishments exist and all zones are in Class II, the influence of any one planned center of highway strip is generally less intense and does not dominate consumers beyond the limit of the zone or a radius of about one mile from the location of the stores and services.

## Community-of-Interest Areas

A fourth stage of development can be projected which would be the formation of more complete community-of-interest areas.  In this stage there would be a full assemblage of the professional services, such as physicians, lawyers, etc., together with a complex of churches, schools, hospitals and various public agencies and recreational facilities, grouped around a major regional shopping center.  Tendencies of this sort are observed around the Levittown Shop-A-Rama in Tullytown and the two adjacent townships in Lower Bucks County as well as in Willingboro around the Willingboro Plaza in Burlington County.  The Cherry Hill Shopping Center and associated developments in Cherry Hill Township in Camden County, outside the study areas, best exemplify this stage of urban development on the metropolitan fringe of the Philadelphia region.  In this example, the pattern of consumer travel is concentrated at one major shopping center and it may be hypothesized that total travel is minimized, especially when trips for educational, social and recreational purposes are combined with the purposes of shopping and personal business.  Such development of a community-of-interest area would seem to be hindered by the dispersed pattern of development in the second instance (Stage Three, Phase Two) mentioned above.

What is involved in this fourth stage of urban expansion is the creation of complete new urban communities based on Class I centers.  Such a center with a two-mile radius of attraction comprises about 12.6 square miles with some 22,200 households and 76,000 to 77,000 inhabitants.[1]  If the radius of attraction is three miles, the area is increased to 28.6 square miles, households to 26,040 and population to about 90,000.[2]  The

---

[1] The household estimate is based on one Class I-A zone (mean area 2.4 square miles), containing 3,840 households, and three Class II zones (mean area of each 3.4 square miles), containing 18,360 households.  Population estimate is based on mean number of 3.44 persons per household obtained in the Census of 1960 (Bucks, Burlington and Gloucester Counties).

[2] The household estimate is based on addition of 16.0 square miles with household density of 240 per square mile, the mean density observed in Class III zones.

empirical data analyzed in the preceding chapters suggest that this is a valid range of territory for proper functioning of an urban community on the metropolitan fringe--the American equivalent of the English "new towns" which have been established purposefully to accomodate metropolitan population expansion. Lacking the English policies of governmental planning and land use control, a program of local community planning under both private and public auspices, aided by county land use zoning, will be necessary to attain the fruits of this kind of urban development in the Philadelphia region. When the center of the larger urban community is an old city or borough which has suffered decline of income and business activity, there must be systematic renewal of its physical facilities and stimulation of its functions as a place for exchange of goods and services.

A rational approach to planning and zoning problems may require realignment of local municipal boundaries in order to bring under one jurisdiction the majority of households in the service area of a Class I center. In the nineteenth century, when compact urban units formed around the higher-order centers in the midst of open country, political separation from the rural townships was necessary for urban dwellers to achieve the municipal improvements and services which farmers would not and could not support through taxation. Now that the old dichotomy between urban and rural has lost its meaning the existence of small municipalities is no longer justified. Public consensus and political action of some sort will be needed to achieve unification and comprehensive development of whole community-of-interest areas on the metropolitan fringe.

# THE UNIVERSITY OF CHICAGO
## DEPARTMENT OF GEOGRAPHY
### RESEARCH PAPERS (Lithographed, 6 × 9 Inches)

*(Available from Department of Geography, Rosenwald Hall, The University of Chicago, Chicago, Illinois, 60637. Price: four dollars each; by series subscription, three dollars each.)*

*1. GROSS, HERBERT HENRY. *Educational Land Use in the River Forest-Oak Park Community (Illinois)*

*2. EISEN, EDNA E. *Educational Land Use in Lake County, Ohio*

*3. WEIGEND, GUIDO GUSTAV. *The Cultural Pattern of South Tyrol (Italy)*

*4. NELSON, HOWARD JOSEPH, *The Livelihood Structure of Des Moines, Iowa*

*5. MATTHEWS, JAMES SWINTON. *Expressions of Urbanism in the Sequent Occupance of Northeastern Ohio*

*6. GINSBURG, NORTON SYDNEY. *Japanese Prewar Trade and Shipping in the Oriental Triangle*

*7. KEMLER, JOHN H. *The Struggle for Wolfram in the Iberian Peninsula, June, 1942—June, 1944: A Study in Political and Economic Geography in Wartime*

*8. PHILBRICK, ALLEN K. *The Geography of Education in the Winnetka and Bridgeport Communities of Metropolitan Chicago*

*9. BRADLEY, VIRGINIA. *Functional Patterns in the Guadalupe Counties of the Edwards Plateau*

*10. HARRIS, CHAUNCY D., and FELLMANN, JEROME DONALD. *A Union List of Geographical Serials*

*11. DE MEIRLEIR, MARCEL J. *Manufactural Occupance in the West Central Area of Chicago*

*12. FELLMANN, JEROME DONALD. *Truck Transportation Patterns of Chicago*

*13. HOTCHKISS, WESLEY AKIN. *Areal Pattern of Religious Institutions in Cincinnati*

*14. HARPER, ROBERT ALEXANDER. *Recreational Occupance of the Moraine Lake Region of Northeastern Illinois and Southeastern Wisconsin*

*15. WHEELER, JESSE HARRISON, JR. *Land Use in Greenbrier County, West Virginia*

*16. MCGAUGH, MAURICE EDRON. *The Settlement of the Saginaw Basin*

*17. WATTERSON, ARTHUR WELDON. *Economy and Land Use Patterns of McLean County, Illinois*

*18. HORBALY, WILLIAM. *Agricultural Conditions in Czechoslovakia, 1950*

*19. GUEST, BUDDY ROSS. *Resource Use and Associated Problems in the Upper Cimarron Area*

*20. SORENSEN, CLARENCE WOODROW. *The Internal Structure of the Springfield, Illinois, Urbanized Area*

*21. MUNGER, EDWIN S. *Relational Patterns of Kampala, Uganda*

*22. KHALAF, JASSIM M. *The Water Resources of the Lower Colorado River Basin*

*23. GULICK, LUTHER H. *Rural Occupance in Utuado and Jayuya Municipios, Puerto Rico*

*24. TAAFFE, EDWARD JAMES. *The Air Passenger Hinterland of Chicago*

*25. KRAUSE, ANNEMARIE ELISABETH. *Mennonite Settlement in the Paraguayan Chaco*

*26. HAMMING, EDWARD. *The Port of Milwaukee*

*27. CRAMER, ROBERT ELI. *Manufacturing Structure of the Cicero District, Metropolitan Chicago*

*28. PIERSON, WILLIAM H. *The Geography of the Bellingham Lowland, Washington*

*29. WHITE, GILBERT F. *Human Adjustment to Floods: A Geographical Approach to the Flood Problem in the United States*

30. OSBORN, DAVID G. *Geographical Features of the Automation of Industry* 1953. 120 pp.

*31. THOMAN, RICHARD S. *The Changing Occupance Pattern of the Tri-State Area, Missouri, Kansas, and Oklahoma*

*32. ERICKSEN, SHELDON D. *Occupance in the Upper Deschutes Basin, Oregon*

*33. KENYON, JAMES B. *The Industrialization of the Skokie Area*

*34. PHILLIPS, PAUL GROUNDS. *The Hashemite Kingdom of Jordan: Prolegomena to a Technical Assistance Program*

*35. CARMIN, ROBERT LEIGHTON. *Anápolis, Brazil: Regional Capital of an Agricultural Frontier*

*36. GOLD, ROBERT N. *Manufacturing Structure and Pattern of the South Bend–Mishawaka Area* 1954. 224 pp. 6 folded inserts. 2 maps in pocket.

*37. SISCO, PAUL HARDEMAN. *The Retail Function of Memphis*

*38. VAN DONGEN, IRENE S. *The British East African Transport Complex*

*39. FRIEDMANN, JOHN R. P. *The Spatial Structure of Economic Development in the Tennessee Valley*

*40. GROTEWOLD, ANDREAS. *Regional Changes in Corn Production in the United States from 1909 to 1949*

*41. BJORKLUND, E. M. *Focus on Adelaide—Functional Organization of the Adelaide Region, Australia*

*42. FORD, ROBERT N. *A Resource Use Analysis and Evaluation of the Everglades Agricultural Area*

*43. CHRISTENSEN, DAVID E. *Rural Occupance in Transition: Sumter and Lee Counties, Georgia*

*44. GUZMÁN, LOUIS E. *Farming and Farmlands in Panama*

* Out of print.

*45. ZADROZNY, MITCHELL G. *Water Utilization in the Middle Mississippi Valley*
*46. AHMED, G. MUNIR. *Manufacturing Structure and Pattern of Waukegan–North Chicago*
*47. RANDALL, DARRELL. *Factors of Economic Development and the Okovango Delta*
    1956. 282 pp. (Research Paper No. 3, Program of Education and Research in Planning, The University of Chicago.)
 48. BOXER, BARUCH. *Israeli Shipping and Foreign Trade*  1957. 176 pp.
 49. MAYER, HAROLD M. *The Port of Chicago and the St. Lawrence Seaway*
*50. PATTISON, WILLIAM D. *Beginnings of the American Rectangular Land Survey System, 1784–1800*
    1957. 2d printing 1963. 260 pp. Available from Ohio Historical Society.
*51. BROWN, ROBERT HAROLD. *Political Areal-Functional Organization: With Special Reference to
    St. Cloud, Minnesota.*
*52. BEYER, JACQUELYN. *Integration of Grazing and Crop Agriculture: Resources Management Prob-
    lems in the Uncompahgre Valley Irrigation Project.*  1957. 131 pp.
 53. ACKERMAN, EDWARD A. *Geography as a Fundamental Research Discipline*  1958. 40 pp. $1.00.
*54. AL-KHASHAB, WAFIQ HUSSAIN. *The Water Budget of the Tigris and Euphrates Basin*
*55. LARIMORE, ANN EVANS. *The Alien Town: Patterns of Settlement in Busoga, Uganda*  1958. 210 pp.
 56. MURPHY, FRANCIS C. *Regulating Flood-Plain Development*  1958. 216 pp.
*57. WHITE, GILBERT F., *et al. Changes in Urban Occupance of Flood Plains in the United States*
*58. COLBY, MARY MC RAE. *The Geographic Structure of Southeastern North Carolina*  1958. 242 pp.
*59. MEGEE, MARY CATHERINE. *Monterrey, Mexico: Internal Patterns and External Relations*
 60. WEBER, DICKINSON. *A Comparison of Two Oil City Business Centers (Odessa-Midland, Texas)*
    1958. 256 pp.
 61. PLATT, ROBERT S. *Field Study in American Geography*  1959. 408 pp.
 62. GINSBURG, NORTON, editor. *Essays on Geography and Economic Development*  1960. 196 pp.
 63. HARRIS, CHAUNCY D., and FELLMANN, JEROME D. *International List of Geographical Serials*
    1960. 247 pp.
*64. TAAFFE, ROBERT N. *Rail Transportation and the Economic Development of Soviet Central Asia*
    1960. 186 pp.
*65. SHEAFFER, JOHN R. *Flood Proofing: An Element in a Flood Damage Reduction Program*
    1960. 190 pp.
 66. RODGERS, ALLAN L. *The Industrial Geography of the Port of Genova*  1960. 150 pp.
 67. KENYON, JAMES B. *Industrial Localization and Metropolitan Growth: The Paterson-Passaic Dis-
    trict.*  1960. 250 pp.
 68. GINSBURG, NORTON. *An Atlas of Economic Development*
    1961. 119 pp. 14 × 8½″. Cloth $7.50. University of Chicago Press.
 69. CHURCH, MARTHA. *Spatial Organization of Electric Power Territories in Massachusetts*
    1960. 200 pp.
 70. WHITE, GILBERT F., *et al. Papers on Flood Problems*  1961. 234 pp.
 71. GILBERT, E. W. *The University Town in England and West Germany*
    1961. 79 pp. 4 plates. 30 maps and diagrams.
 72. BOXER, BARUCH. *Ocean Shipping in the Evolution of Hong Kong*  1961. 108 pp.
 73. ROBINSON, IRA M. *New Industrial Towns of Canada's Resource Frontier*
    1962. (Research Paper No. 4, Program of Education and Research in Planning, The University of Chicago.) 192 pp.
 74. TROTTER, JOHN E. *State Park System in Illinois*  1962. 152 pp.
 75. BURTON, IAN. *Types of Agricultural Occupance of Flood Plains in the United States*
    1962. 167 pp.
 76. PRED, ALLAN. *The External Relations of Cities during 'Industrial Revolution'*  1962. 124 pp.
 77. BARROWS, HARLAN H. *Lectures on the Historical Geography of the United States as Given in 1933*
    Edited by WILLIAM A. KOELSCH.  1962. 248 pp.
 78. KATES, ROBERT WILLIAM. *Hazard and Choice Perception in Flood Plain Management*
    1962. 157 pp.
 79. HUDSON, JAMES. *Irrigation Water Use in the Utah Valley, Utah*  1962. 249 pp.
 80. ZELINSKY, WILBUR. *A Bibliographic Guide to Population Geography*  1962. 257 pp.
*81. DRAINE, EDWIN H. *Import Traffic of Chicago and Its Hinterland*
*82. KOLARS, JOHN F. *Tradition, Season, and Change in a Turkish Village*
    NAS-NRC Foreign Field Research Program Report No. 15. 1963. 205 pp.
 83. WIKKRAMATILEKE, RUDOLPH. *Southeast Ceylon: Trends and Problems in Agricultural Settlement*
    1963. 163 pp.
 84. KANSKY, K. J. *Structure of Transportation Networks: Relationships between Network Geometry
    and Regional Characteristics*  1963. 155 pp.
 85. BERRY, BRIAN J. L. *Commercial Structure and Commercial Blight*  1963. 254 pp.
 86. BERRY, BRIAN J. L., and TENNANT, ROBERT J. *Chicago Commercial Reference Handbook*
    1963. 178 pp.
 87. BERRY, BRIAN J. L., and HANKINS, THOMAS D. *A Bibliographic Guide to the Economic Regions
    of the United States*  1963. 128 pp.
 88. MARCUS, MELVIN G. *Climate-Glacier Studies in the Juneau Ice Field Region, Alaska*  1964. 128 pp.
 89. SMOLE, WILLIAM J. *Owner-Cultivatorship in Middle Chile*  1964. 176 pp.
*90. HELVIG, MAGNE. *Chicago's External Truck Movements: Spatial Interaction between the Chicago
    Area and Its Hinterland*  1964. 132 pp.

    * Out of print.

\*91. HILL, A. DAVID. *The Changing Landscape of a Mexican Municipio, Villa Las Rosas, Chiapas*
NAS-NRC Foreign Field Research Program Report No. 26. 1964. 121 pp.

92. SIMMONS, JAMES W. *The Changing Pattern of Retail Location* 1964. 202 pp.

93. WHITE, GILBERT F. *Choice of Adjustment to Floods* 1964. 150 pp.

94. MCMANIS, DOUGLAS R. *The Initial Evaluation and Utilization of the Illinois Prairies, 1815–1840*
1964. 109 pp.

95. PERLE, EUGENE D. *The Demand for Transportation: Regional and Commodity Studies in the United States* 1964. 130 pp.

96. HARRIS, CHAUNCY D. *Annotated World List of Selected Current Geographical Serials in English* 1964. 32 pp. $1.00

97. BOWDEN, LEONARD W. *Diffusion of the Decision To Irrigate: Simulation of the Spread of a New Resource Management Practice in the Colorado Northern High Plains* 1965. 146 pp.

98. KATES, ROBERT W. *Industrial Flood Losses: Damage Estimation in the Lehigh Valley*
1965. 76 pp.

99. RODER, WOLF. *The Sabi Valley Irrigation Projects* 1965. 213 pp.

100. SEWELL, W. R. DERRICK. *Water Management and Floods in the Fraser River Basin* 1965. 163 pp.

101. RAY, D. MICHAEL. *Market Potential and Economic Shadow: A Quantitative Analysis of Industrial Location in Southern Ontario* 1965. 164 pp.

102. AHMAD, QAZI. *Indian Cities: Characteristics and Correlates* 1965. 184 pp.

103. BARNUM, H. GARDINER. *Market Centers and Hinterlands in Baden-Württemberg* 1966. 172 pp.

104. SIMMONS, JAMES W. *Toronto's Changing Retail Complex* 1966. 126 pp.

\*105. SEWELL, W. R. DERRICK, *et al. Human Dimensions of Weather Modification* 1966. 423 pp.

106. SAARINEN, THOMAS FREDERICK. *Perception of the Drought Hazard on the Great Plains.* 1966. 183 pp.

107. SOLZMAN, DAVID M. *Waterway Industrial Sites: A Chicago Case Study.* 1967. 138 pp.

108. KASPERSON, ROGER E. *The Dodecanese: Diversity and Unity in Island Politics.* 1967. 184 pp.

109. LOWENTHAL, DAVID, editor, *Environmental Perception and Behavior.* 1967. 88 pp.

110. REED, WALLACE E., *Areal Interaction in India: Commodity Flows of the Bengal-Bihar Industrial Area.* 1967

111. BERRY, BRIAN J. L. *Essays on Commodity Flows and the Spatial Structure of the Indian Economy.*
1966. 334 pp.

112. BOURNE, LARRY S. *Private Redevelopment of the Central City, Spatial Processes of Structural Change in the City of Toronto.* 1967. 199 pp.

113. BRUSH, JOHN E., and GAUTHIER, HOWARD L., JR., *Service Centers and Consumer Trips: Studies in the Philadelphia Metropolitan Fringe.* 1967. 182 pp.

114. CLARKSON, JAMES D., *The Cultural Ecology of a Chinese Village, Cameron Highlands, Malaysia.*
1967

\* Out of print